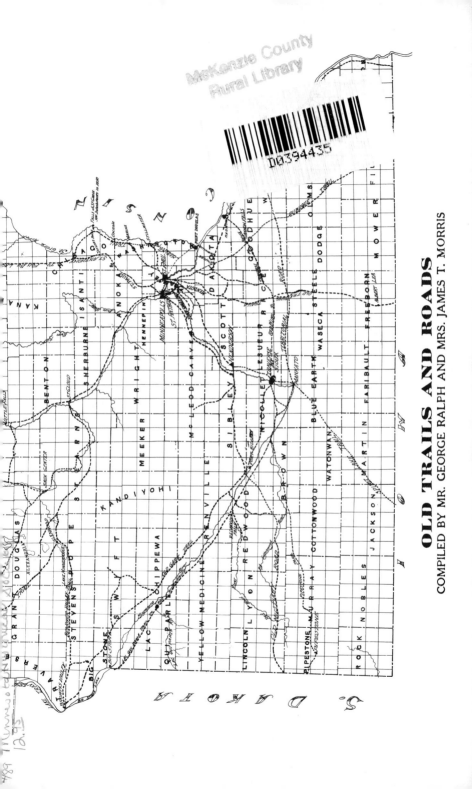

OLD TRAILS AND ROADS

COMPILED BY MR. GEORGE RALPH AND MRS. JAMES T. MORRIS

Publications of the

MINNESOTA HISTORICAL SOCIETY

RUSSELL W. FRIDLEY
Director

JUNE D. HOLMQUIST
Assistant Director
for Research and Publications

LUCY LEAVENWORTH WILDER MORRIS
Originator of "Old Rail Fence Corners."

Old Rail Fence Corners

FRONTIER TALES
TOLD BY MINNESOTA PIONEERS

Edited by LUCY LEAVENWORTH WILDER MORRIS

REPRINT EDITION

With an Introduction by MARJORIE KREIDBERG

MINNESOTA HISTORICAL SOCIETY PRESS
ST. PAUL • 1976

New material copyright © 1976
By the MINNESOTA HISTORICAL SOCIETY
   First edition 1914
   Second edition 1915
   Reprint edition 1976

First published in 1914 as *Old Rail Fence Corners: The A.B.C.'s of Minnesota History* by The Book Committee, a subcommittee of the Old Trails and Historic Spots Committee, Minnesota Society of the Daughters of the American Revolution

Library of Congress Cataloging in Publication Data
Daughters of the American Revolution. Minnesota.
   Old Trails and Historic Spots Committee.
   Old rail fence corners.
   (Publications of the Minnesota Historical Society)
   Reprint of the 2d ed., 1915, printed by
F. H. McCulloch Print. Co., Austin, Minn., under
title: Old rail fence corners: the A.B.C.'s of
Minnesota history.
   Includes bibliographical references and index.
   1. Frontier and pioneer life—Minnesota.
2. Minnesota—History, Local. 3. Pioneers—
Minnesota—Biography. 4. Minnesota—Biography.
I. Morris, Lucy Leavenworth Wilder, 1865–1935.
II. Title. III. Series: Minnesota Historical
Society. Publications.
F606.D34   1976   977.6'04   76-30262

International Standard Book Number: 0-87351-108-5
   (cloth cover)
   0-87351-109-3
   (paper cover)

Contents

Introduction

In the twenty-year period before 1865, Minnesota became the home of about 265,000 people who chose to live
on the frontier. Some of these pioneers arrived in the late
1840s, when Minnesota was a youthful territory. Many arrived in the 1850s and inflated the population figures from a
sparse 6,077 at the beginning of the decade to about 40,000
by 1855. Others arrived about 1860, just two years after
Minnesota had become the thirty-second state and the
population had mushroomed to 172,023. They traveled to
Minnesota from as far away as the eastern states and as
nearby as neighboring Wisconsin and Iowa. A few arrived
directly from the Old World. Sometimes the men of the
families ventured west first to discover for themselves what
the land offered. Often several families made the journey
together, bringing with them their worldly possessions, including household goods and livestock. Some had saved
money for as long as three years before they had enough to
pay their way west. Others arrived with little in their pockets. Among the pioneers were future leaders in government and politics, agriculture, lumbering, milling, bank-
ing, and newspapering. Far more numerous were those
whose role was to build Minnesota with hard work and little
fanfare.[1]

The stories of how many settlers traveled to Minnesota,
what they found when they arrived, and how they coped
with the rigors of frontier life were first collected over sixty

[1] William W. Folwell, *A History of Minnesota*, 2:64, 344 (Revised ed.,
St. Paul, 1961); *Minnesota Pioneer* (St. Paul), March 27, 1850; Joseph A.
Wheelock, *Minnesota: Its Place Among the States*, 125, 126 (Minnesota
Bureau of Statistics, *First Annual Report* — Hartford, Conn., 1860).

years ago and published in a book entitled *Old Rail Fence Corners*. The tales reveal that, arriving by steamboat or prairie schooner, the pioneers usually stopped first at a river settlement. To a young girl from Maine who came up the Mississippi River in 1850, St. Paul looked at first appearance "like a little town that had been left." Winona, recalled an elderly woman, was a collection of only a dozen families in 1854, and Duluth was remembered as a "cotton-town" because so many people lived in tents or in log houses roofed with canvas. St. Anthony, the embryo of the state's largest city, was described as a New England village. In those days $100 paid for 260 acres of "fine wooded land," located just south of Minneapolis, and it was more the bargain for having Minnehaha Creek running through it and a partly finished house standing on it. So great was the demand for building materials that people stood in line at sawmills, eager to "grab the boards as they came from the saw."[2]

It was a time when "battalions" of wild geese, ducks, and pigeons darkened the spring skies, and a man could easily catch several hundred pounds of pike, bass, and pickerel and salt them away for winter use. Rural families walked miles to the nearest post office to fetch their mail and to "hear the postmaster read the news from the weekly St. Paul paper." Women bought sewing threads in "hanks." Children's dolls were fashioned from grass and flowers. Cold weather was forecast by the presence of "dog moons" at night and "dog suns" by day. Lead was melted in a ladle over the heat of a cookstove and formed into bullets.[3]

This was life on the Minnesota frontier as recalled by

[2] Lucy L. W. Morris, ed., *Old Rail Fence Corners: The A.B.C.'s of Minnesota History*, hereafter abbreviated as *ORFC*, 33, 38, 55, 56, 69, 184, 240 (Second ed., Austin, [1915]).

[3] *ORFC*, 21, 100, 141, 174, 187, 265, 278.

those who lived it. These recollected images, and hundreds more like them, are captured in the collection of incomparable personal stories told in *Old Rail Fence Corners*. Although its compilers offer no explanation for the title, it brings to mind leaves blown by the wind into the corners of an old rail fence and was probably meant to suggest the accumulated memories gathered in this volume. The book, first published in 1914 and reprinted in 1915, is a magnificent human record, a microcosm of the very essence of the frontier experience. It was the inspiration of its discerning editor, Lucy Leavenworth Wilder Morris, who recognized in the early 1900s that the exceptional legacy of the pioneers — their "precious reminiscences" — would soon be lost. In 1911 she conceived the idea for the book and began to interview and record the recollections of early Minnesotans. Overwhelmed by the task she had set for herself, she enlisted twenty-two fellow members of the Daughters of the American Revolution in Minnesota to help in the effort. They called themselves "The Book Committee" and they represented sixteen chapters of the D.A.R. — six in Minneapolis, two in Duluth and St. Paul, and one each in Mankato, Winona, Rochester, Faribault, Northfield, and St. Peter. Together the women collected the "simple anecdotes" of 62 men and 92 women, and Mrs. Morris interviewed more than half of them herself. She also edited the collection of "authentic incidents gleaned from the old settlers" and guided its evolution into the book she entitled *Old Rail Fence Corners: The A.B.C.'s of Minnesota History.*[4]

The volume, published late in 1914, met with immediate

---

[4] *ORFC*, title page, [5]; Mary Dillon Foster, *Who's Who Among Minnesota Women*, 223 (n.p., 1924); advertising card for *ORFC*, second edition, in Lucy L. W. Morris Papers, Minnesota Historical Society, hereafter abbreviated as MHS.

acceptance from both critics and the public. "A remarkable book," wrote a reviewer in the *Minneapolis Sunday Tribune*, "at once a labor of love and a contribution to history" whose "picturesque narratives" make possible a personal contact with the "state-builders of yesterday." The writer called the stories "Plain . . . disconnected, fragmentary, just as these old, white-haired persons might really tell them to the grandchildren on their laps . . . tales of the stirring days when they and their fathers and mothers, their sons and daughters, were carving an empire out of the Indian-peopled, deer-run woods and buffalo-bounded prairies." Echoing an appreciation of this personal quality of the book, the *Christian Science Monitor* pointed out that the "work serves to give an intimate knowledge of the life of those who conquered the forests and prairies of Minnesota and laid the foundation for a great state." Writing in *The Bellman*, a Minneapolis magazine, a reviewer praised *Old Rail Fence Corners* as "one of the most remarkable 'first-hand' histories ever published in America. First hand, because these little anecdotes are printed in the exact words of the narrators with very little editing." He commended the "uncanny wisdom which made the compilers permit their native Homers to sing in 'their own unvarnished way.' " He urged that any writer "who is striving to produce a novel of real American life or a novel of real life of any sort, if he should chance upon this book, would do well to read it carefully, not even skipping the occasional bad grammar." His suggestion was well taken, and at least one internationally famous author — Sinclair Lewis — not only read the book for his own benefit but placed "the admirable Minnesota chronicles" in the hands of Carol Kennicott, the major character in *Main Street*.[5]

[5] *Minneapolis Sunday Tribune*, December 6, 1914, section (13), p. 3, 5; *Christian Science Monitor*, March 31, 1915; *The Bellman*, 18:694

Because the book is a "history written by the history makers," it is still a rich source for modern researchers and writers who want to characterize a time and a people. Its vivid descriptions re-create an era when homes were sod huts, log cabins, or a simple frame dwelling; when a family often shared its cramped quarters with those in need, and when contact with Native Americans was frequent. The Indians roamed freely, entered cabins, ate bread and molasses, pancakes, dried-apple pies, or any other food in sight. Dakota children played lacrosse with the children of the newcomers and went fishing and hunting with them. Some pioneers learned that an unlocked door developed a spirit of mutual respect. When a family was to be gone from the house a stick was propped against the door to indicate their absence and, simultaneously, to assure the Indians of their trust in them.[6]

Like frontier people everywhere, Minnesota pioneers made do with what they had. Coffee was made from corn meal or browned beets. Cabin walls were plastered with mud then decorated with wallpaper when it was available. Farmers traded a peck of potatoes or six of their wives' doughnuts for a pair of beaded Indian moccasins. School desks in a Fillmore County settlement were made from black walnut because the trees were native to the area. Frontier pragmatism is also revealed by the man who bundled his three youngsters into sacks on a winter night then put them to sleep on straw beds laid on the dirt floor with more straw piled on top to keep them warm. A pioneer woman considered her blue-black silk dress with the leg-

(November 28, 1914); Sinclair Lewis, *Main Street: The Story of Carol Kennicott*, 151 (New York, 1920). Copies of the reviews are in Morris Papers.

[6] *Minneapolis Sunday Tribune*, December 6, 1914, section (13), p. 5; *ORFC*, 38, 64, 100, 101, 210.

of-mutton sleeves "Cheaper to wear than calico because it would never wear out." [7]

Fragments of a larger history appear in the stories too — the Civil War and the Dakota War of 1862, steamboat travel up the Mississippi River, the agitation that preceded the coming of the railroads, and the evolution of a road system and of the milling industry. The great financial disaster of 1857 is recalled by many people, among them a woman who said that "money was scarcer than teeth in a fly. We never saw a penny sometimes for a year at a time," and a Mankato resident who commented that cash was loaned to the hard-pressed settlers at 36 to 60 per cent interest a year. Lucy Morris regarded each personal story in *Old Rail Fence Corners* as "a mesh in a priceless lace fabric, that fabric Minnesota History." Although she realized that some statements were historically inaccurate, she nonetheless had the foresight to recognize the contribution of the collected reminiscences to the over-all pattern of the past. [8]

The number of books printed in the first edition is not known, but at $1.50 per copy the work was "sold all over the world," and within six months a second edition was planned. Mrs. Morris supplied corrections and additions to the F. H. McCulloch Printing Company in Austin, Minnesota, and on August 19, 1915, a thousand books were shipped to Miss Louise Clifford in Minneapolis who was the agent for the Minnesota D.A.R. Book Committee. This "illustrated second edition," which cost $400 to produce, sold for $1.75 a copy. Its content is not fundamentally different from that of the first edition. The title page and copyright notice mistakenly carry a publication date of 1914. Although the first edition contained a list of nine errors, only five of them were corrected in the second printing. These

[7] *ORFC*, 72, 86, 90, 96, 102, 117, 215, 300.
[8] *ORFC*, [6], 118, 170.

included changing the spelling of several names and transposing the order of names of book committee members on one page. The pioneers among those interviewed who had died before the 1915 edition was readied were named on a new memorial page. A fold-out map of "Old Trails and Roads" appeared in both editions, but its title is absent in the first. The map was compiled by Mrs. Morris and George Ralph, a former state drainage engineer, using information gathered from pioneers, old maps, and government-issued plats.[9]

Perhaps the most significant addition to the second edition, at least for today's readers, are seven illustrations. Almost all of the photographs have the quality of snapshots in a family album, and it is easy to wish there were more of them to acquaint us with those who speak from the book's pages. Fittingly, the first of the photographs found between the leaves is a portrait of the editor, Lucy Morris.

Like *Old Rail Fence Corners*, Mrs. Morris was considered by many to be "remarkable." She was, noted a contemporary, a woman "of indefatigable energy, and boundless enthusiasm, intensely interested in and so keenly alive to the accomplishment of whatever might have been the subject of her interest at the moment, that she was able to spur others to an equal enthusiasm." Born in Evanston, Illinois, about 1862, Lucy Leavenworth Wilder was educated at the Rockford seminary. At the age of sixteen she moved to Houston County, Minnesota, where she taught in the graded and ungraded schools. In the early 1880s she

[9] *The Bellman*, 18:694; F. H. McCulloch to Mrs. J. T. Morris, May 25, August 19, 1915; invoice statement from F. H. McCulloch Printing Company, dated August 19, 1915; advertising card for *ORFC*, second edition — all in Morris Papers; "Errata," in *ORFC*, [327] (First ed., 1914). George Ralph is identified in *Christian Science Monitor*, March 31, 1915. The original map on tracing cloth is in the MHS Division of Archives and Manuscripts; it was presented by Mrs. Morris in 1921.

went to LaCrosse, Wisconsin, to further her education. She returned permanently to Minnesota in 1890, after her marriage to Minneapolitan James T. Morris, who was then engaged in the lumber business and who later became an expert in the "general credit and adjustment business." The couple made their home in Minneapolis.[10]

Within a few years Mrs. Morris was deeply involved in many activities, among them travel, writing, and history. European journeys inspired her to write and publish a 64-page guide for travel-hungry ladies with limited funds. In the pocket-sized booklet, entitled *European Primer for the Penniless: A Book for Women*, she offered explicit advice on how to manage six "very enjoyable months traveling wherever you wish in Europe" for only $500, including steamer passage. Her purpose was not to tell readers what to see but rather what kind of clothes to take, how to pack, when and how much to tip, how to avoid unnecessary expense, where to find accommodations, and the ins and outs of train travel. "Find out what your rights are," she advised train passengers, "and quietly but firmly insist upon them."[11]

The former school teacher also wrote children's stories and informative articles, some of which were published locally. One of her instructive works is entitled *Story of a Caterpillar*, which describes the transformation of a caterpillar into a hawk moth. In an article accepted by

[10] Lois N. Jordan, "Tribute to Mrs. James T. Morris," 1, a manuscript dated March 12, 1936, in the Minnesota Society of the D.A.R. Papers, Sibley House, Mendota; Foster, *Who's Who Among Minnesota Women*, 223; letter of recommendation signed by D. C. Cameron, superintendent of Houston County schools, March 14, 1881, in Morris Papers. No record of Mrs. Morris' exact birth date has been found. On James T. Morris, see *Minneapolis Journal*, November 1, 1917, p. 2.

[11] Morris, *European Primer for the Penniless: A Book for Women*, 36, 64 (Minneapolis, n.d.).

the *Northwest Magazine*, a St. Paul publication that paid her five dollars for the piece, Mrs. Morris promoted the harvesting of "The Neglected Crop," shaggy-mane and horse mushrooms. Her writing reached a wider audience in 1897, when the *National Magazine* published a touching narrative sketch of the widow of a seafaring man.[12]

While the subjects of her interest were diverse, a substantial number grew out of her activities in the D.A.R., which she joined in 1894, just four years after its founding. Her eligibility was established by her great-grandfather's service in the Revolutionary War. She also noted on her membership application that she was a distant cousin of Colonel Henry Leavenworth, the United States Army officer who commanded troops of the Fifth Infantry assigned in 1819 to build Fort Snelling in Minnesota. For several years, Mrs. Morris was a member of the Colonial Chapter of the D.A.R. in Minneapolis before transferring to member-at-large status early in 1913. In October of that year she became Organizing Regent of the Old Trails Chapter, whose primary purpose was to identify and commemorate historic places and trails in the Minneapolis vicinity. Four years later she was named State Regent and in June, 1920, she was installed as a Vice President General of the National Society of the D.A.R. for a three-year term. Mrs. Morris was named an Honorary Vice President General in 1933, a distinction awarded for life.[13]

[12] Morris, *Story of a Caterpillar* (Minneapolis, 1897); in *Northwest Magazine*, 16:10 (November, 1898); "Grass Pinks," in *National Magazine*, April, 1897, p. 88; Stephen Conday to Morris, January 14, 1899 — all in Morris Papers. Also among the Morris Papers is a card sent by the Library of Congress in July, 1916, to notify Mrs. Morris that copyright had been approved for a book entitled *Our Tree*, a copy of which has not been found.

[13] See Mrs. Morris' "Application for Membership" to the D.A.R., May 2, 1894, in Registrar General files, National Society of the D.A.R., Washington, D.C.; Mrs. Wakelee R. Smith to author, July 16, 1976; Jordan, "Tribute to Mrs. J. T. Morris," 1.

In September, 1915, when Lucy Morris was active in the Old Trails Chapter, the organization placed a bronze tablet, dedicated to the memory of Colonel Leavenworth and his command, on the Round Tower at Fort Snelling. Mrs. Morris was the featured speaker at the unveiling ceremonies, and she presented what was described as a "thrilling historic review" of the fort and of Colonel Leavenworth.[14]

Pursuing her "chief work" of "preserving places of historic interest," Mrs. Morris began in 1920 a formal effort to establish a national military park at Yorktown, Virginia, to save the site of the Revolutionary battlefield where Cornwallis was defeated in 1781. At the time, she was the D.A.R.'s national chairman of historic sites. With the unanimous endorsement of the organization's Continental Congress, she sought and received backing from two of Minnesota's congressional leaders, Representative Walter H. Newton and Senator Frank B. Kellogg, who agreed to sponsor a bill creating the park. She also won the support of Secretary of War John W. Weeks, who directed that the proposed park area be surveyed and a map drawn to locate the battlefield. Then, "with a willing heart but often most unwilling legs," Mrs. Morris "walked miles on the cement floors of the Government offices" to win approval of the park bill from "uninterested Congressmen." Her efforts were crowned with success; Congress passed the bill and President Warren G. Harding signed it on March 2, 1923. The War Department then named a national commission to establish the military park at Yorktown and appointed Mrs. Morris one of the four commissioners. She proudly announced to the D.A.R. Continental Congress meeting in Washington, D.C., in April, that "They say this is the first

[14] *Minneapolis Sunday Tribune*, September 12, 1915, p. 7.

time that a woman has been appointed on a Commission for National Military Parks."[15]

Mrs. Morris' interest in the development of the park at Yorktown continued, and as chairman of the D.A.R. Yorktown Sesquicentennial Committee she completed in 1931 a long-term project to verify the names of 133 French soldiers who fought there with the Americans. The D.A.R. prepared two bronze tablets — one bearing the names of the Americans and the other the names of the Frenchmen — and they were placed at the base of the Yorktown battle monument. In appreciation, the French government awarded Mrs. Morris the badge of the Legion of Honor at ceremonies in Paris on October 19, 1932.[16]

While Lucy Morris served as a national officer of the D.A.R., she continued her leadership of efforts to preserve historic sites in Minnesota. In the fall of 1922, the Minnesota Society of the Daughters of American Colonists was organized in her home. The group's first project, suggested by William Watts Folwell, Minnesota historian and one-time president of the state university, was to mark the site from which Father Louis Hennepin first viewed the Falls of St. Anthony in 1680. Located on the bank of the Mississippi River at the foot of Sixth Avenue Southeast, the site was, according to Mrs. Morris, "the dirtiest and most desolate spot in the whole city of Minneapolis. Erosion had taken away what had probably been verdant banks in 1680, and dump carts had filled in with old boilers, wringers, tin cans

[15] Mrs. E. G. Bowman, "Mrs. James T. Morris, Honorary Vice President General, N.S.D.A.R.," a typed copy (with several incorrect dates) is in the files of the Minnesota Society of the D.A.R., Sibley House; National Society of the D.A.R., *Proceedings of the Thirty-second Continental Congress*, 111 (Washington, D.C., April, 1923).

[16] Bowman, "Mrs. James T. Morris"; Jordan, "Tribute to Mrs. J. T. Morris," 3.

and whiskey bottles, etc. Underneath, the bank was found to be engine ashes, and beneath that, shale, not one single thing was growing there, and it looked as though nothing ever would."[17]

Undaunted, the women launched a successful campaign of persuasion. The owner of the property granted the society an easement, vigorous support of the project was secured from Theodore Wirth, Minneapolis superintendent of parks, and full co-operation was obtained from the city's park board. The society ordered a large, inscribed bronze tablet, which was to be placed on a huge boulder moved to the site at a cost of fifty dollars. Needing more money to complete the project, the society hosted a fund-raising party for 800 guests and took in $700 for the supporting fund.

In September, 1924, the tablet was dedicated, even though the park grounds were not fully in order. During ceremonies that included an address by Dr. Folwell and "thrilling music" played by a fife and drum corps, it was announced that the historic area would be named Lucy Wilder Morris Park to honor the society's founding regent. The women continued to develop the park — building a surrounding fence and a stairway to the river ("No one but a rocky mountain goat could get down that almost perpendicular slope," Lucy noted); installing a water system that was a gift in memory of James T. Morris, who died in 1917; and planting "memorial trees" for Dr. Folwell and Maria Sanford, a well-known University of Minnesota teacher.

[17] For a list of historic markers erected by the D.A.R. in the state to 1964, see D.A.R., Minnesota, "Memorial Markers in Minnesota," a typed copy in the MHS Library. On the establishing of Lucy Wilder Morris Park by the Daughters of the American Colonists, here and the following paragraphs, see a typed text of an address by Mrs. Morris to the State Assembly of the Minnesota Society, D.A.C., September 26, 1929, in files of the Minnesota Society of the D.A.R., Sibley House.

Unfortunately, the beautiful park of which Lucy Morris could be justly proud was to have an uncertain future. Over the years the memorials disappeared or were vandalized, and the grounds became unkempt. Now the Hennepin County Historical Society holds the easement to the small parcel of land. In 1971 the little park was absorbed into a newly established public area called Father Hennepin Bluffs. At that time the Riverfront Design Team of the Minneapolis City Planning Department installed a new inscribed plaque giving the history of the site.[18]

Lucy Morris experienced many personal satisfactions and triumphs during her lifetime. Along with her accomplishments in the D.A.R. and its history-related activities, she was "long identified with varied efforts for social betterment." Among the latter were those to promote Americanization and citizenship of the foreign born and, during World War I, to provide for the health and comfort of soldiers. As State Regent of the Minnesota D.A.R., she led the women in sending to patients in military hospitals "wonderful home made grape juice and jelly," selling Liberty Bonds, preparing surgical dressings, and knitting garments for use by navy personnel at sea. When she died on November 1, 1935, a *Minneapolis Journal* editorial called her death "a notable loss" to Minneapolis and lauded her work in historic preservation that benefitted the entire state and nation.[19]

[18] Information on the present status of the former Lucy Wilder Morris Park was provided by Mrs. Donna Lind, Hennepin County Historical Society.

[19] *Minneapolis Journal*, November 3, 1935, p. 4; Mrs. A. W. Abbott *et al* to "Madam Regent," National Society of the D.A.R., December 26, 1919, Morris Papers; Mrs. E. J. Edwards, "An Appreciation of the Work of Mrs. J. T. Morris," May 28, 1920, in Morris Papers; A. Schuyler Clark to Mrs. J. T. Morris, October 18, 1918; John E. Struthers to Mrs. James T. Morris, November 2, 1918, both in Morris Papers.

After six decades, *Old Rail Fence Corners* remains as "monumental evidence" of Lucy Morris' "zeal for the preservation of local history."[20] As the years have gone by, the book's wide-ranging, richly detailed, firsthand accounts of early Minnesota have become an increasingly valued and respected source of information on a long-vanished era. The collection, which was never intended to capture history in headlines, serves to fill the gaps left in other historical works dealing primarily with major events, well-known people, and broad social movements, but seldom mentioning the daily life lived by nameless pioneers, their hopes, fears, joys, and indomitable spirit. In these reminiscences, the old settlers offer concrete details about the houses they built, the foods they ate, the gardens they planted, the illnesses they suffered, and the home remedies they administered. They describe in colorful, unself-conscious language the squeaking Red River oxcarts, swarms of voracious grasshoppers that obscured the sun and destroyed crops, hailstorms, revival meetings, howling wolves, the wild fruits of summer, and much more. This is a people's record of the past, as genuine as a homemade preserve. It is a major source of women's history, too, for nearly two-thirds of the stories are told by the wives, mothers, and daughters of pioneers. Although it speaks specifically of Minnesota, it also tells something of the national experience that was often repeated as the frontier moved westward.

Long out of print and much sought after, *Old Rail Fence Corners* is again made available to a new generation of readers. The present reprint was produced from the second edition. The map of "Old Trails and Roads" that was inserted in the first two editions appears here as end sheets in a slightly reduced size. Added to the reprint edition are this

[20] Jordan, "Tribute to Mrs. J. T. Morris," 2.

introduction, a contents page, and a comprehensive index that makes the book even more useful to researchers and general readers.

The Minnesota Historical Society Press expresses its thanks to the Minneapolis Public Library and the St. Paul Public Library for their co-operation in supplying copies of the earlier book.

St. Paul, Minnesota   MARJORIE KREIDBERG
November 1, 1976

OLD RAIL
FENCE CORNERS

THE A. B. C's. OF
Minnesota History

SECOND EDITION

AUTHENTIC INCIDENTS GLEANED FROM
The Old Settlers
By The Book Committee
1914

Title page of the second edition

Explanatory

How little we know about what we don't know!

During my search for a map of the Old Trails and Roads of Minnesota, public libraries were thoroughly investigated, but no book or map could be found showing these old highways. A few old maps in the Historical Library bore snatches of them, but in their entirety they had disappeared from books and maps, as well as from our state.

They might be the foundations for modern roads, but only the names of those modern roads survived, so they were lost.

Months of this research work failed to resurrect them, although a map was made from the fragmentary pieces on old maps, filled out by what the pioneers who had traveled those roads could furnish. All old maps seemed to have disappeared from the state.

"We had one of the new territory of Minnesota when it was admitted in '49, but just threw it out when we cleaned house lately. I think it came from Washington," said one dear old pioneer woman.

"What do you want of those old roads anyway," said another. "If you had been over them as I have, you would know how much better these roads are, and be glad they are gone,"

It was hard to locate them from hearsay for when we asked "Did it go through Alexandria," the answer was, "There was no town on it after leaving St. Cloud, so I can't say just where it went, but we went to Fort Garry and crossed the river at Georgetown."

Finally, after nearly a year's hard work, as we were on our way to the Capitol to look over the first government surveys, Mr. George Ralph was met, became interested, and drew part of these trails from the old plats for this map.

When a surveyor goes into a new country to make a government survey, he is required to place on that plat every trail, road or plowed field—John Ryan, who worked in the forties was the only one we found who always followed these directions. He would survey several townships, and there would be the much-wanted road. Some other surveyor would do the one below and there would be a break, but John would take hold again a little further on and the trail could be joined from the direction shown.

Later this map made was compared with old maps since destroyed at the Army Building in St. Paul and found correct.

The three great routes for the Red River carts to St. Paul, the great fur market, which used to come down by the hundreds from the Pembina and Fort Garry country are shown. One through the Minnesota Valley; one through the Sauk Valley, and the most used of all through the Crow Wing Valley by way of Leaf Lake. They used to come to the head waters of the Mississippi in 1808* The Wabasha Prairie Road, called Winona Trail on this map, was a very old one, as also were those leading to the sacred Pipestone Quarries and the sacred Spirit Lake. There is a tradition that there was a truce between all tribes when these trails were followed.   Mrs. J. T. M.

* From Captain Alexander Henry's diary about the Red River country in 1801, presented to Ottawa. He also says there were 1500 of these carts there in 1808

The Book Committee

A sub-committee of the Old Trails and Historic Spots Committee, Daughters of the American Revolution, Appointed by the Chairman.

Mrs. James T. Morris.
Mrs. William J. Morehart
Mrs. E. C. Chatfield
Mrs. S. R. Van Sant
Miss Beatrice Longfellow
Miss Rita Kelly
Mrs. F. W. Little
Mrs. O. H. Shepley
Mrs. Alonzo Phillips
Mrs. Guy Maxwell
Miss Marion Moir
Mrs. E. A. Welch
Miss Ida Wing
Mrs. Mary E. Partridge
Mrs. Ell Torrance
Miss Stella Cole
Mrs. C. A. Bierman
Mrs. Chas. Keith
Miss Emily Brown
Mrs. G. C. Lyman
Mrs. A. B. Kaercher.
Mrs. W. S. Woodbridge
Miss K. Maude Clum

The Reason

When I was a child my grandmother, Lucy Leavenworth Sherwood, used to show us a little map drawn on the back of a cotillion invitation, by her cousin Henry Leavenworth, the first officer at Fort Snelling. He was there in 1819.

It was yellow with age, but showed Fort Snelling, Lake Harriette, named for his wife, other lakes and two rivers. That yellow bundle of letters read to us and the stories she told of this, her favorite cousin, as he had told them to her never failed in breathless interest. Few of them remain with me. The painted Indian in his canoe on the river, the Indian runner, stand out vividly, but the valuable stories contained in those old letters are gone. Nothing was ever a greater surprise than the loss of those stories when I tried to recall them years later. The Bible with the map and all those letters were burned when the home was destroyed by fire.

These valuable data have disappeared. The knowledge that this was so, made me listen with the greatest attention to stories told by the old settlers and record them. All at once the realization came that they, too, were fast disappearing, taking their stories with them. It was impossible for me to get all these precious reminiscences before it was too late. It must be done at once by a large number of interested women. These were found in our committee who have gathered these data most lovingly and financed this book. The proceeds are for patriotic work in Minnesota as deemed best by the committee.

It is hoped that our first work will be the raising of a monument to the Pioneer Women of our State. Those unsung heroines should not their heroism be heralded while some still live?

We thank these dear friends who have made this little volume possible by their warm interest. Every item in this book has been taken personally from a pioneer.

Each one is a mesh in a priceless lace fabric, that fabric Minnesota History.

If each mesh is not flawless, if age has weakened them, does not the pattern remain?

LUCY LEAVENWORTH WILDER MORRIS.

In Memoriam

Mr. Eli Pettijohn
Mrs. Missouri Rose Pratt
Mr. James McMullen
Mrs. Samuel B. Dresser
Mr. William W. Ellison
Mr. Henry Favel
Major Benjamin Randall
Mrs. Duncan Kennedy
Major S. A. Buell
Mrs. Helen Horton
Mrs. Mary Massolt
Mrs. J. M. Paine
Mr. Chas. Watson
Mrs. C. W. Gress

OLD RAIL FENCE CORNERS

OLD TRAILS CHAPTER

Minneapolis

LUCY LEAVENWORTH WILDER MORRIS

(Mrs. J. T. Morris)

Mr. Eli Pettijohn—1841.

Mr. Pettijohn, now ninety-five years old, clear in memory, patriarchial in looks, says:

I came to what is now Minnesota, but was then a part of Wisconsin Territory April sixteenth, 1841. I was on my way to work for the Williamsons, missionaries, at Lac qui Parle. I landed from the large steamer, the Alhambra, at the Fort Snelling landing. I climbed the steep path that led up to the fort, circled the wall and came to the big gate. A sentinel guarded it. He asked me if I wanted to enlist. I said, "No, I want to see the fort, and find a boarding place." He invited me in. I looked around this stone fort with much interest and could see Sibley House and Faribault house across the Minnesota river at Mendota. There were no large trees between the two points so these houses showed very clearly. The ruins of part of the first fort which was of wood, were still on the bluff about one block south of the new fort.

I asked where I could find a boarding place, and was directed to the St. Louis house, near where the water tower now stands. Before proceeding there, I stood and watched the Indians coming to the fort. I was told they were from Black Dog's, Good Road's and Shakopee's villages. The trail they followed was deeply worn. This seemed strange as they all wore moccasins. Their painted faces looked very sinister to one who had never before

---

* All pioneers over ninety are so introduced as we feel sure no state can show so large a number who have the same mentality

seen them, but later I learned to appreciate the worth of these Indians, who as yet were unspoiled by the white man's fire water.

I was told that the St. Louis House had been built after the fort was, by Mr. Baker, a trader, to accommodate people from the south, who wanted to summer here. It was now deserted by its owners and any one of the sparse settlers or traders would occupy it. He said a trader by the name of Martin McLeod was living there and that Kittson, another trader, lived at his trading post about fifty yards away from the house. There was a good wagon road about where the road is now. My friend, for such he later became, told me it led to the government mill at the Falls of St. Anthony, but that it took longer to walk it than it did the Indian trail that led along the bank of the Mississippi. So I took this as advised. There were many Indians on the trail going and coming. All at once I heard a great commotion ahead of me. Indians were running from every direction. When I came to the place where they all were, I heard lamentations and fierce imprecations. I saw the reason there. Two of their warriors were lying dead and scalped, while clambering up the opposite bank of the river, three of the Sioux's sworn enemies, three Chippewas, could be seen. The slain were head men in the tribe. The guns and arrows of the Sioux could not carry across the river, so they escaped for the time being. I was afraid the Sioux vengeance would fall on me, but it did not.

I soon came to the St. Louis house. While there, I saw Walter McLeod, then a baby.

McLeod, the father, had fled from Canada at the time of one of the rebellions, in company with others, but was the only one to survive a terrible blizzard and reach Mendota. Mr. Sibley at once employed him as he was well educated. When he was married later, he gave him some fine mahogany furniture, from his own home, to set up housekeeping with.

OLD RAIL FENCE CORNERS

While at the St. Louis House, I walked with a soldier along the Indian trail that followed the river bank to the government mill at the Falls of St. Anthony. On our way, we went down a deep ravine and crossed the creek on a log. We could hear the roaring of falls and walked over to see them. They were the most beautiful I had ever seen and were called Brown's Falls, but General LeDuc in 1852 gave them the name Minnehaha. I thought I had never seen anything quite so pretty looking as the river and woods. The deer were everywhere and game of all kinds bountiful. The soldier told me that no white man could settle here anywhere for ten miles as it was all in the Fort Snelling reservation. That is why the town of St. Anthony was built on the east side of the river instead of on the west side and why there was no town on this side of the river for many years after. We saw some Sioux teepees and met the Indians constantly. They were a fine sturdy race, with fine features and smiling faces. The soldier said they could be depended on and never broke a promise. The old mill was on the river bank about where we used to take the cars in the old Union Station. It was not then in use, as the rocks had broken off, leaving it perhaps forty or fifty feet from the Falls. A flume had to be constructed before it could again be used.

The Falls were a grand sight. We heard their roaring long before we could see them and saw the spray sparkling in the sunlight. There was a watchman living in a little hut and he gave us a nice meal. A few Sioux wigwams were near.

On the other side, we could see smoke 'way up above where the suspension bridge now is. He said some Frenchmen and halfbreeds lived there. The place was called St. Anthony. We did not go over. He also said there were many white people, French, Scotch and English living in the country upon the Red River. Some were called Selkirk settlers. He did not know why. He said Martin McLeod had been one of these.

OLD RAIL FENCE CORNERS

We passed some squaws in a big dugout. It was thirty feet long. There were fourteen of them in the boat.

There was no boat leaving the fort for some time so I went to Mendota, crossing the Minnesota River in a canoe ferry. My business at Mendota was to present a letter of introduction to Mr. Sibley, Manager of the American Fur Trading Co., from the missionary board of Ohio and see how I could reach Lac qui Parle. I arrived at Mr. Sibley's home just about noon. He told me he had a boat leaving in two weeks and that I could go on her. He said he had several of these boats plying to Traverse des Sioux. He was a gentlemanly looking man and very pleasant spoken. With the courtliness that always distinguished him, he asked me if I had dined and being informed that I had not, invited me to do so; I replied, "I am obliged to you sir." I was told that the furniture of massive mahogany had been brought up the river by boat.

The table was waited upon by an Indian woman. The meal was bountiful. I had a helping of meat, very juicy and fine flavored, much like tenderloin of today, a strip of fat and a strip of lean. My host said, "I suppose you know what this is?" I replied, "Yes, it is the finest roast beef I have ever tasted." "No," said Mr. Sibley, "this is what we call 'boss' of buffalo and is the hump on the back of a young male buffalo." "Whatever it is, it is the best meat I have ever tasted," I declared.

Some dried beef on a plate on the end of the table was also delicious. Mr. Sibley again challenged me to tell what this was;—My reply being "dried beef." "No," said Mr. Sibley, "This too, is something you have never tasted before—it is boned dried beaver's tail. Over five thousand of them, as well as the skins have been brought in here during the year." There was also O'Donnell crackers and tea, but no bread. The tea, I was told, had been brought hundreds of miles up the river.

OLD RAIL FENCE CORNERS

I bade my host farewell, thanking him for his entertainment and thinking I had never met a more courteous gentleman. Mr. Sibley, too, had told me that the St. Louis house was the best place I could stay, so I returned there.

For my journey down the river, I had brought with me a tarpaulin and a few of my worldly goods. I hired a man with an ox-cart to take these to the boat before dawn the day it was to leave, preparatory to my early start at sunup. The boat was about sixty feet long and propelled only by hand power, furnished by French halfbreeds who pushed it with long poles from the front, running rapidly and then taking a fresh start to push it again. These boats could make about twenty miles a day. They almost reached Shakopee the first day. At ten o'clock the boat tied up and breakfast was served. This was a very hot, thick soup made of peas and pork which had been cooked all night over hot coals in a hole in the ground, covered snugly over with earth. It had been wrapped in a heavy tarpaulin and buffalo robe and when served was piping hot, as it came from this first fireless cooker. Hardtack was served with this soup and made a most satisfactory meal. The other meal consisted of bacon and hardtack and at the end of the eighth day, had become quite monotonous. Whenever these meals were prepared, the boat was tied to the bank.

The mosquitoes, even in the daytime were so terrible that it was almost impossible to live. I looked forward to the time when we would tie up for the night, with great apprehension on this account. However, the clerk of the boat came to me and asked me if I had a mosquito net with me and when I said, "No" invited me to sleep under his as he said it would be unbearable without one. Just before they tied up for the night the clerk came to me saying that he was sorry, but he had forgotten that he had a wife in this village. I spent the night in misery under my tarpaulin, almost eaten alive by the mosquitoes. The half breeds did not seem to mind them at all. I again looked forward to a night under the mosquito bar and was again told the same as the night before. During the eight days which this journey consumed, I was only able once to sleep a night under the friendly protection of this mosquito bar, as it was always required for a wife.

When the boat tied up at Traverse des Sioux, Mr. Williamson met me. The trader sent a man to invite the three white men to dine with him. The invitation was accepted with great anticipation. The trader's house was a log cabin. The furniture consisted of roughly hewn benches and a table. An Indian woman brought in first a wooden bowl full of maple sugar which she placed on one end of the table with bowls and wooden spoons at the three places. We were all eyes when we saw these preparations. Last, she brought in a large bowl of something which I could see was snow-white and put that in the center of the table. All were then told to draw up to the table and help themselves. The bright anticipations vanished when the meal was seen to consist solely of clabbered milk with black looking maple sugar.

Mr. Williamson left me at Traverse to go East. Before going he helped me load all our supplies into the two Red River carts which he had brought. There were six hundred pounds on each. The trail was very easy to follow and I walked along by the side of the slow going oxen. By keeping up until late, and getting up at daybreak, I made the trip in seven days. For the first four days I was followed by a great gaunt shape that made be uneasy. I knew if it was a dog it would have come nearer. I slept under the cart the first night, but was conscious of its presence as the cattle were restless. On the fourth day of its enforced company, I met a little caravan of carts owned by a Frenchman who was with the half breeds. I told him of my stealthy companion, and he sent some of the half breeds after it with their bows and arrows. They followed it four miles into a swamp and then lost it. They seemed suspicious about this particular animal, and went after it half heartedly. The trader gave me a piece of dough and told me if it came again to put this in meat and drop it. He said "Kill him quick as one gun."

My sister, Mrs. Huggins, wife of the farmer at Lac qui Parle, was overjoyed to see me. Think what it must have meant to a woman way off in the wilderness in that early day to see anyone from civilization, let alone her brother. I had not seen her in several years. They had a nice little garden and quite a patch of wheat, which I was told was fine for the climate. The seed came from the craw of a wild swan that they had shot. It was supposed to have come from the Pembina country for those people had wheat long before the missionaries came. It was always called "Red River Wheat."

Pemmican, which I first tasted on this journey was made by boiling the flesh of any edible animal, usually that of buffalo or deer, pounding it fine and packing it tight into a sack made of the skin of a buffalo calf, then melting the fat and filling all interstices. When sewed up, it was absolutely air tight and would keep indefinitely. It was the most nourishing food that has ever been prepared. For many years it was the chief diet of all hunters, trappers, explorers and frontiersmen.

Pemmican was also made by drying the meat and pulverizing it. The bones were then cracked and the marrow melted and poured into this. No white man could ever make pemmican right. It took a half breed to do it.

The Red River people had cattle very early. The stock at the mission at Lac qui Parle came from there.

I returned to Illinois in the summer of '43 and threshed. In the Fall I returned and built a house for Gideon Pond. It was a wooden house where their brick house now stands.

In 1844, I was building a mission building at Traverse. An Indian came in one day and told me there was a very sick man about twenty miles away at his camp. I went back with him and we brought the white man to the mission. After he was better, he told me that he was one of six drovers who had been bringing a herd of three hundred cattle from Missouri to Fort Snelling. They had lost their compass and then the trail and wandered along until they found a road near what is now Sauk Center. There they met a band of Sioux. The Indians killed a cow and when the drovers remonstrated, they killed one of them and stampeded the cattle. The drovers all ran for their lives. Two of them managed to elude the Indians, and took the road leading east. Our man was one, the other was drowned while crossing the river on a log raft, the rest were never found. Many of the cattle ran wild on the prairies. The Indians used often to kill them and sell the meat to the whites. One of the claims at Traverse de Sioux was for these cattle from the owners of the herd.

Mrs. Missouri Rose Pratt—1843.

In 1842 my father was going to the Wisconsin pineries to work, so mother and we children went along to keep house for him. We came from Dubuque to Lake Pepin. Mr. Furnell, from the camp, had heard there were white people coming so he came with an ox team down the tote road to meet us and our baggage, and take us to camp. We found a large log house which we thought most complete. We lived there that winter and Mr. Furnell and some others boarded with us. A romance was started there.

The next Spring we took our household goods in a cabin built on a raft, floated down to Nauvoo and sold the lumber to the Mormons. Joseph Smith was a smart speaker, mother said, when she responded to the invitation to hear the "Prophet of the Most High God" preach. The children of these people were the raggedest I have ever seen. Mr. Furnell had his raft lashed to ours and sold his lumber to them too.

We went to St. Paul on the Otter. Mr. Furnell went with us. When mother saw "Pig's Eye" as St.

OLD RAIL FENCE CORNERS

Paul was then called, she did not like it at all. She thought it was so much more lonesome than the pineeries. She begged to go back, but father loved a new country. On landing, we climbed up a steep path. We found only six houses there. One was Jackson's. He kept a store in part of it. In the kitchen he had three barrels of liquor with spigots in them. The Jackson's were very kind and allowed us to live in their warehouse which was about half way down the bluff. We only slept there nights for we were afraid to cook in a place with powder stored in it, the way that had, so we cooked outside.

My sister Caroline had light hair, very, very blue eyes and a lovely complexion. The Indians were crazy about her. It was her fairness they loved. She was engaged to Mr. Furnell and wore his ring. The Indian braves used to ask her for this and for a lock of her hair to braid in with theirs but of course, she would never let them have it. She was afraid of them. The interpreter told her to be careful and never let them get a lock of her hair for if they did and braided it in with theirs, they would think she belonged to them. One day when she was alone in the warehouse, an Indian came in his canoe and sat around watching her. When he saw she was alone, he grabbed her and tried to cut off some of her hair with his big knife. She eluded him by motioning to cut it off herself, but instead, ran shrieking to father at Jackson's. He came with a big cudgel but the Indian had gone in his canoe.

In the election of '43 in St. Paul, every man there got drunk even if they had never drunk before and many of them had not. Early in the evening, Mr. August Larpenteur came into Mrs. Jackson's kitchen to get a drink of liquor. He was a very young man. She said, "August, where's the other men?" just as he was turning the spigot in the barrel. He tried to look up and tell her, but lost his balance and fell over backward while the liquor ran over the floor. Then he laughed and laughed and told her where they were.

OLD RAIL FENCE CORNERS

We built a cabin a few miles out of town. Our nearest neighbors were the Denoyers who kept a halfway house in a three roomed log cabin. Their bar was in the kitchen. Besides this, there was a scantily furnished sitting room and bed room. Mrs. DeNoyer was a warm hearted Irish woman when she had not been drinking, but her warm heart never had much chance to show. They bought their liquors at Jackson's.

Our house was made from logs hewed flat with a broadax. My father was a wonder at hewing. The ax was eight inches wide and had a crooked hickory handle. Some men marked where they were to hew but father had such a good eye that he could hew straight without a mark. The cracks were filled with blue clay. For windows, we had "chinkins" of wood. Our bark roof was made by laying one piece of bark over another, kind of like shingles. Our floor was of puncheons. This was much better than the bark floors, many people had.

I used to take much pleasure in watching and hearing the Red River carts come squawking along. They were piled high with furs. The French halfbreed drivers would slouch along by them. It seemed as if the small rough coated oxen just wandered along the trail. Sometimes a cow would be used. I once saw one of these cows with a buffalo calf. It seemed to be hers. Was this the first Cataloo?

When I was nine years old my father sent me to the spring for a pail of water. I was returning with it, hurrying along as father had just called to me to come quick, when I was surrounded by a band of Sioux warriors on their way to Shakopee to a scalp dance. They demanded the water but I would not let them have it and kept snatching it away. It tickled them very much to see that I was not afraid. They called to the chief, Little Crow, and he too ordered me to give it to them, but I said, "No, my father wants this, you can't have it." At this the chief laughed and said, "Tonka Squaw" meaning brave woman and they left. They had on everything fancy that an Indian could—paint and warbonnets and feathers. They always wore every fancy thing they had to a dance, but in actual war, they were unpainted and almost naked.

The first soldiers I saw in 1843 were from Fort Snelling. They had blue uniforms with lots of brass buttons and a large blue cap with a leather bridle that they used to wear over the top. Their caps were wide on top and high. The soldiers used to come to De-Noyer's to dinner so as to have a change. Mrs. De-Noyer was a good cook if she would stay sober long enough.

We had splint bottom chairs made out of hickory and brooms made by splitting it very fine too. These were all the brooms we had in '43. Our hickory brooms were round but Mr. Furnell made a flat one for my sister.

Once when father was roofing our house, a storm was coming and he was very anxious to get the shakes on before it came. We had had a bark roof that was awful leaky. Some Indians came along on the other side of the river and made motions that he should come and get them with his boat, "The Red Rover." He sometimes ferried the soldiers over. As he did not answer or get off the house, they fired several shots at him. The bullets spattered all around him. He got down from the house and shot at them several times. After that, my mother was always afraid that they would come and shoot us when father was not home.

I have seen Indians run from Jackson's at sight of a soldier. They were afraid of them always.

My father brought some beautiful pieces of red morocco to Minnesota and the last piece of shoemaking he did, was to make that into little shoes for me. They had low heels such as the children have today.

My sister was married the first day of January in '44. We lived on the Main Road between St. Paul and St. Anthony. It just poured all day, so that none of the guests could come to the wedding. Mr. Jackson did get there on horseback to marry them, but Mrs. Jackson had to stay at home. The bride, who was a beautiful girl, wore a delaine dress of light and dark blue with a large white lace fichu. Her shoes were of blue cloth to match and had six buttons. She wore white kid gloves and white stockings. Her bonnet was flat with roses at the sides and a cape of blue lute-string. The strings were the same. Wasn't she stylish for a girl who was married New Years day in 1844?

The wedding dinner was fish, cranberry sauce and bread and butter.

One day a lot of Sioux Indians who were on their way to fight the Chippewas borrowed my sister's washtub to mix the paint in for painting them up. They got their colored clay from the Bad Lands. They were going to have a dance.

Hole-in-the-Day used to stay all night with us. He always seemed to be a friend of the whites. When the Indians first came to the house, they used to smoke the peace pipe with us, but later, they never did.

Bears and wolves were very plentiful. We had an outdoor summer kitchen where we kept a barrel of pork. One night a bear got in there and made such an awful noise that we thought the Indians were on a rampage. We often saw timber wolves about the house. They would come right up to the door and often followed my father home.

A French woman by the name of Mrs. Traverse lived near us. She came from Little Canada. Her husband bought some dried apples as a treat and she served them just as they were. Poor thing! She was very young when her baby came and she used to get wildly homesick. One day, she started to walk to Little Canada carrying her baby. A cold rain came on and she was drenched when she was only half way there. She took cold and died in a few weeks from quick consumption. Strange how so many who had it east, came here and were cured, while she got it here.

OLD RAIL FENCE CORNERS

In the Spring when the wheat was sprouting, the wild ducks and geese would light in the field and pull it all up. They would seize the little sprouts and jerk the seeds up. They came by batallions. I have seen the fields covered with them. They made a terrible noise when rising in the air. I have seen the sun darkened by the countless myriads of pigeons coming in the spring. They would be talking to each other, making ready to build their nests. In the woods, nothing else could be heard.

We had one wild pair of almost unbroken steers and a yoke of old staid oxen. The only way father could drive the steers was to tie ropes to their horns and then jump in the wagon and let them go. They would run for miles. I was always afraid of them. They were apt to stampede and make trouble in finding them if there was a bad storm. One evening father was away and a bad storm approached. I took the ropes and told mother I was going to tie the oxen. She begged me not to, as she feared they would hurt me. I had a scheme—I opened the front gate and as they came through the partly opened gate, threw the ropes over them and quickly tied them in the barn. The old oxen, I got in without any trouble. I tied them and went to reach in behind one, to close the barn door and bolt it. He was scared and kicked out, knocking me with his shod hoof. I did not get my breath for a long time. The calk of the iron shoe was left sticking in the barn door.

Some drovers stayed near us with a large drove of cattle in '45 or '46. They were on their way to the Red River of the north country. We kept the cattle in our yard and used to milk them. I picked out a cow for Mr. Larpenteur to buy as I had milked them and knew which gave the richest milk. He put her in a poorly fenced barnyard. She was homesick and bellowed terribly. The herd started on and was gone two days when she broke out and followed them and the Larpenteurs never saw her again. They had paid thirty dollars for her.

OLD RAIL FENCE CORNERS

I was very anxious to see the Falls of St. Anthony so in the summer of 1844, my brother borrowed an old Red River cart and an old horse from Mr. Francis who lived in St. Anthony. He drove it over to our house in the evening. The next day, Sunday, we put a board in for a seat and all three climbed onto it. We drove over and saw the Falls which roared so we could hear them a long way off and were high and grand. We did not see a person either going or coming the six miles although we were on what was called the Main Road.

The French people always kissed all the ladies on the cheek on New Year's day, when they made calls.

In the early day, Irvine built a new house of red brick. A little boy, Alfred Furnell, took a hatchet and went out to play. He got to hewing things and finally hewed a piece about a foot long out of the corner of that red brick house making it look very queer. His father asked him who did it. Unlike George Washington, he could tell a lie and said, "A little nigger boy did it." His father 'tended to the only little boy that was near, regardless of color.

Once there was a Sunday school convention in St. Paul. When lunch was called, Mr. Cressey, the minister, said, "Now, we will go out and have refreshments provided by the young girls who will wait on us. May God bless them, the young men catch them and the devil miss them."

They used to call my sister-in-law, "Sweet Adeline Pratt."

Mrs. Gideon Pond—1843, Ninety years old.

"In 1843 in Lac qui Parle, we had a cow. We paid thirty dollars to the Red River men for her. She had short legs and a shaggy black and white coat. She was very gentle. She was supposed to have come from cattle brought to Hudson Bay by the Hudson Bay traders.

In 1843 we visited the Falls of St. Anthony. There was only a little mill there, with a hut for the soldier who guarded it. The Falls were wonderful. I thought I had never seen anything more beautiful. The spray caught the sun and the prismatic colors added to the scene. The roaring could be heard a long way off.

We raised a short eared corn, that was very good and grew abundantly. I have never seen any like it since. Our flour was sent to us from way down the Mississippi. When we got it, it had been wet and was so mouldy that we had to chop it out with an ax. It took so much saleratus to make anything of it. We learned to like wild rice. It grew in the shallow lakes. An Indian would take a canoe and pass along through the rice when it was ripe shaking it into the boat until he had a boat full—then, take it to the shore to dry.

I was out to dinner with Mr. Scofield and his wife who came in '49. It was dark and stormy. Mrs. Scofield was first taken home and then Mr. Scofield started for our home. We soon found we were lost and drove aimlessly around for some time. We came to a rail fence. I said "Perhaps I can find the way". I examined this fence carefully and saw that one of the posts was broken, then said to Mr. Scofield, "I know just where we are now. I noticed this broken post when I was going to meeting Sunday." I soon piloted the expedition home.

In '43 when I was Mrs. Hopkins I was standing with Mrs. Riggs and Mrs. Huggins on the steps of the St. Louis house. The Gideon Ponds were then living in vacant rooms that anyone could occupy in this old hotel. Little three year old Edward Pond was standing with us. He and the little Riggs boy had new straw hats that we had bought of the sutler at the Fort. The wind blew his hat off suddenly. We did not see where it went but we did hear him cry. We could not find it in the tall grass. Mrs. Riggs took her little boy and stood him in the same place and we all watched. When the wind blew his hat off we went where it had blown and sure enough, there lay the other little hat too. The Indians standing around laughed long and loud at this strategy.

OLD RAIL FENCE CORNERS

Captain Stephen Hanks—1844, Ninety-four years old.

Captain Hanks, now in his ninety-fifth year, hale, hearty, a great joker and droll storyteller, as an own cousin of Abraham Lincoln should be, says: "In the spring of 1840, when a youth, I came north from Albany, Illinois, with some cattle buyers and a drove of eighty cattle, for the lumberjacks in the woods north of St. Croix Falls. We came up the east bank of the river following roads already made. In the thick woods near the Chippewa Falls, I found an elk's antlers that were the finest I ever saw. I was six feet, and holding them up, they were just my height. The spread was about the same. Of course, we camped out nights and I never enjoyed meals more than those on that trip. The game was so delicious.

In our drove of cattle was a cow with a young calf. When we came to a wide river, we swam all the cattle across, but that little calf would not go. We tried every way that we knew of to make it, then thought we would let it come over when it was ready. We rested there two days. The mother acted wild and we tied her up. The morning we were going to start, just as it was getting light, she broke away and swam the river. The calf ran to meet her but the mother just stood in the water and mooed. All at once, the calf took to the water and swam with the mother to the other side where it made a hearty breakfast after its two days fast. I thought I had never seen any animal quite so human as that cow mother.

When we got to St. Croix Falls, I thought it was a metropolis, for it was quite a little town. I was back and forth across the river on the Minnesota side too. In 1843, I helped cut the logs, saw them, and later raft them down the river to St. Louis. This was the first raft of logs to go down the St. Croix river. Lumber rafts had gone before. Our mill had five saws—four frame and one muley. A muley saw was a saw without a frame. It took a good raftsman to get a raft over the Falls. It took four St. Croix rafts to make one Mississippi raft. I got sixteen dollars a month and found, working on a raft. I was raised to twenty after a while and to two dollars a day when I could take charge.

In 1844 we had been up in the woods logging all winter on the Snake River. The logs were all in Cross Lake in the boom waiting for a rain to carry them down to the boom at St. Croix. There was a tremendous amount of them, for the season before, the water had been so low that it was impossible to get many out and we had an unusual supply just cut. One day in May, there was a regular cloudburst. We had been late in getting out the logs as the season was late. The Snake River over-ran its banks and the lake filled so full that the boom burst and away went all those logs with a mighty grinding, headed straight for the Gulf of Mexico.

They swept everything clean at the Falls. Took the millrace even. The mill was pretty well broken up too. We found some of them on the banks along and some floated in the lake. We recovered over half of them. We built a boom just where Stillwater is to-day, in still water. Joe Brown had a little house about a mile from there. There were the logs, and the mill at St. Croix was useless. McCusick made a canal from a lake in back and built a mill. The lumbermen came and soon there was a straggling little village. I moved there myself one of the first.

I used to take rafts of lumber down the river and bring back a boat for someone loaded with supplies. The first one I brought up was the Amulet in 1846. She had no deck, was open just like a row boat. She had a stern wheel.

In 1848, Wisconsin Territory was to be made a State. The people there wanted to take all the land into the new state that was east of the Rum River. We fellows in Stillwater and St. Paul wanted a territory of our own. As we were the only two towns, we wanted the capitol of the new territory for one and the pene-tentiary for the other. In the Spring—in May, I think, I know it was so cold that we slept in heavy blankets, the men from St. Paul sent for us and about forty of us fellows went over. We slept that night in a little hotel on one of the lower bluffs. It was a long building with a door in the middle. We slept on the floor, rolled up in blankets. The next day, we talked over the questions before mentioned and it was decided that we should vote against the boundary as proposed and have a new territory and that St. Paul should have the capitol and we the penetentiary. This decision was ratified at the convention in Stillwater, the last of August 1848.

The hottest time I ever had in a steamboat race was in May, 1857, running the Galena from Galena to St. Paul. A prize had been offered, free wharfage for the season, amounting to a thousand dollars, for the boat that would get to St. Paul first that year. I was up at Lake Pepin a week before the ice went out, waiting for that three foot ice to go. It was dreadful aggravating. There was an open channel kind of along one edge and the ice seemed to be all right back of it. There were twenty boats all waiting there in Bogus Bay. I made a kind of harbor in the ice by chopping out a place big enough for my boat and she set in there cozy as could be. I anchored her to the ice too. The Nelson, a big boat from Pittsburg was there with a big cargo, mostly of hardware—nails pretty much. There were several steamers that had come from down the Ohio. When the ice shut in, it cut the "Arcola" in two just as if it was a pair of shears and she a paper boat. She sank at once. It shoved the "Falls of St. Anthony" a good sized steamer way out of the water on the niggerheads. The "Pioneer" sank. It broke the wheels of the "Nelson" and another boat and put them out of commission. I stayed in my harbor until morning, then steamed away up the little new channel. The "War Eagle" locked us at the head of the lake and held on. I was at the wheel. When we came to Sturgeon Bay, I took a cut in through the bar. I had found it when I was rafting so I knew they did not know about it. That little advantage gained the day for us. As it was, we burned several barrels of resin and took every chance of meeting our Maker. We got to St. Paul at two o'clock in the morning. Such a hullaballoo as there was—such a big tar barrel fire. We could plainly see "Kaposia" six miles away.

Christmas the company sent me one hundred dollars which came in handy, as I was just married.

Mr. Caleb Dorr—1847, Ninety years old.

I came to St. Anthony in 1847 and boarded at the messhouse at first. Later I was boarding with the Godfrey's and trouble with the Indians was always feared by the new arrivals. One night we heard a terrible hullabaloo and Mrs. Godfrey called, "For the Lord's sake come down, the Indians are here." All the boarders dashed out in scant costume, crying, "The Indians are upon us," but it turned out to be only the first charivari in St. Anthony given to Mr. and Mrs. Lucien Parker. Mrs. Lucien Parker was a Miss Huse.

Mrs. Dorr was never afraid of the Indians, although they seemed very ferocious to her with their painted faces, stolid looks and speechlessness. One day she was frying a pan of doughnuts and had finished about half of them when she glanced up to see seven big braves, hideously painted, standing and watching her with what she thought was a most malevolent look. She was all alone, with nobody even within calling distance. One of the number looked especially ferocious and her terror was increased by seeing him take up a knife and test it, feeling the edge to see if it was sharp, always watching her with the same malevolent look. Quaking with fear, she passed the doughnuts, first to him. He put out his hand to take the whole pan, but she gave him a jab in the stomach with her elbow and passed on to the next. This occasioned great mirth among the rest of the

OLD RAIL FENCE CORNERS

Indians who all exclaimed, "Tonka Squaw" and looked at her admiringly. When they had finished, they left without trouble.

Once I was spending the evening at Burchineau's place when a number of the Red River cart men were there. As they were part Indian and part white, I looked down on them. One of them challenged me to see who could dance the longest. I would not let him win on account of his color, so danced until my teeth rattled and I saw stars. It seemed as if I was dancing in my sleep, but I would not give up and jigged him down.

I remember a dance in the messhouse in '48 when there were ten white girls who lived in St. Anthony there. They were wonderfully graceful dancers— very agile and tireless. The principal round dance was a three step waltz without the reverse. It was danced very rapidly. The French four, danced in fours, facing, passing through, all around the room, was most popular. The square dances were exceedingly vigorous, all jigging on the corners and always taking fancy steps. We never went home until morning, dancing all the time with the greatest vim. This mess house stood between the river and the front door of the old Exposition Building.

The Red River carts used to come down from Fort Garry loaded with furs. There had been a white population in that part of the country and around Pembina long before there was any settlement in what is now Minnesota. The drivers were half-breeds, sons of the traders and hunters. They always looked more Indian than white. In the early days, in remote places, where a white man lived with the Indians, his safety was assured if he took an Indian woman for his wife. These cart drivers generally wore buckskin clothes, tricked out so as to make them gay. They had regular camping places from twelve to fifteen miles apart, as that was a day's journey for these carts.

As there was not much to amuse us, we were always interested to see the carts and their squawking was endured, as it could not be cured. It could be heard three miles away. They came down the Main Road, afterwards called the Anoka road.

The lumber to face the first dam in '47 came from Marine. There had been a mill there since 1834, I believe.

We used to tap the maple trees in the forest on Nicollet Island. We had to keep guard to see that the Chippewas did not steal the sap.

The messhouse where I boarded, was of timber. It was forty feet square. It had eight or ten beds in one room.

Mrs. Mahlon Black—1848.

When I came to Stillwater in 1848, I thought I had got to the end of the line. I came up on the Sentinel with Captain Steve Hanks. He was captain of a raft boat then. It took ten days to come from Albany, Illinois. There was nothing to parade over in those days. We took it as it come and had happy lives. Stillwater was a tiny, struggling village under the bluffs—just one street. A little later a few people built in the bluffs and we would climb up the paths holding onto the hazelbrush to help us up. Stillwater was headquarters for Minnesota lumbering then. We would all gather together and in about two minutes would be having a good time—playing cards or dancing. The mill boarding house had the largest floor to dance on and we used to go there often. We used to waltz and dance contra dances. None of these new jigs and not wear any clothes to speak of. We covered our hides in those days; no tight skirts like now. You could take three or four steps inside our skirts, and then not reach the edge. One of the boys would fiddle awhile and then someone would spell him and he could get a dance. Sometimes they would dance and fiddle too.

We would often see bears in the woods. They were very thick.

When we staged it to St. Paul down the old Government Road, we would go down a deep ravine and up

again before we really got started. We paid a dollar
each way. Once they charged me a dollar for my little girl sitting in my lap. We used to pass Jack Morgan's.

Once we moved out on the Government Road,
three miles from Morgan's. It was a lonesome place.
The Chippewas and Sioux were on the warpath as
usual. A large party of Sioux camped right by us.
They were dressed for what they were going after, a
war dance, and were all painted and feathered. They
were looking in the windows always. It used to make
me sick to see their tracks where they had gone round
and round the house. My husband was on the survey
most of the time so I was there alone with my baby
a great deal. One Sunday I was all alone when a lot
of bucks come in—I was so frightened I took my
baby's little cradle and set it on the table. She had
curly hair and they would finger it and talk in their
lingo. When they left I took the baby and hailed the
first team going by and made them come and stay
with me. It was the Cormacks from St. Anthony. I
made my husband move back to Stillwater the next
day.

The Sioux killed a Chippewa father and mother
and took the son, twelve years old, captive. They had
the scalp dance in Stillwater and had the poor child
in the center of the circle with his father's and
mother's gory scalps dangling from the pole above
him. I never was so sorry for a young one.

Old Doctor Carli was our doctor. Our bill was
only one dollar for a whole year. If he had not had
money laid back, he could never have lived.

Once in the winter, Mrs. Durant and I were going
along, I was behind her. The boys were coasting and
went 'way out onto Lake St. Croix. They struck me
full tilt and set me right down in one of their laps and
away we went. I have always gone pell-mell all my
life. If it comes good luck, I take it—if bad luck, I
take it. Mrs. Durant went right on talking to me.
Finally she looked around and I had disappeared. She

was astonished. Finally she saw me coming back on that sled drawn by the boys and could not understand it. She only said, "Lucky it did not break your legs," when I explained.

Mr. James McMullen—1849.

Mr. McMullen, in his ninetieth year says—I started from Maine by the steam cars, taking them at Augusta. As I look back now, I see what a comical train that was, but when I first saw those cars, I was overpowered. To think any man had been smart enough to make a great big thing like that, that could push itself along on the land. It seemed impossible, but there we were, going jerkily along, much faster than any horse could run. The rails were wood with an iron top and after we had bumped more than usual, up came some of that iron through the floor. One lady was so scared that she dropped her traveling basket and all the most sacred things of the toilet rolled out. She just covered them quickly with the edge of her big skirt and picked them up from under that. The piece of iron was in the coach, but we threw it out.

We went by boat to Boston, then by rail to the Erie canal. We were ten days on a good clean canal boat and paid five dollars for board and our ticket. I don't remember how long we were on the lakes or what we paid. I should say two weeks. We landed at Chicago. It was an awful mudhole. The town did not look as big as Anoka. A man was sending two wagons and teams to Galena, so I hired them, put boards across for seats and took two loads of passengers over. We got pretty stiff before we got there. I was glad to get that money as I was about strapped. It just about bought my ticket up the river.

We bought tickets to St. Paul. Three of us took passage on the Yankee. She was really more of a freight than a passenger boat. She only made three trips to St. Paul that year. We bought wood along the way, anywheres we could see a few sticks that some settler had cut. The Indians always came down to see us wherever we stopped. I did not take much of a fancy to them devils, even then. It was so cold the fifteenth day of October that the Captain was afraid that his boat would freeze in, so would go no further and dumped us in Stillwater. Cold! Well, I should say it was pretty durned cold!

I had been a sailor, so knew little about other work. On the way up, I kept wondering, am I painter, blacksmith, shoemaker, carpenter or farmer? On voyages, the sailors always got together and discussed the farm they were to have when they saw fit to retire. Said farm was to be a lot with a vine-wreathed bungalow on some village street. Having talked this question over so much with the boys, I felt quite farmerfied, though I had never used shovel, hoe or any farm tool. I said to myself, I must find out what I am at once for I only have four shillings. My brother-in-law borrowed this, for it was agreed that he should go on to St. Paul. As I walked along the one street in Stillwater with its few houses, I saw a blacksmith shop with the smith settin' and smokin' and stopped to look things over. There were three yoke of oxen standing ready to be shod. They were used to haul square timbers. The smith asked me if I could shoe an ox and then slung one up in the sling 'way off the ground. I did not see my way clear to shoe this ox, so saw I was not a blacksmith. I could see that there were not houses enough around to make the paintin' trade last long so gave that up too. In a little leanto I saw a man fixing a pair of shoes. I watched him, but saw nothing that looked possible to me so said to myself, "Surely I am no shoemaker." Further I met a young man sauntering along the road and asked him about farming. Said he, "You can't raise nothing in this here country. It would all freeze up; besides the soil is too light." Well, thinks I, it takes money to buy a hoe anyway, so I guess I'm no farmer.

I went up to the hotel and stayed all night. My brother-in-law had left a tool chest with me. I was much afraid they would ask for board in advance, but they did not. In the morning, the proprietor said, "I have a job of work I want done—is that your chest?" I said, "Here is the key." "Then", said he, "you are a carpenter." I had worked a little at boat building so I let him say it. I worked sixteen days for him building an addition out of green timber. At the end of that time he asked what I wanted for the work. I did not know so he gave me $25.00 in shin plasters. It was Grocers Bank, Bangor, Maine money. All of the money here was then.

As soon as I got it, I hiked out for St. Anthony, where I took to building in earnest. I helped build the Tuttle mill on the west side in '50 and '51. Tuttle moved from the east side over to the government log cabin while it was building and I boarded with them there. I also built the mill at Elk River.

The first Fourth of July I was driving logs up above what is now East Minneapolis. We had a mill with two sash saws, that is, saws set in a sash. Settlers were waiting to grab the boards as they came from the saw. How long it took those saws to get through a log! A mill of today could do the same work in one-tenth the time. We could only saw five thousand feet a day working both saws all the time.

I helped build the Governor Ramsey which plied above the Falls and up the river. She was loaded with passengers each trip going to look over sites for homes. I also helped build the H. M. Rice. After the railroad was built, these boats were moved on land over the Falls and taken by river to the south where they were used in the war.

I first boarded at the messhouse of the St. Anthony Water Power Company. This messhouse was on a straight line with the front door of the Exposition Building on the river bank. All butter and supplies of that nature were brought a long distance and were not in the best of condition when received, so this messhouse was called by the boarders, "The Soap

Grease Exchange," and this was the only appellation it was known by in old St. Anthony.

The first sawmills put up in St. Anthony could saw from thirty to forty logs apiece, a day.

As there were absolutely no places of amusement, the men became great wags. One of the first things that was established by them was a police court of regulations with Dr. Murphy as judge. As there were no sidewalks, a stranger would be run in and have to pay a fine, such as cigars for the crowd, if he was found spitting on the sidewalks. Lawyer Whittle was fined two pecks of apples and cigars for wearing a stovepipe hat and so the fun went on, day after day.

Mr. Welles ran for Mayor and, as there was no opposition, the before mentioned wags decided to have some. A colored man, called Banks, had a barbershop that stood up on blocks. The boys told him he must run for Mayor in opposition. They told him he must have a speech, so taught him one which said, "Down, Down, Down!" and he was to stand in the door and deliver this. Just as he got to the last "Down" these wags put some timbers under the little building and gently turned it over in the sand. It took them half a day to get it up and get everything settled again, but in a town where nothing exciting was going on, this was deemed worth while.

If you had half a pint of whiskey in those days, and were willing to trade with the Indians, you could get almost anything they had, but money meant nothing to them.

I remember seeing tame buffalo hitched to the Red River carts. They seemed to have much the same disposition as oxen, when they were tame. The oxen on the Red River carts were much smaller than those of today and dark colored. The most carts I remember having seen passing along at one time, was about one hundred. These carts were not infrequently drawn by cows. The drivers were very swarthy, generally dressed in buckskin with a bright colored knit sash about the waist and a coonskin cap with a tail hanging down behind or a broad brimmed hat.

In '51 I built a mill at Elk River. Lane was the only white man living there. It was right among the Winnebagoes. They were harmless, but the greatest thieves living. They came over to our camp daily and would steal everything not nailed down. We used to feed them. We had a barrel full of rounds of salt pork. By rounds of pork, I mean pork that had been cut clear around the hog. It just fittted in a big barrel. Eli Salter was cooking for us. One night he had just put supper on the table. It was bread, tea and about twenty pounds of pork—about two rounds. There were seven of us and just as we were sitting down, four squaws came in. Nowadays they sing, "All Coons look Alike to me," but at this time all squaws looked alike to us. We could never tell one from the other. They ate and ate and ate. Eli said, "They seemed like rubber women." The table was lighted with tallow dips, four of them. Just as Salter was going to pick up that pork, each squaw like lightning wet her fingers and put out the candles. When we got them lighted again, them squaws and the pork was together, but not where we were. We just charged it to profit and loss.

Among them Indians was Ed, the greatest thief of all. He had been for yea at a school in Chicago and had been their finest scholar. The Indians were all making dugout canoes and found it hard with their tools. I had a fine adz and Ed stole it. I could not make him bring it back. I used to feed the chief well and one day I told him Ed had stolen my adz. He said, "I make him bring it back." Sure enough, the next day at dusk Ed sneaked up and thinking no one was looking, threw it in a pile of snow about two feet deep. We saw him do it, so got it at once. We never knew how the chief made him do it.

Once when I was building a mill up at Rum River we had to go to Princeton to get some things, so I started. I had to pass a camp of those dirty Winnebagoes. They had trees across for frames and probably two hundred deer frozen and hanging there. I was sneaking by, but the old chief saw me and insisted on my coming in to eat. I declined hard, saying I had had my dinner, but I knew all the time they knew better. I had on a buffalo overcoat and a leather shortcoat inside. In the tepee, they had a great kettle of dog soup, as it was a feast. Each one had a horn spoon and all ate out of the kettle. They gave me a spoon and I started in to eat. I did not touch it but poured it inside my inside coat for a couple of times. When I left the chief went and picked out one of the thinnest, poorest pieces of venison there was and insisted on my taking it. I was disgusted but did not dare refuse. A short distance away, I threw it in the snow which was about two feet deep off the trail. Shortly afterward I met the chief's son and was frightened, for I thought he would notice the hole and find what I had done. I watched him, but he was too drunk to notice and as it soon began to snow, I was safe. I guess the dogs got it.

Mrs. James McMullen—1849.

Mrs. McMullen says: When I first came to St. Anthony in 1849, there were no sandburrs. They did not come until after a flock of sheep had been driven through the town. We always thought they brought them. The sand was deep and yielding. You would step into it and it would give and give. It would seem as if you never could reach bottom. It would tire you all out to walk a short distance. We soon had boards laid down for walks. Lumber was hard to get, for the mills sawed little and much was needed. The sidewalk would disappear in the night. No one who was building a board house was safe from suspicion. They always though he had the sidewalk in his house.

When we first built our house I wanted a garden. My brother said, "You might as well plant seeds on the seashore," but we did plant them and I never had seen such green stuff. I measured one pumpkin vine and it was thirty feet long.

OLD RAIL FENCE CORNERS

Whenever the Red River carts came by, I used to tie the dog to the doorlatch. I did not want any calls from such rough looking men as they were. Those carts would go squawking by all day. Later they used to camp where the Winslow house was built. There would be large numbers there, a regular village. Once when I was driving with Mr. McMullen, one of them stopped by us and I said, "Oh, see that ox is a cow!"

In '49 or '50 the old black schoolhouse was the site of an election. I lived near enough to hear them yell, "To Hell mit Henry Siblee—Hurrah for Louis Robert." If those inside did not like the way the vote was to be cast, they would seize the voter and out the back window he would come feet first, striking on the soft sand. This would continue until the voter ceased to return or those inside got too drunk or tired to throw him out. The town was always full of rough lumberjacks at these early elections and for the day they run the town.

I used always to make twenty-one pies a week. One for every meal. I had two boarders who were friends of ours. Not that I wanted boarders, but these men had to stay somewhere and there was no somewhere for them to stay. Each took her friends to help them out. I was not very strong and cooking was hard on me. There was no one to hire to work. After a very hot day's work, I was sick and did not come down to breakfast. One of the boarders was not working. I came down late and got my breakfast. I set half of a berry pie on the table and went to get the rest of the things. When I came back, it was in the cupboard. The boarder sat reading. I thought I had forgotten and had not put it on, so set it on again and went for the tea. When I came back again, the pie was again in the cupboard and the boarder still studying the almanac. I said, "What are you doing to that pie?" He said, "Keeping it from being et! After this you make seven pies instead of twenty-one and other things the same and you won't be all wore out, we'll

37

only have them for dinner," and so it was. I suppose there were more pies on the breakfast tables of that little village of St. Anthony than there would be now at that meal in the great city of Minneapolis, for it was then a New England village.

Dr. Lysander P. Foster—1849.

I came to Minneapolis on the Ben Franklin. She was a wood burner and every time that her captain would see a pile of wood that some new settler had cut, he would run ashore, tie up and buy it. A passenger was considered very haughty if he did not take hold and help.

My father built his house partly of lumber hauled from Stillwater, but finished with lumber from here, as the first mill at the foot of First Avenue Southeast was then completed. It had one saw only and so anxious were the settlers for the lumber, that each board was grabbed and walked off with as soon as it came from the saw.

The first school I went to as a boy of fourteen, was on Marshall Street Northeast, between Fourth and Sixth Avenues. It was taught by Miss Backus. There were two white boys and seven half-breed Bottineaus. It was taught much like kindergarten of to-day—object lessons, as the seven half-breeds spoke only French and Miss Backus only English. McGuffy's Reader was the only text book.

The Indians were much like white people. The Sioux boys at their camp at the mouth of Bassett's Creek were always my playfellows. I spent many happy days hunting, fishing and playing games with them. They were always fair in their play. The games they enjoyed most were "Shinny" and a game played on the ice in the winter. A stick with a long handle and heavy smooth curved end was thrown with all the strength possible. Some could throw it over a block. The one throwing it farthest beat. I suppose what I call "shinny" was really La Crosse.

OLD RAIL FENCE CORNERS

What is now Elwell's Addition was a swamp. I have run a twelve foot pole down in many parts of it without touching bottom.

Mr. Secomb, the father of Methodism in Minneapolis, was going to St. Paul to preach. He took a dugout canoe from the old board landing. His friend, Mr. Draper, was with him. It was below the Falls where the river had rapids and rocks. They tipped over and were so soaked that St. Paul had to get along that day without them. It was considered a great joke to ask the dominie if he was converted to immersion, now that he practiced it.

The peculiarity of the swamp land in St. Paul was that it was all on a ledge and was only about two feet deep. You could touch rock bottom anywhere there, but here a swamp was a swamp and could be any depth.

In 1848 halfbreeds had gardens and raised famous vegetables up in what is now Northeast Minneapolis.

I once took my sister over on the logs to pick strawberries on the end of what is now Eastman Island. They were large, very plentiful and sweet. Almost every tree that grew anywhere in the new territory grew there. Black walnut grew there and on Nicollet Island.

Mrs. Silas Farnham—1849.

Mrs. Silas Farnham says: I came to St. Anthony in 1849. My husband had a little storehouse for supplies for the woods, across from our home on the corner of Third Avenue and Second Street, Southeast. A school house was much needed so they cleared this out and Miss Backus taught the first school there. It was also used for Methodist preachin'. Our first aid society was held there in '49.

I well remember the first Fourth of July celebration in 1849. The women found there was no flag so knew one must be made. They procured the materials from Fort Snelling and the flag was made in Mrs. Godfrey's house. Those working on it were Mrs. Caleb Dorr, Mrs. Lucien Parker, Misses Julia and

39

Margaret Farnham, Mrs. Godfrey and myself. I cut all the stars. Mr. William Marshall who had a small general store was orator and no one could do better. That reminds me of that little store. I just thought I'd laugh out loud the first time I went in there. There were packs of furs, all kinds of Indian work, hats and caps, tallow dips and more elegant candles, a beautiful piece of delaine for white women and shoddy bright stuff for the squaws, a barrel of rounds of pork most used up, but no flour, that was all gone. There was a man's shawl, too, kind of draped up. You know men wore shawls in them days; some hulled corn the Indians done, too, I saw. But to return to that first Fourth—it seemed a good deal like a Farnham Fourth, for the music which was just soul stirrin' was sung by them and the Gould boys. When the Farnhams all got out, it made a pretty big crowd for them days. Perhaps their voices wan't what you call trained, but they had melody. Seems to me nowadays some of the trained high-falutin voices has just got that left out. Seems so to me—seems so. All the Farnhams just sung natural, just like birds. Old Doctor Kingsley played the bass viol so it was soul stirrin' too. Margaret Farnham, the president of our first aid society married a Hildreth—Julia a Dickerson.

In '49 my husband paid a ten cent shin plaster for three little apples no bigger than crabs. I tried to make these last a long time by just taking a bite now and then, but of course, they couldn't hold out forever.

The Indians was always around, but we never minded them—always lookin' in the windows.

General William G. Le Duc—1850, Ninety-two years old.

I arrived at St. Paul on the steamboat Dr. Franklin. Among the travelers on board the boat were Mr. and Mrs. Lyman Dayton and a brother of Goodhue, the Editor of the Pioneer Weekly Newspaper. The principal, if not the only hotel at that time, was the Central, a frame building about twenty-four by sixty

feet, two stories kept by Robert Kenedy. It was used
as a meeting place for the legislature, court, and public offices, until something better could be built. Here
I found quarters, as did Mr. and Mrs. Dayton.

A few days after my arrival, I was walking along
the high bank of the river in front of the Central
House in conversation with a large robust lumberman
who had come out of the woods where he had been
all winter logging and was feeling very happy over his
prospects. Suddenly he stopped and looking down on
the flowing waters of the Mississippi, he exclaimed,
"See those logs." A number of logs were coming down
with the current. "What mark is on them? My God,
that is my mark!—the logs are mine! My boom has
broken! I am a ruined man." He went direct to the
hotel and died before sun down of cholera, the Doctor
said. He was hurriedly buried and there was a cholera panic in St. Paul. The next day while walking
in front of the hotel, Mrs. Dayton called from an open
window excitedly to me, "Come and help me quick.
Mr. Baker has the cholera!" (Mr. Baker was a boarder
at the Central and a school teacher at that time.) Mrs.
Dayton was frightened and said she had given him all
the brandy she had and must have some more. I got
more brandy and she insisted on his taking it, altho
he was then drunk. He recovered next day and I
have never heard of a case of cholera in Minnesota
since that time.

I hired a little board shack about twelve by sixteen feet at the Northeast corner of Third and Roberts
Streets, St. Paul, and put out my sign as Attorney and
Counselor at Law, but soon discovered there was little law business in St. Paul, not enough to sustain the
lawyers already there and more coming with every
boat. My business did not pay the monthly rent,
$9.00, so I rented a large house on the southwest
corner and started a shop selling books and stationery,
and in this succeeded in making a living.

On the 22nd day of July '50, a number of citizens
of St. Paul and some travelers chartered a little stern

wheel steamboat, the Yankee, and intended to explore the St. Peter River, now the Minnesota, if possible to its source, Big Stone Lake. We invited the ladies who wished to go, promising them music and dancing. A merry time was anticipated and we were eager to see the fertile valley, knowing it was to be purchased of the Indians and opened for settlement to the frontier settlers. The passengers were men mostly, but enough women went to form three or four cotillion sets. The clergy was represented by Rev. Edward Duffield Neill; the medical fraternity by Dr. Potts; statesmen by one who had been an Aide to General Harrison and later Ambassador to Russia; another was a graduate of Yale Law School and of West Point Military Academy; another, one of the Renvilles, had been interpreter for Nicollet; another was an Indian Trader, Joe La Framboise, who was returning to his post at the mouth of Little Cottonwood. He was noted for his linguistic ability and attainments and could acquire a talking acquaintance with an Indian language if given a day or two opportunity; another was a noted Winnebago halfbreed, Baptiste, whose Indian dress and habits attracted much attention.

As we entered the sluggish current of the St. Peters at Mendota, the stream was nearly bank full and it seemed like navigating a crooked canal. The first stop was at an Indian village, fifteen or twenty miles from the Mississippi, called Shakopee, or Little Six village. Our boat attracted a crowd of all kinds and conditions of Indian village population, not omitting Little Six who claimed toll for permission to navigate his river. His noisy demand was settled by the trader by some trifling presents, including some whiskey and we proceeded on our voyage up the river. The next stop was at Traverse des Sioux. Here there was a Missionary station in charge of Mr. Hopkins, from whom we bought the rails of an old fence for fuel. Next we landed at a beautiful level grassy meadow called Belle Prairie, where we tried to have a dance. The next landing was at the mouth of the Blue Earth River, called Mankato, where a tempting grove of young ash trees were cut for fuel. Here the passengers wandered about the grove while the boat hands were cutting and carrying the wood. Leaving the Blue Earth we slowly ascended the stream, hoping to arrive at the Cottonwood where La Frambois promised some fuel for the boat, but night overtook us and Captain Harris tied up to the bank and announced the voyage ended for want of fuel and that early in the morning he would return. Millions of mosquitoes invaded the boat. Sleep was impossible. A smudge was kept up in the cabin which gave little relief and in the morning all were anxious to return. I stationed myself on the upper deck of the boat with watch and compass open before me and tried to map the very irregular course of the river. It was approximately correct and was turned over to a map publisher in New York or Philadelphia and published in my Year Book.

Some time during this summer, I had occasion to visit the Falls of St. Anthony, a village of a few houses on the east side of the Mississippi River, ten miles Northwest of St. Paul. I crossed the river to the west side in a birch bark canoe, navigated by Tapper, the ferryman for many years after, until the suspension bridge was built. Examining the Falls, I went down to an old saw mill built by and for the soldiers at Fort Snelling and measured the retrocession of the fall by the fresh break of the rock from the water race way and found it had gone back one hundred and three feet which seemed very extraordinary until examination disclosed the soft sandstone underlying the limestone top of the falls.

Events and persons personally known to me or told me by my friend, Gen. Henry Hastings Sibley, who was a resident of Minnesota, years before it was a territory. He was the "Great Trader" of the Indians, a partner of the American Fur Co., and adopted into the Sioux Tribe or nation, the language of which he spoke as well or better than the Indians. He told

me that Little Crow, the chief of the Kaposia Band
of Sioux, located on the west side of the Mississippi
river, six miles below St. Paul, was a man of unusual
ability and discernment, who had chivalric ideas of
his duty and that of others. As an instance he told
me the following story. A medium of the tribe had a
dream or vision and announced that he would guide
and direct two young members of the tribe, who were
desirous of winning the right to wear an eagle's
feather, as the sign to all that they had killed and
scalped an enemy, to the place where this would be
consummated. He conditioned that if they would agree
to obey him implicitly, they would succeed and return
safely home to their village with their trophies. Little
Crow's eldest son, a friend of the whites, much beloved by all, and another young man were interested
in the venture. He took them into the Chippewa
country. They concealed themselves in some dense
bushes along a trail used by the Chippewas traveling
from camp to camp. Instructions were given that they
should fire from cover and on no account show themselves or pursue the Chippewa. They awaited silently in their ambush until two Chippewas came unsus-
pectedly along the path. When opposite, the Sioux
boys fired and the Chippewa in the lead fell dead. The
one in the rear fled with his gun over his shoulder and
was pursued instantly by young Little Crow with
tomahawk in hand. The Chippewa discharged his
gun backward as he ran and killed the young man as
he was about to bury his tomahawk in the Chippewa's
brain. Little Crow's comrade took the scalp of the dead
Chippewa, returned to Kaposia, reported to Little
Crow the death of his son and that his body had been
left where he fell. Little Crow at once summoned a
number of his tribe and went to the place where the
body lay, dressed it in Indian costume, placed the
corpse with his face to the Chippewa country in sitting position against a large tree; laid across his knees
the best double barreled gun in the tribe and left the
body in the enemies' country. When he came to Men-

dota and reported the facts to the "Great Trader," Sibley said, "Little Crow, why did you give your best gun and fine blankets and all that your tribe prize so highly to the Chippewas. Your son was dead; why leave his body to his enemies." Little Crow replied, "He was killed in the enemies' country and according to the custom of Indian warfare his enemies were entitled to his scalp; therefore I left his body. I left the gun and blankets that they might know they had killed a man of distinction."

Some years subsequently, Little Crow came to his death by carelessness on returning from a duck hunting expedition. Having stepped ashore from his canoe, he drew his gun out from the canoe, taking it by the muzzle. The gun was discharged into the bowels of the unfortunate chieftain. He was carried to his tent and sent a message to Sibley to come to him and bring with him the surgeon then stationed at Fort Snelling. When they arrived he said, "First I will see the surgeon," to whom he said, "I am not afraid of death. Examine my wound and tell me truly if there is a chance for life." The surgeon told him he had no possible chance for recovery; that he could do nothing but give him some medicine to relieve the pain. "For that I care not. I will now talk with the 'Great Trader,'" to whom he said, "My friend, I wish you to be present while I talk with my son to whom I must leave the care of my tribe." The son, the "Little Crow" who is known as the leading devil in the massacre of the the whites in 1862, was then a grown boy. The old chieftain said to him, "My boy, I must now die and you will succeed to the chieftaincy of the tribe. I thought it would have been the duty of your older brother, who was a good boy in whom I trusted and who I hoped would prove a good leader to the people, but he is dead, and I also must die, and leave you to succeed me. You have always been a bad boy, and I have asked the 'Great Trader' my friend to attend and listen to my last instructions to you and to advise you in all matters of interest to the tribe, and I wish you to take heed to his advice; he is my friend and the friend of my people and in all matters of importance I desire you to listen to his advice and follow his directions. Especially, I charge you never to quarrel with the whites. You may go now my son, and remember what I have said to you."

Then to Sibley, he said, "My friend, you have heard me talk to my wayward son. For my sake, look after his conduct and the welfare of my people, for I feel impressed to tell you that that boy will be the ruin of his people." The boy was the leader in the massacre of twelve hundred white men, women and children on the Minnesota frontier in 1862 and was shot and killed near the town of Hutchinson in 1863.

Another story of early time I had from Genl. Sibley concerned the claimant of the land and property which afterwards became and is now a part of the city of St. Paul, but was then known as Pigs Eye, so called because the eyes of the old voyageur for whom it was named were inclined somewhat in the manner of a pig.

Jospeh R. Brown had a trading post on Gray Cloud Island, sixteen miles below St. Paul and was a Justice of the Peace with unlimited jurisdiction. Pigs Eye, an old toughened voyageur and a young fellow, both claimed the same quarter section of land and agreed to refer their quarrel to Brown. Accordingly both appeared at his place on Gray Cloud and stated their cases to Brown. Brown knowing that he had no jurisdiction over land titles and seeing an opportunity for a joke, informed them that the one who first put up a notice that he would write and give them, would be entitled to possess the land. They must strip for the race and he would give them a fair start, which accordingly he did, by marking a line and causing them to toe the line, and then solemnly giving the word "Go" started the sixteen mile race and retired to his cabin to enjoy the joke. The young man started off at his best speed, thinking he had an easy victory before him, but the experienced old Pigs Eye, knowing it was a sixteen mile race took a stride he could keep up to the end and placed his notice first on the property; hence the first name of St. Paul was Pigs Eye. The second and real name was given by the Missionary Priest, Father Gaultier, who told me that having occasion to publish the marriage notice of Vitale Guerin, he had to give the little log confessional on the hill some name, and as St. Croix and St. Anthony and St. Peter had been honored in this neighborhood, he thought St. Paul should receive the distinction.

Mr. Reuben Robinson—1850.

Mr. Reuben Robinson, ninety-five years old, says: I came to St. Anthony and worked at the mill near St. Anthony Falls. A fine bathing place had been discovered near the mill and was much used by the few women and men of St. Anthony who came over in boats for the purpose. One day when I was at work I heard hollering and thought someone must have gone beyond his depth. I went out and looked around, saw nobody, but still heard the calling. I finally looked at a pile of logs near the Falls and there saw a man who was calling for help. I threw a rope to him several times which he finally was able to grasp and I hauled him in hand over hand. His clothing was all wet and bedraggled, but a straw hat was still on his head although it was so wet that the green band had run into the straw. No trace of his boat was ever found. As soon as he landed, he took a whiskey flask from his pocket and took a long pull, which disgusted me very much. I discovered that these long pulls were what was accountable for his trouble, as he had taken a boat when he was drunk and had gone too near the Falls.

When we came through Chicago, the mud was up to the hubs everywhere. Much of the time the bottom of the stage was scraping it. In one deep hole where the old road had been, a big scantling stuck up with these words painted on it, "They leave all hope who enter here."

OLD RAIL FENCE CORNERS

I remember killing a snake over seven feet long down near Minnehaha Falls. Snakes were very abundant at that time.

When I was in the Indian war, one of the Indian scouts showed me how to find the Indians' underground store houses. Only an Indian could find these. The soldiers had hunted for days without success, but the Indian succeeded in a short time and found a community store house holding several hundred bushels of corn. This was six feet under the ground and looked exactly like the rest of the ground except that in the center a small tuft of grass was left, which to the initiated showed the place.

I had a serious lung trouble and was supposed to have consumption as I was always coughing. After I was married my wife induced me to take the water cure. She kept me wrapped in wet sheets for several days. At the end of that time an abscess of the lungs was relieved and my cough was cured. This climate has cured many of lung trouble.

I have to laugh when I think how green I was about these western places. Before I left my old home at Troy, New York, I bought twelve dollars worth of fishing tackle and a gun, also quantities of cartridges. I never used any of them for the things here were much more up to date. When I went to church I was astonished. I never saw more feathers and fancy dressing anywhere.

In 1860 hogs were $2.00 a hundred and potatoes 14c a bushel.

Mrs. Samuel B. Dresser—1850.

We took a steamer from Galena to Stillwater, as everyone did in those days.

They were paying the Sioux Indians at Red Wing. A noble looking chief in a white blanket colored band with eagles feathers colored and beautifully worked buckskin shirt, leggings and moccasins was among them. He stands out in my mind as the most striking figure I ever saw. There was so much majesty in his look.

OLD RAIL FENCE CORNERS

We took a bateau from Stillwater to Clouse's Creek. My uncle came the year before and had a block house where Troutmere now is, four miles from Osceola and we visited him.

A little later when I was seven years old, we went to Taylor's Falls, Minnesota, to live. There were only three houses there. We rented one end of a double block house and school was held in the other end. Our first teacher in '51 and '52 was Susie Thompson. There were thirty-five scholars from St. Croix Falls and our own town. Boats came up the river to Taylor's Falls on regular trips.

In our house there was a large fireplace with crane hooks, to cook on. These hooks were set in the brick. We hung anything we wanted to cook on them. The fire was directly under them. My mother brought a crane that was a part of andirons, with her, but we never used that.

I was married when I was sixteen. My husband built a house the next year. The shingles were made by hand and lasted forty years. The enamel paint came from St. Louis and was as good as new fifty years afterward. The paper, too, which was a white background with long columns with flowers depending from the top, was good for forty years.

In Osceola there was a grist mill that cracked the grain.

The Delles House looks the same now as it did in '52 when I first remember it.

In '52 I saw a party of Chippewa Indians hiding in the rough ground near Taylor's Falls. They said they were going to fight the Sioux. Some white men came and drove them away. They killed a Chippewa. A Sioux warrior, looking for Chippewa scalps found the dead Indian, skinned his whole head and rode away with the white men, with the scalp in his hand, whooping and hollering.

There was a road from Point Douglas through Taylor's Falls to Fond du Lac. It went through Stillwater and Sunrise Prairie, too. I used to watch it as the Indians passed back and forth on it and wish I could go to the end of it. It seemed to me that Adventure waited there.

We used to go to dances and dance the threestep waltz and French four with a circle of fours all around the room, and many other old style dances, too. We put in all the pretty fancy steps in the cotillion. No prettier sight could be than a young girl, with arms circled above her head, jigging on the corners.

My wedding dress was a white muslin, made very full around the bottom and plaited in at the waist. My traveling dress was made the same. It was a brown and white shepherd check and had eight breadths of twenty-seven inch silk. That silk was in constant wear for fifty years and if it was not all cut up, would be just as good today. My shoes were brown cloth to match and had five or six buttons. I had another pair that laced on the outside. Nothing has ever fitted the foot like those side-lace shoes. My traveling cape was of black net with bands of silk—very ample looking. I wore a white straw bonnet trimmed with lavender. The strings were white lutestring and the flowers in front of the flaring rim were small and dainty looking. There was a wreath of them on the crown too. When I tied this bonnet on, I felt very grown up for a sixteen year old bride.

Mr. Luther Webb, Indian agent, used to visit us often.

The Indians were always very curious, and spent much of the time before our windows watching everything we did. In time we were as calm with those glittering black eyes on us as we would have been if a gentle old cow had been looking in.

Mrs. Rufus Farnham—1850.

I moved to the farm on what is now Lyndale Avenue North, sixty-four years ago. The Red River carts used to pass along between my home and the river, but I was always holding a baby under one arm and drawing water from the well, so could not tell which way they went. I only saw them when they were straight in front of me. Women in those days never had time to look at anything but work.

Sugar came in a large cone. It was cracked off when needed. When purchased, a blue paper was wrapped around it. This when boiled, made a dye of a lovely lavender shade. It was used to dye all delicate fabrics, like fringe or silk crepe. I have a silk shawl which I dyed in this way in '56 that still retains its color. Later I paid 50c for three teacups of sugar. This just filled a sugar bowl.

My mother used to live on First Street North. Once when I was spending the day with her a dog sled from Fort Garry, now Winnipeg, passed the house. There were never many of these after we came for it seemed that the Red River carts had taken their places. There were six dogs to this team. They laid down and hollered just in front of the house. I suppose they were all tired out. The halfbreed driver took his long rawhide whip and give them a few cracks and they got up and went whimpering on to St. Paul. When they were rested, they would come back from St. Paul, like the wind. It only took a few days for them to come and go, to and from the fort, while it took the carts many weeks. The drivers would have suits of skin with the hair inside. They never forgot a bright colored sash. A bridal couple came with a dog team once, after I moved here, but the sled I saw only had a load of fine furs.

I made sour emptyings bread. Very few could make it. I stirred flour, sugar and water together until it was a little thicker than milk, then set it aside to sour. When it was thoroughly sour, I put in my saleratus, shortening and flour enough to make it stiff. It took judgment to make this bread, but everyone thought there was nothing like it.

Captain John Van der Horck—1850.

I always relied on an Indian just as I did on a white man and never found my confidence misplaced. I often went hunting with them on the sloughs out of St. Paul. Game was very plentiful. My Indian com-

panion and I would both have a gun. He would pad-
dle the frail canoe. We would see the game. "Bang!"
would go my gun. "Bang!" would go his. I would be
loading while he was shooting. All game was plenty,
plenty.

Well I remember the woodcock, long bill, big, big
eyes—look at you so trustingly I never could shoot
them.

There were such mighty flocks of ducks and geese
in season that their flight would sound like a train of
cars does now. Once I went deer hunting and saw
six does. They turned their beautiful faces towards
me and showed no fear. I could not shoot them.

I have seen strings of those Red River carts and
many, many in a string, loaded with furs coming from
Fort Garry or Pembina.

Mrs. James Pratt—1850.

My father moved to Minnesota Territory in '50.
We lived with my uncle, Mr. Tuttle, who had a mill
for some time on this side. He was living in a small
house belonging to the government, but my father and
he added two more rooms so we could stay with them.
In the spring my father took up land and built a house
down by the river not far from the Minnehaha Falls.
He began to work on the Godfrey mill at Minnehaha.
My mother was very timid. The sight of an Indian
would nearly throw her into a fit. You can imagine
that she was having fits most of the time for they were
always around. Timber wolves, too, were always
skulking around and following the men, but I never
knew them to hurt anyone. Father said it used to
make even him nervous to have them keep so near
him. They would be right close up to him, as close as
a dog would be. He always took a lively gait and
kept it all the time. One night father was a little late
and mother had seen more terrifying things than usual
during the day, so she was just about ready to fly.
She always hated whip-poor-wills for she said they
were such lonesome feeling things. This night she
stood peering out, listening intently. Then she, who

had tried so hard to be brave, broke into wild lamentations, saying, she knew the wolves or Indians had killed father and she would never see him again. My grandmother tried to calm her, but she would not be comforted until father came, then he had a great time getting her settled down. She said the whip-poor-wills seemed to say as she looked out in the blackness of the night, "Oh, he's killed—Oh, he's killed." What these timid town bred women, used to all the comforts of civilization, suffered as pioneers, can never be fully understood. After that, whenever father was late, little as I was, and I was only four, I knew what mother was going through and would always sit close to her and pat her.

Our home only had a shake roof and during a rain it leaked in showers. My little sister was born just at this time during an awful storm. We thought it would kill mother, but it did not seem to hurt her.

The Indians used to come and demand meat. All we had was bacon. We gave them all we had but when they ate it all up they demanded more. We were much frightened, but they did not hurt us. Father used to tap the maple trees, but we could not get any sap for the Indians drank it all. That winter we lived a week on nothing but potatoes.

Our nearest neighbor was Mrs. Wass. She had two little girls about our ages. They had come from Ohio. We used to love to go there to play and often did so. Once when I was four, her little girls had green and white gingham dresses. I thought them the prettiest things I had ever seen and probably they were, for we had little. When mother undressed me that night, two little green and white scraps of cloth fell out of the front of my little low necked dress. Mother asked at once if Mrs. Wass gave them to me and I had to answer, "No." "Then," she said, "in the morning you will have to take them back and tell Mrs. Wass you took them." I just hated to and cried and cried. In the morning, the first thing, she took me by the hand and led me to the edge of their plowed field and made me go on alone. When I got there, Mrs. Wass came out to meet me. I said, "I've come to bring these." She took me up in her arms and said, "You dear child, you are welcome to them." But my mother would not let me have them. I never took anything again.

We had a Newfoundland dog by the name of Sancho, a most affectionate, faithful beast. A neighbor who had a lonely cabin borrowed him to stay with his wife while he was away. Someone shot him for a black bear. No person was ever lamented more.

In '54 my father built the first furniture factory at Minnetonka Mills. Our house was near it. The trail leading from Anoka to Shakopee went right by the house and it seemed that the Indians were always on it. There were no locks on the doors and if there were, it would only have made the Indians ugly to use them. Late one afternoon, we saw a big war party of Sioux coming. They had been in a scrimmage with the Chippewas and had their wounded with them and many gory scalps, too. We ran shrieking for the house but only our timid mother and grandmother were there. The Sioux camped just above the house, and at night had their war dance. I was only seven years old at the time, but I shall never forget the awful sight of those dripping scalps and those hollering, whooping fiends, as they danced. I think they must have been surprised in camp by the Chippewas for they had wounded squaws, too, with them. One old one was shot through the mouth. The men were hideously painted. One side of one's face would be yellow and the other green. It seemed no two were exactly alike.

One Sunday morning I was barefoot, playing in the yard. There were bushes around and I heard a queer noise like peas rattling in a box. I could not see what made it, so finally ran in and told father. He came out and lifted up a wide board over two stones. He jumped back and called to me to run in the house, then grabbed an ax and cut the head off a huge rattlesnake. It had ten rattles. We never saw its mate.

The first school taught in Minneapolis proper was taught by Clara Tuttle, a niece of Calvin Tuttle, in one of the rooms of the government log cabin where we were living in '51. The pupils were her cousins. Miss Tuttle returned to the east the next summer and died of consumption. My cousin Luella Tuttle, the next year used to go over to St. Anthony to school, on the logs, jumping from one to the other, rather than wait for the ferry.

In '58 we returned to Minneapolis to live. Old Dr. Ames was our doctor. He was one of the finest men that ever lived. I had terrible nose bleeds. His treatment was to whittle pine plugs and insert them in the nostrils. It always cured. No matter how poor a patient was, Dr. Ames always did his best. No child was ever afraid of him. He was very slow in his movements.

Mrs. Mary Harrison—1850.

I came to Minnesota from Maine. I had never been on the railroad or seen a train, so when I saw what I thought then was the most awe inspiring and stupendous mechanism there was ever going to be in the world, I took my seat with elation and bumped along on that crazy track with the greatest joy. I took no thought of danger. Now I should want an insurance of $100,000 to ride a block under those circumstances. The rails were of wood, with an iron top. I have heard my friends say that these iron pieces sometimes came up through the floor. We went by water to Boston, again by rail and then by the Erie Canal and Great Lakes.

We landed at Milwaukee. It was a little town. They were just building their first sidewalks then. I can shut my eyes and see those little narrow walks now. We drove in wagons with boards across for seats from Milwaukee to Galena. Weren't those seats easy!

Somewhere in Wisconsin we stopped at a little log hotel over night. We knew that rattlesnakes abounded in this region as we had seen them on our way. There were holes all around the base of the room. We took off our petticoats, of which every little girl had several, and stuffed them in the holes, shaking them carefully the next morning to see that there were no enquiring friends of the snake tribe rolled up in them.

We took the Nominee at Galena. After the high bluffs began, the scenery was magnificent. At a trading station called La Crosse, fifty Indians came on board. One chief in a white blanket I have always remembered. He was certainly majestic looking. A little two year old tot had his ears pierced from top to bottom and common wire with three cornered pieces of shiny tin run through all the places. His eyes were very black, shiny and bright, but we could not raise a smile from him. That chief was all porcupine quill and bead embroidery. He was painted, too, as were all the rest. St. Paul, after we had climbed that awful flight of stairs up the bluff, looked like a little town that had been left. Our carriage to St. Anthony was a light express wagon with more boards across for seats. When we came to University Hill in St. Paul, there were no houses in sight, but oh! what a beautiful place it was! We did enjoy that drive. We stopped at De Noyers to water the horses. This was a little tavern between the two little towns.

When we came to the ravine in St. Anthony, with its little cascades, father said, "I have not a doubt that the time will come when it will be settled through here." We all thought it was very grand of father to take such a long shot as that.

When we reached St. Anthony, the people were lovely to us. We did begin to feel at home at once. We had to find a place to live. One of them went with us to the "Stranger's House," a slab house standing near the falls. Anyone who came and had no place to live was welcome to live in this house until they had a home of their own. This was why it was called the "Stranger's House.". The Mousseau's, a

OLD RAIL FENCE CORNERS

French Red River family were living in one half of it. We scrubbed it out and moved in. Mother sewed some loops on some quilts and made two bedrooms. We told her she was a fine carpenter. We did have lots of fun in our family. The floor was rough boards, but we planed them off by scrubbing with white sand. When the floor was dry, we always sprinkled it with white sand. The slabs were put on lengthwise, and there were always rows of bright Indians' eyes like beads on a string watching us through these cracks. My brother had smallpox in this house. We never knew how it came, but come it did. Dr. Murphy when he first saw him said it was measles or smallpox, but he vaccinated us all. It took just lovely. In those days they used a scab from the arm of someone who had been vaccinated. My brother took quantities of penny-royal tea and no other medicine. He came through fine.

On the Fourth of July we went to a dancing party or ball at the hotel. We did have a beautiful time— Mrs. Northrup was a lovely cook. I remember the butter was in the shape of a pineapple with leaves and all. We danced contra dances, such as "The Tempest" and Spanish dances. The waltz, too, with three little steps danced very fast, was popular. We took hold of our partner's elbows.

I taught the first school at Shingle Creek when I was a girl of seventeen. My school house was a claim shanty reached by a plank from the other side of the creek. My boarding place was a quarter of a mile from the creek. The window of the school house was three little panes of glass which shoved sideways to let in the air.

One afternoon just before time to dismiss the school, the windows were darkened by the faces of savages looking in. Each carried a gun and the terror inspired by them was very great as they were not the friendly faces of the Indians we were used to. The children all flocked around me. I went on hearing their lessons and then told them to sing. The Indians appeared delighted with this and laughed and talked with each other. After school, with the children clustered around me, I took an atlas and went out and showed the Indians the pictures. I knew they were very fond of looking at pictures. They all stayed until the last picture had been shown and the leaves turned again and again and then with a friendly glance at me and my little flock, strode off and I never saw them again.

The only time I ever fished was when I was teaching this school. I went with friends to the mouth of Shingle Creek. I did not know how to go at it when the pole and line were given to me. I asked what I should do and they told me if I felt my line pulling, to throw it over my head as quickly as I could. I was standing before some thick hazel brush and when I felt a tug, I did as I was told, landing on my back in the hazel brush at the same time. However, the largest black bass that the fishermen had ever seen was on my hook in the hazel brush. They thought it weighed over four pounds.

My little sister was taken to a revival meeting in the old church in St. Anthony. She was about as big as a minute and understood nothing of what was going on but was very wise looking. The minister did not slight even this atom, but asked her if she had found Jesus. She said hastily, "I didn't know he was lost."

Mr. William W. Ellison—1850.

Mr. Ellison now in his ninety-third year, with a perfect memory says:

I came to Minnesota with a determination to lead an outdoor life as my lungs were giving me much trouble. One of the first things I did was to take a yoke of oxen to Traverse to meet Mr. Williamson who was a missionary at Lac qui Parle. It was in November. I was new at this kind of work. The oxen were delivered to me at Fort Snelling. I crossed the river in a canoe and swam the oxen across to Mendota. Then I went on towards Shakopee. There was a well worn Indian trail leading along the Minnesota River and I followed that. I went through Black Dog's village. I started late in the afternoon.

A young couple had been married at Mendota a few days before and had gone on ahead. I expected to catch up with them. My oxen were most tractable and the country through which I passed very beautiful. The trail led along a ridge.

My Uncle, Mr. Williamson, had always told me to make my camp early while there was plenty of light, so not seeing or hearing anything of the other wagon, I made my camp where an old Indian camp had been and prepared to spend a comfortable night in the woods. I cooked my supper and then turned in. The wind had come up and I soon became very chilly, so I looked around for a warmer place. I found a windfall and made myself a nice little fire by crossing the trunks and building a fire under them. I spent the next four hours in comfort, though it was very cold. My uncle had told me to start with the first rays of the sun. I had no timepiece, so when I saw a glow in the east, I got up, ate my breakfast and started. It was not long before I saw that my dawn was a prairie fire. I had not gone far when I heard a horse neighing and soon found my Mendota friends. They had not understood how to camp so were nearly frozen to death. Their wagon had broken down when they were in a swamp. They had taken what little bedding they had and camped on a knoll in this swamp. I surely was sorry for that bride. Her husband had had a chill early in the evening before they camped. She had been up with him all night and now thought he was dying. I thought he was too. I tried to make a fire out of the wet willow wood there, but could not and he got bluer and bluer. We used all the blankets we had. Finally I said, "You lie down on one side of him and I will on the other." After some time his teeth stopped chattering and his color returned. I think it would have been the last of him if I had not found them as I did.

I tried to fix the cart but could not. A half breed who was driving for them had gone on to Shakopee for help, taking one horse the night before. I started on with my oxen to bring help. When I got nearly to Shakopee, I met a half breed, John Moores, going to their help. I waited for them in Shakopee. McLeod's boat came along and they took that as they could not get their cart mended well. I could make about twenty miles a day walking with my oxen. I stayed one night in the big woods at Belle Plaine. The wolves were very thick, so I hung my food on a sapling and leaned it against a tree. When I got to the crossing at Traverse, it was dark. I hollered. I could hear someone say, "That must be Ellison." Then they came over for me. The Hopkins' and Huggins' had the mission station there then. It did seem good to get where I had a square meal. I had been living principally on a sweet biscuit my Aunt, Mrs. Williamson, the missionary's wife at Kaposia made. Don't ever take anything sweet to eat for any length of time.

Martin McLeod met the boat with a string of Red River carts. They were loaded with furs and were to take supplies back. It was very interesting to me to watch the loading and unloading of this boat. I was not yet familiar with those half breed drivers. They seemed sociable fellows, among themselves, laughing, joking and talking in their lingo.

The boat had brought a barrel of flour, one of pork and other supplies for the Mission at Lac qui Parle, so after spending a week at Traverse waiting for the train to start, I took these in a cart drawn by one ox and started with the rest on Monday morning. The Dressers had their cart which I had managed to fix and their team of horses. I started with them and the string of carts. I could see the trail two miles ahead. It had to go around the sloughs. The cart train of course followed it. I soon saw the sloughs were frozen and would bear my ox and wide wheeled cart where it was not deep, so I cut across. When Mrs. Dresser was getting dinner, I appeared and ate with them. They could not understand how I could keep up with horses. The train was several miles back. We all camped together at night. The first night was spent on the border of Swan Lake. The trail followed a straight line from Traverse to Lac qui Parle, except for these sloughs.

Saturday night we camped at Black Oak Lake, twelve miles from Lac qui Parle. In the morning, McLeod and his train went on, but we stayed and kept the Sabbath, arriving the next day.

The first Indian I ever shook hands with was Little Crow at Kaposia, his village. He was common looking even for an Indian. My uncle, Dr. Williamson said, "He is the smoothest Indian I know. Usually when I am told a lie once, I look out for that liar and never trust him again, but Little Crow has fooled me with his lies a dozen times and I suppose he will a dozen times more."

When I first knew John Otherday he was a savage with all a savage's instincts. My uncle, Mr. Williamson said to me one night, "We'll lock the cattle up tonight; Oupeto Topeca, later Otherday, is back from Washington and feels very much abused. He might kill them." When he became a Christian all this was changed. He never forgot his religion for a moment. At the time of the outbreak he led a party of refugees at the greatest risk to himself through the back country to Shakopee. I think there were over forty in the party.

I used to walk fifty miles a day with ease, and could keep it up for several days. I never walked in moccasins, for they gave no support to the feet; but a soldier's shoe, bought at the fort for $2.00 was ideal to wear. It had a long, heavy sole leather sole, a very low heel and heavy leather all hand sewed, for the uppers.

The Northwestern Fur Company's trail started from New Cave, now St. Paul, and followed the Mississippi River through St. Anthony to Anoka. It forded the Rum River at Anoka, near the Mississippi, fol-

OLD RAIL FENCE CORNERS

lowing as nearly as possible that river to St. Cloud, where it crossed at a ford. It then followed the Sauk River about eleven miles; then turned to the right and crossed Big Bend forty-five miles, striking the river again four miles north from Sauk Center. Then it passed through the timber to Alexandria. It crossed Red River near Fort Abercrombie; then went directly north to Pembina, passing from point to point of the Red River of the North. The Red River carts had wheel rims eight inches wide. I have seen them with solid wheels cut from a single round of a tree. I have heard that the carts around Pembina were formerly all like this, but in my day they generally had spokes. I suppose they were lighter. It was the width of wheel and sagacity of the animal that made it possible to go with security over the most impossible roads. They usually carried eight hundred pounds. When they reached St. Paul they camped where Larpenteur's home now is.

I never knew an Indian who had been converted to go back on the whites. Some people would sell them a pair of pants, for a Christian Indian could vote and then say as they saw them so dressed, "There is a Christian Indian." It took more than a pair of pants to Christianize an Indian, but when they were once converted, they stayed so, as the many people who were saved by them in the massacre could testify.

Mr. D. E. Dow—1850.

In 1850 when I first came to Minnesota, I took a claim at Lake Harriet near where the pavilion now stands. The ruins of the old Steven's Mission were on my claim. It had been built in 1834. I did not keep this claim long, though I built a log cabin there and kept bachelor's hall, but soon took a claim where my present house stands in Hopkins. I built a cabin here but boarded with a widow and her children. All the food we had was game, pork and buckwheat cakes. The buckwheat they had brought from their home and it was all ground in the coffee mill then sifted through a horsehair sieve before it could be used. There were

seven in the family to grind for, so it kept one person
grinding all the time.

I was supposed to live alone in my cabin but
hardly ever spent a night without the companionship
of some Sioux Indians who were hunting around
there. I gladly received them as they were friendly,
and their company was much better than none. One
winter they came in such numbers that at night the
floor was entirely covered by their sleeping forms.
Early in the morning, they would go out and all day
hunt the deer, with which the woods abounded. It
was very cold and the slain deer froze immediately.
They stacked them up, making a huge pile. Suddenly
all the Indians left. One morning shortly after, I was
working in the clearing around my cabin, when I saw
a line of squaws which I think was a block long, coming over the trail which led from Shakopee to Hopkins.
The squaws went to the pile of deer. Each took one
on her back and silently trudged away over the trail
toward Shakopee. Some of the squaws were so small
that the frozen carcass had to be adjusted by another
squaw or it would drag on the ground. They were
two weeks removing this pile of deer and had to walk
twenty-eight miles with each one before they got
home with it.

When I first made my way to Minnetonka, I came
out at Gray's Bay. There were vast numbers of Indian mounds there and bark sheds for drying fish.
This was in '53.

An Indian trail led along the shore of Lake Calhoun just above where the street car track is now. It
continued on the high ground to the Mission at Lake
Harriet. I killed a deer at what had been the Mission
ground the first time I ever saw the lake. The trail
continued on the high ground around Lake Harriet.
There were fishing trails, too, around the lakes near
the water, but the trails ordinarily used were on high
ground where there was no fear of ambush. Another
trail was north of Lake Calhoun and led to Hopkins,
then to Shakopee, Little Six Village. The opposite

shore was a big swamp. Another much used trail followed along the highlands of the Mississippi River to the fort sawmill which stood near where the old Union Station was in Minneapolis. The reservation on which the fort stood was ten miles square and included all the present site of Minneapolis. This is why that city was so long without settlers, although the water power was the finest to be found anywhere.

Mrs. Elizabeth Clifford—1850.

My father had asthma terribly and was advised to come to Minnesota for his health. He arrived in Stillwater with his family and a stock of goods in 1850. He exchanged these for land six miles out of that town and two and one half miles off the main traveled road leading to Marine. We had a very fine barn and comfortable home made of lumber from the Stillwater Mills. Our nearest neighbor was two and one-half miles away, Mr. Morgan who kept the halfway house, but I cannot remember that I was ever lonesome.

We spent much time in the woods, where we found the most wonderful wild flowers. There was not a tame flower known to us whose counterpart we could not find in our woods. Of vegetables I remember best a small pink eyed potato, the most delicious I have ever tasted. As they baked, they could be heard popping in the oven. They are not raised now. The wild plum found in the woods my father cultivated and they were as large as small eggs and looked like small peaches.

One day as I glanced from the window, I saw a body of Indian warriors coming on the trail that led around the lake near us. As they came up, I saw they were in full war paint and feathers. They entered, examined everything, but took nothing. They asked for and ate bread and molasses, as they had seen the children doing when they came in. They all had guns and big bowie knives sticking in their belts. One particularly villainous looking one took out his knife and felt the edge, looking wickedly at us. One was exceptionally pleasant looking and I thought he would protect

SURVIVORS WHO WERE AT TRAVERSE DES SIOUX AT THE
TIME OF THE TREATY IN 1851.

Mrs. Richard Chute, General William G. Le Duc and Mrs. Gideon Pond.
Mrs. Morris is standing by General Le Duc.

Taken at a Celebration given in their honor July 17, 1914, by the
Old Trails Chapter, at the home of Mrs. M. W. Savage.

us if the rest got ugly. They finally went away. They were followed in the afternoon by a band of Chippewa braves who asked if the Sioux warriors had been that way that day. When told they had, they rode hurriedly after them. They said the Sioux had taken some Chippewa scalps.

Mrs. Richard Chute—1851.

I came to Minnesota a bride in 1851 and with my husband shortly afterwards took the steamer for Traverse de Sioux, where a great treaty with the Indians was to be signed. With us we took a tent, provisions and a French man to cook. I was the only woman in all the company.

It was all so wonderful to me—the beautiful country through which we passed and the preparations made for all the company on landing.

The Indians, a great concourse of them were down to see the boat come in. To see them scamper when the boat whistled was a sight to be remembered. Some fell in the water, but fled as soon as they could get themselves out. I think this was the first steamboat they had ever seen. They were frightened and curious at the same time.

Ten years before, at my home in Ohio, I had seen the Indians often as they would stop at our house for food on the way to Fort Wayne. My mother always cooked corn dodgers for them and gave them milk to drink. They loved her and knew she was their friend. They always gave me strings of vari-colored glass beads. I think I had one of every color.

These Indians at Traverse made me feel at home at once and I gave them a friendly smile. The glances they returned were shy, but friendly. Their painted faces and breasts and gaudy clothes were different from our Indians. Their tepees stretched as far as the eye could see. It seemed that the squaws must have had instruction in embroidery from some civilized teacher. Their patterns were so intricate. Their colors so well placed. Their moccasins were always beautifully done with beads and colored porcupine quills; their best petticoats, too. As for their liege lords, their best suits, if suits they might be called, were beautifully done. A young squaw, instead of pouring out her love in song, would pour it out in embroidery and her husband would be very gay, indeed.

Mrs. Hopkins, wife of the missionary, met us and took us home with her where we were very well cared for. She was a charming little woman, full of missionary zeal and greatly loved. I never heard her complain. Her husband, too, was greatly beloved by the Indians.

We took our stores and cooked there and with fresh vegetables from the little farm worked by Mr. Huggins, fish and game, we had choice meals.

I used to ride horseback, or rather "pony back," every day, always with my husband and frequently with Mr. Sibley. My pony was borrowed from the Indians. Mr. Chute and Mr. Sibley rode large horses. Every Indian brave, who came, came on a pony. His tepee, household goods and children were drawn by one. There were so many that they seemed more than the blades of grass. Literally thousands of these ponies were grazing some distance back of the encampment. We three rode out to see them. As we neared them, and they smelled my pony, that vast herd, with one accord, started towards us and almost at once literally engulfed me. The men called, "For God's sake, don't get off. Hold on for your life." I took the pony around the neck with both arms and did hold on. The men came after me as fast as they could and rode their big horses on either side of me. The Indians rushed in on their ponies and after some time succeeded in turning that vast multitude and letting the prisoner escape. I was cool and collected while the danger menaced, but when it was over, trembled and shook. My taste for horseback riding at Traverse was gone.

Mr. Sibley, Mr. Chute and I, with a guide, went to see a miniature Minnehaha. We walked all day going there and back—crossing the little stream many times. My husband took off his boots to ford the stream. He always carried me over. He cut his foot badly and could hardly get to the commission tent. Mr. Sibley urged us not to go to the Hopkins', but to stay there, but Mr. Chute wanted to go. It was bright moonlight, and I walked three quarters of a mile to Mr. Hopkin's to get a pony to take my husband back. I passed a little lake on the prairie. Mr. Chute and I always walked arm in arm as was then the custom for married people. Mirrored in the lake I could see reflected many, many Indian lovers walking as they had seen the pale faces do. I laughed to myself as I thought what mimics these children were. It was their following the customs of the white man, drinking as they saw him drink, that degraded them so.

On the Fourth of July there was to be a great celebration. The Indians were to have all their dances. Early in the morning, Mr. Hopkins went out to bathe in the river. He did not return. A little Indian girl said she had seen him go under the water and only two hands come above it. His body was not found for two days. A great crowd of squaws surrounded the house, showing by their sad looks what the loss was to them. At the burial, the Indians, a vast number of them, sang the hymns in Sioux. This funeral, way off in the wilderness, with these crowds of savage mourners, could never be forgotten.

Mr. Charles Bohanon—1851.
I moved to the farm where I am now living in '53. My father first took up a claim in 1851 where the Central Market now stands, but while he was in the woods, Old Man Stimson squat on that, so he took a claim at what is now Camden Place. He built a small house there. The farm was covered with brush and "oak openins". Everyone of these trees had to be grubbed out. One of my earliest recollections is the Red River carts that used to go squawking by on this side of the river as well as on the St. Anthony side. They were called the Red River Band. They

were one of the loudest bands ever brought together, as their music, that of wood rubbing against wood, could be heard three miles. While my father was in the woods, the Indians used to come and sleep in the dooryard. Sometimes it would be full of painted Sioux. They never stole anything or begged, but would gratefully take anything offered them. They were very friendly and kind and full of curiosity, as their looking in the windows at all times showed.

My father had brought a fine pair of horses from Galena. One day when he was mowing wild hay on a meadow, he left them unhitched and was excitedly told by a neighbor that they had got in the river. He ran and saw one swimming near the other shore but as the other had turned over with his feet in the air, the combined weight of the horse and wagon was too much for him and before help came, he sank. We recovered the running gear of the wagon later when all came upon a sandbar, but the harness had been stolen. What the loss of this team was to a pioneer farmer, we can hardly conceive.

The countless number of pigeons which migrated here every spring could never be estimated. At all hours of the night their cry of "Pigie, Pigie, Pigie," could be heard. They could be seen in countless numbers on the "slab trees," that is, old, dead trees. Anyone could kill hundreds in a day and thousands killed, seemingly made no impression. They flew very low and in dense masses. Ducks and geese were exceedingly plentiful. I have never seen wild swan here, but many in Minnesota in the Red River country.

On our farm was a thicket of plums which probably came up from the stones from one tree. Some were blue, some red, others yellow and red. Some were sour, some bitter, others tasteless, while others still, were sweet and of an exquisite flavor. These trees soon ran out and I think all of this best variety are gone. I remember picking raspberries, blackberries and wild strawberries in quantities. Every summer we would go up to Anoka and spend a week camping and picking blueberries.

We sold our corn which was our first crop, to Alexander Moore in St. Anthony. At that time, he was the only one buying corn. Two bushel baskets made a bushel. This sold for 15c. Mr. Moore had much larger baskets than those ordinarily in use and measured the corn in these. When the farmers demurred, he said, "If you don't like my measure, take your corn home." He knew there was no one else for us to take it to, so was very brave. There were very few scales so farm produce was generally sold by measure.

I never saw a pair of shoes until after the war. Everyone wore boots.

In the northern part of the State I have seen men start out in the morning with an ox team and return at night, blind themselves and the oxen, too, from the sting of the buffalo gnat. The mosquitoes came in great clouds and were everywhere.

Every little clear space of a hundred acres or more was called a prairie.

When I first saw Duluth it was only a cotton-town. That is, log houses with canvas roofs or tents. Most mail carriers used dog teams. Three dogs hitched tandem was the common sight. I have seen three dogs haul a dead horse.

In our expedition against the Indians only thirty-seven of the eight hundred horses we took, came back with us. The rest starved to death. Unlike the Red River stock which would paw through the deep snow to the long grass, fill themselves and then lie down in the hole and sleep, they knew nothing of this way and so could not forage for themselves. This campaign was with Hatch's Independent Battalion.

Lieut. Grosvenor who was new to the Red River country was married and on his wedding trip was to stop at McCauleyville. He sent word ahead that he wanted a private room. When he got there, he was shown into the only room there was—full of halfbreed sleepers. He hastened to the propiretor and said, "I ordered a private room." His answer was, "There are only six beds in there, what more could you want?"

Mr. Austin W. Farnsworth—1851.

We came to Fillmore County in the Fall of 1851 from Vermont. We were strapped. Not one cent was left after the expenses of the trip were paid. A neighbor took my father with him and met us at McGregor Landing with an ox team hitched to a prairie schooner. We were four days getting to Fillmore County, camping on the way. The nearest town, only a post office, was Waukopee. Father had come the previous spring and planted two acres of wheat, two acres of corn and one-half acre of potatoes. The potatoes all rotted in the ground.

I was only nine years old and my brother thirteen, but we made all the furniture for that cabin out of a few popple poles and a hollow basswood log. For beds, beams were fitted in between the logs and stuck out about a foot above the floor and were six feet long. To these we fastened cross pieces of "popple" and on this put a tick filled with wild hay and corn stalk leaves. It made a wonderful bed when you were tired as everyone was in those days, for all worked. After we had cut off a section of our big log by hand, we split it in two and in one half bored holes and fitted legs of the unpeeled popple for the seat. The other half made the back and our chair was done. As we had no nails, we fitted on the backs with wood pegs. Our table was made of puncheons split with a wedge and hewed with a broadax. The cabin would have been very homelike with its new furniture if it had not been for the smoke. My mother had to do all the cooking on a flat stone on the floor with another standing up behind it. She nearly lost her sight the first winter from the smoke. Our attic was filled with cornstalks to make the cabin warmer.

Our fare was good, as game was very plentiful and we had corn meal and a coarse ground wheat more like cracked wheat. There was a little grist mill at Carimona, a tiny town near. My mother made coffee from corn meal crusts. It would skin Postum three ways for Sunday.

When I was nine years old I killed a buffalo at Buffalo Grove near us. That grove was full of their runs. Elk were very plentiful, too, and deer were so plenty they were a drug in our home market. I have counted seventy-five at one time and seven elk. Pigeons were so thick that they darkened the sky when they flew. Geese and ducks, too, were in enormous flocks. In season, they seemed to cover everything. We used the eggs of the prairie chickens for cooking. They answered well.

Once my brother shot a coon and my mother made him a cap with the tail hanging behind and made me one too, but she put a gray squirrels tail at the back of mine. She knit our shoes and sewed them to buckskin soles. I was twelve, when I had my first pair of leather shoes. They were cowhide and how they did hurt, but I was proud of them. None of the country boys wore underclothing. I was nineteen before I ever had any. Our pants were heavily lined and if it was cold, we wore more shirts. I never had an overcoat until I went in the army. Before we left Vermont, my mother carded and spun all the yarn and wove all the cloth that we wore for a long time after coming to Minnesota.

We found the most delicious wild, red plums, half the size of an egg and many berries and wild crab-apples.

The timber wolves were plenty and fierce. My sister was treed by a pack from nine o'clock until one. By that time we had got neighbors enough together to scatter them. I was chased, too, when near home, but as I had two bulldogs with me, they kept them from closing in on me until I could get in the house.

There was a rattlesnake den near us and once we killed seventy-eight in one day. They were the timber rattlesnakes—great big fellows. I caught one by holding a forked stick over its head and then dropped it in a box. I kept it for a pet. It was seven feet, one and a half inches long. I used to feed it frogs, mice and rabbits. I thought it was fond of me, but it struck at me and caught its fangs in my shirt when I was careless, so I killed my pet.

The only time I ever went to school was for two months in '55, to John Cunningham. Wilbur made our desks out of black walnut lumber, cut in Buffalo Grove. It was very plentiful there.

Later we used to go to dances. I was great for cutting pigeon wings and balancing on the corner with a jig step. We used to dance the whirl waltz, too. Some called it the German waltz. We spun round and round as fast as we could, taking three little steps.

Mr. Elijah Nutting—1852.

We came to Faribault in 1852 and kept the first hotel there. It was just a crude shanty with an upstairs that was not partitioned off. Very cold too. I rather think there never was anything much colder. But it was very well patronized, as it was much better than staying outside.

There were many Indians whose home was in our village. We used to have good times with them and enjoyed their games and seeing them dance. Families were moving in all the time. Finally winter was over and spring with us.

We began to think how near the Fourth was and how totally unprepared we were for its coming. We decided to have a minstrel show. We had seen one once. My brother was to be end man and black up for the occasion. But he was a little tow head and we did not see our way clear to make nice kinky black wool of his hair.

Unfortunately for her, a black sheep moved into town in an otherwise white flock. We boys would take turns in chasing that sheep and every time we could get near her, we would snatch some of the wool. When sewed on to cloth, this made a wonderful wig. The proceeds from this entertainment, we saved for

72

firecrackers. Then we bought some maple sugar of the Indians—very dark and dirty looking. It looked very inadequate for a young merchant's whole stock of goods, but when it was added to by scrapings from the brown sugar barrel, when mother's back was turned, it sold like wild fire.

We felt like Rockefeller when we entrusted the stage driver with our capital to buy the coveted fire crackers in Cannon City, which then was much larger than Faribault. They cost forty cents a bunch, so we only got three bunches. The size of the crackers depressed us considerably for they were the smallest we had ever seen. We feared they would not make any noise. We put them away in a safe place. Brother was a natural investigator. Every time I was gone, he would fear those crackers were not keeping well and try one. He wanted no grand disappointment on the Fourth.

Joe Bemis, son of Dr. Bemis, always trained with us fellows and never backed down. We were going to have a circus in the barn. Joe said, "I'll ride a hog." The hogs were running around loose outside. They were as wild as deer. We laid a train of corn into the barn and so coaxed one old fellow with great tusks into it, and then closed the door. Joe ran and jumped on his back. Like lightning the hog threw him and then ripped him with his tusk. Joe yelled, "For God's sake let him out." We did. We laid Joe out on a board and Dr. Bemis came and sewed him up. He said, "Joe won't ride a hog very soon again, boys. Neither will you, I guess."

Mr. Charles Rye—1853.

Mr. Rye, eighty-six years old, hale and hearty, who still chops down large trees and makes them into firewood for his own use, says:

I left England in a sailing vessel in 1851 and was five weeks on the voyage. My sister did not leave her bunk all the way over and I was squeamish myself, but I see the sailors drinking seawater every morning, so I joined them and was never sick a minute after.

OLD RAIL FENCE CORNERS

We brought our own food with us and it was cooked for us very well and brought to us hot. We did not pay for this but we did pay for any food furnished extra. Some ships would strike good weather all the way and then could make a rapid voyage in three weeks, but usually it took much longer. I stayed in the east two years and came to St. Anthony in 1853.

The best sower in our part of England taught me to sow grain. After three days he came to me and said, "Rye, I don't see how it is, but I can see you beat me sowing." I hired out to sow grain at $1.00 a day as soon as I came here and had all the work I could do. I would put the grain, about a bushel of it, in a canvas lined basket, shaped like a clothes basket and fastened with straps over my shoulders, then with a wide sweep of the arm, I would sow first with one hand and then with the other. It was a pretty sight to see a man sowing grain. Seemed like he stepped to music.

Once I saw twenty-five deer running one after another like Indians across my sister's farm where St. Louis Park now is. I was watchman for the old mill in St. Anthony the winter of '53. It was forty degrees for weeks. I kept fire in Wales bookstore, too, to keep the ink from freezing.

I made $34.00 an acre on the first flax I sowed. A man had to be a pretty good worker if he got $15.00 a month and found in '53. Most farm hands only got $12.00.

I used to run the ferry with Captain Tapper. It was a large rowboat. Once I had eight men aboard. When I got out in the river, I saw the load was too heavy and thought we would sink. "Boys", I said, "don't move. If you do, we'll all go to the bottom." The water was within one inch of the top of the boat but we got across.

I graded some down town, on Hennepin Avenue when it was only a country road. There was a big pond on Bridge Square. The ducks used to fly around there like anything early in the morning.

OLD RAIL FENCE CORNERS

I cut out the hazelbrush on the first Fair Ground. It was on Harmon Place about two blocks below Loring Park. We cut a big circle so that we could have a contest between horses and oxen to see which could draw the biggest load. The oxen beat. I don't remember anything else they did at that Fair.

Mr. James M. Gillespie—1853.

I remember that our first crop on our own farm at Camden Place in 1853 was corn and pumpkins. The Indians would go to the field, take a pumpkin, split it and eat it as we do an apple with grunts of satisfaction.

There was an eight acre patch of wild strawberries where Indians had cultivated the land on our new claim about where our house stands today. They were as large as the small cultivated berries with a most delicious flavor. Everyone that we knew picked and picked but wagon loads rotted on the ground.

A good strong, quick stepping ox could plow two acres a day but much oftener they plowed one and one half acres only. The pigeons flew so low in '54 that we could kill them with any farm implement we happened to be using. They seemed to be all tired out. We killed and dried the breasts for winter.

Miss Nancy Gillespie—1853.

I remember a pear shaped wild plum which grew along the river bank. It was as large as the blue California plum and of a most wonderful color and taste. I have never seen anything like it and have not seen this variety of late years.

Mr. Isaac Layman—1853.

My father came to Minnesota in '52 and bought the land where Layman's Cemetery now is for $1,000.00 of Mr. Dumar. He returned for us January first '53. Snow was two feet on a level and the cold was terrible.

We went with our horses and wagon to Chicago from Peoria. There we bought a bobsled and put the wagon box on it, adding a strong canvas top. We put in a stove and made the twenty-one day journey very comfortably. We came up through Wisconsin. The only spot I remember was Black River Falls. The woods abounded with game. There were thousands of deer and partridges. We killed what we could eat only. We saw many bear tracks. We crossed the Mississippi at St. Anthony and arrived at our cabin.

Our house was only boarded up but father got out and banked it with snow to the eaves, pounding it down hard so it would hold. It made it very comfortable.

In the early days ammunition was very expensive for the farmer boys who loved to shoot. They found that dried peas were just as good as shot for prairie chicken, quail and pigeons, so always hunted them with these. The passenger pigeons were so plentiful that the branches of trees were broken by their numbers. They flew in such enormous flocks that they would often fly in at open doors and windows. They obscured the sun in their flight. Looked at from a distance, they would seem to extend as far up as the eye could reach. I have brought down thirty at a shot. They could be knocked off the branches with a stick while roosting and thousands of them were killed in this way. In these early days, they brought only 10c or 20c a dozen. The ducks used to congregate in such large numbers on Rice Lake that their flight sounded louder than a train of cars.

Mrs. Mary Weeks—1853, Ninety years old.

We came to Minnesota in 1853. My husband went up to our claim and broke from twenty-five to forty acres and sowed rutabagas. It was on new breaking and virgin soil and they grew tremendous. We moved there and bought stock. They seemed never to tire of those turnips and grew very slick and fat on them. We, too, ate them in every form and I thought I had never tasted anything so good. They were so sweet and tasty. The children used to cut them in two and scrape them with a spoon. We said we had "Minnesota apples" when we took them out to eat. It did seem so good to have real brooms to use. In Maine, we had always made our brooms of cedar boughs securely tied to a short pole. They were good and answered the purpose but a new fangled broom made of broom straw seemed so dressy. I can well remember the first one of this kind I ever had. It was only used on great occasions. Usually we used a splint broom which we made ourselves.

I used to do all the housework for a family of seven besides making butter and taking care of the chickens. If help was short, I helped with the milking, too. I made all the clothes the men wore. A tailor would cut out their suits and then I would make them by hand. I made all their shirts too. You should have seen the fancy bosomed shirts I made. Then I knit the stocking and mittens for the whole family and warm woolen scarfs for their necks. My husband used to go to bed tired to death and leave me sitting up working. He always hated to leave me. Then he would find me up no matter how early it was. He said I never slept. I didn't have much time to waste that way. We lived on beautiful Silver Lake. In season the pink lady-slippers grew in great patches and other flowers to make the prairie gay.

For amusement we used to go visiting and always spent the day. We would put the whole family into a sleigh or wagon and away we would go for an outing. We had such kind neighbors—no one any better than the other—all equal.

Mrs. E. A. Merrill—1853, Minneapolis.

My home was where the old Union station stood. In 1853 my father, Mr. Keith, learned that the land near where the Franklin Avenue bridge now is was to be thrown open to settlement. He loaded his wagon with lumber and drove onto the piece of land he wanted and stayed there all night. In the morning he built his home. In the afternoon the family moved in and lived there for three years.

OLD RAIL FENCE CORNERS

Mrs. Martha Thorne—1854.

We started from Davenport, Iowa, for Minnesota Territory in 1854. We had expected to be only two weeks on the trip to the junction of the Blue Earth and Minnesota rivers, but were six weeks on that terrible trip with our ox teams. There had been so much rain that all dry land was a swamp, all swamps lakes, and the lakes and rivers all over everywhere. Sometimes we worked a whole day to get one hundred feet through one of the sloughs. We would cut the tallest and coarsest rushes and grass and pile in to make a road bed. We would seem to be in a sea, but finally this trip ended as all trips, no matter how bad, must, and we came to Lake Crystal where we were to stay.

Such a beautiful spot as it was, this home spot! We camped for three weeks, living in our prairie schooner, while the men put up the wild hay.

We built a log cabin with "chinkins" to let in the air. We filled in the cracks except where these chinkins were, with mud. The roof was made by laying popple poles so they met in the middle and fastening them together. Over this we laid a heavy thickness of wild hay, and over that the popple poles again well tied with hand twisted ropes of wild hay, to those below. It was a good roof, only it leaked like a sieve. The floor was just the ground. Over it we put a layer of the wild hay and then staked a rag carpet over it. A puncheon shelf to put my trunk under, and the furniture placed, made a home that I was more than satisfied with. It took my husband over two weeks with a pair of trotting oxen to go for the furniture to St. Paul.

My baby was born three weeks after we moved in. There was no doctor within a hundred miles. I got through, helped only by my sister-in-law. What do you women nowadays, with your hospitals and doctors know of a time like this? When it rained, and rain it did, plenty, that October, the only dry place was on that trunk under the shelf and many an hour baby and I spent there. Whenever there was sunshine that carpet was drying.

We were much troubled with what the settlers called "prairie dig." It was a kind of itch that seemed to come from the new land. It made the hands very sore and troublesome. We did everything but could find no cure. The Dakota Sioux were our neighbors and were very friendly. They had not yet learned to drink the white man's firewater. A squaw came in one day and when she saw how I was suffering, went out and dug a root. She scraped off the outer bark, then cooked the inner bark and rubbed it on my hands. I was cured as if by magic. She buried all parts of the root, so I think it was poison.

The next year we raised the first wheat on the Des Moines River. We put the sacks in the bottom of the wagon, then our feather beds on top of them. The children were put on these and we started for the mill at Garden City, one hundred and thirty miles away. We had two yoke of oxen; the leaders were white with black heads and hoofs and great, wide spreading horns. They were Texas cattle and were noble beasts, very intelligent and affectionate. I could drive them by just calling "Gee and Haw". They went steadily along. My husband and I spelled each other and went right along by night as well as day. We were about forty hours going. The moonlight, with the shadows of the clouds on the prairie was magnificent. We never saw a human being. We had our wheat ground and started back. As I was walking beside the oxen while my husband slept, I started up a flock of very young geese. I caught them all and they became very tame. They once flew away and were gone three weeks, but all returned. When we got home, we had a regular jubilation over that flour. Twenty of the neighbors came in to help eat it. They were crazy for the bread. I made three loaves of salt rising bread and they were enormous, but we never got a taste of them.

OLD RAIL FENCE CORNERS

The Indians were always kind neighbors. They learned evil from the whites. The father of Inkpadutah used to hold my little girl and measure her foot for moccasins. Then he would bring her the finest they could make and would be so pleased when they fitted. The Indians always had wonderful teeth. They did not scrub the enamel off. They used to ask for coffee and one who had been to school said, "Could I have a green pumpkin?" and ate it raw with a relish.

We had a carpet sack for stockings. An Indian orator used to look at it with covetous eyes. One day he came in, laid two mink skins on the table, took the stockings out of the bag and stepping right along with victory in his eye, bore that sack away.

We lived on salt and potatoes for five weeks that first winter. We paid $1.00 for three pounds of sugar and $18.00 for a barrel of musty flour that we had to chop out with an ax and grate. That was in the winter of '55. During the Inkpadutah outbreak, the soldiers ate everything we had.

During the outbreak of '62 we moved to Mankato. I belonged to the ladies aid and we took care of the wounded and refugees sent from New Ulm. We made field beds on the floor for them. One poor German woman went to sleep while carrying a glass of water across the room to her husband, who was wounded. She just sank down in such a deep sleep that nothing could arouse her. I never could imagine such exhaustion. Old man Ireland had sixteen bullet holes, but had never stopped walking until he got to us. Mrs. Eastlake, that wonderful woman, was in this hospital. She was the woman who crawled all those miles on her hands and knees.

Mrs. Nancy Lowell—1854.

I came to Faribault in 1854 and boarded at the hotel kept by the Nuttings the first winter.

One evening I stepped to the door to throw out a washbasin of water and saw a large dog standing there. I put the dish down and was going out to call him. When my husband saw me going toward the door he said, "What are you going to do?" I said, "Call in a dog." It was bright moonlight. He said, "Let me see him." He looked and hastily closed the door saying, "The biggest kind of a timber wolf. Be careful what kind of pets you take in here."

The upper part of the hotel where we lived the first winter, was all in one room. I was the only woman, so we had a room made with sheeting. Sometimes there were twenty people sleeping in that loft. We did not have to open the windows. Most windows in those days were not expected to be opened anyway. The air just poured in between the cracks, and the snow blew in with gusto. It was not at all unusual to get up from under a snow bank in the morning.

I brought many pretty dresses and wore them too. Those who first came, if they had money and were brides, were dressed as if they lived in New York City.

We had a dance one night in our little log hotel. It was forty degrees below zero, and very cold anywhere away from the big stove. The women wanted to dance all the time and so set the table and put on the bread and cake before the company came. Five hours afterward when we went to eat, they were frozen solid. The dish towels would freeze too, as they hung on the line in the kitchen over the stove, while the stove was going, too.

One morning, after we were keeping house, my husband said, "I guess we have some spring company. You better go in and see them." I did and in the parlor was the biggest kind of an ox standing there chewing his quid. He had just come in through the open door to make a morning call. All kinds of animals ran at large then.

Mrs. William Dow—1854, Little Falls.

We came to Little Falls and built this house we are now living in in 1854. It was built right on an Indian trail that paralleled the Red River cart trail. You see that road out there? That is just where the old Red River cart road went. That is Swan River and it went between us and that. Our back door was right on their foot trail. You could step out of our door onto it. There is a big flat rock on the river up about four miles where the Chippewa and Sioux signed treaties to behave themselves. After this they were killing each other before they got out of town. You know our Indians were the Chippewas. They were woods Indians. The prairies belonged to the Sioux. They had always been enemies. Hole-in-the-Day was head chief here and a pretty good chief, too. His tribe got suspicious of him; they thought he was two-faced, so shot him, as they did his father before him. He had married a white woman, so the real chief now is a white man. I think he was on the square though. He used often to drop in for a piece of pie or anything to eat. He is buried upon the bluff here.

Swan River Ferry was three miles from Little Falls. It was on the direct road through Long Prairie to Fort Abercrombie. The Red River Cart Trail crossed the Mississippi River at Belle Prairie. There was a mill at that little place.

When the lumber jacks were driving logs they used to have their wamigans tie up in the river just outside that front door.

The Indians were camped all around here. They used to fill their moccasins with rabbit hair to take the place of stockings. Once I was standing by the river and I saw a squaw come out with a new born baby. She wasn't making any fuss over it. First she took it by the heels and plunged it in the river; then by the head and soused it in that way.

Mrs. Salome was a squaw who had married a white man. Her husband went to the war. I used to write her letters to him and she would sign them with her cross. She became very fond of me. At the time of the outbreak she said to me, "Kinnesagas?" meaning, "are you afraid?" I did not reply. Then she said "If you are, I'll hide you." She made a wigwam by the side of hers and wanted me to go into it with my children, but I would not. I liked her, but I remembered how when the Indians had had a scalp dance, I had seen her shake one of the scalps in her teeth. This was after she had married a white man. I asked her if she did not like the Indians better than the whites and she said in Chippewa, "If I do, why do I not stay with them?"

At the beginning of the outbreak the Sioux were sending runners all the time to get the Chippewas to join them. One of our men, William Nichols, spoke the Indian language as well as English. He had lived with them when he was a fur trader. He used to disguise himself as an Indian and go to the councils, so we all knew just what was going on. Old Buffalo, a chief, said, "If you go to war, I'll be a white man; I won't be an Indian any more. I'll go away and stay by myself always." We knew at once when they fully decided not to join the Sioux.

Finally I yielded to the entreaties of my friends and went down to St. Cloud to stay with friends until the danger should be over. My husband was in the war. One day someone coming from Little Falls said, "There's someone living in your house." "Well," said I, "if anyone can, I can," so back I went. I found an old friend from further up the country there. We joined forces and lived there until the war was over.

One day in war time I looked out of my window and could see Mr. Hall milking his cow in the pasture. It had a rail fence around it. I could see what he could not—some Indians sitting in one of the corners of the fence stretching Sioux scalps over withes. When they finished, they got up all at the same time, giving a blood curdling war-whoop. The cow kicked over the milk and fled bellowing. I think that Mr. Hall made even better time and he never even looked around.

The squaws would often have ear rings made of wire with three cornered pieces of tin dangling all around their ears. It was not how good, but how much, with them. How these Indians ever lived through a winter the way they dressed, I don't see. They wore only leggings, shirts, breech clouts and a blanket. Their legs were no barer than a Scotchman's though. Our Indians used to tuck things in the bosom of their shirt, as well as in their belts. They used to tuck butcher knives in their leggings. If they were ever going to go on a tear and get drunk, when we first came, they would always get my husband to take charge of all their guns and knives.

When the squaws wore mourning, they were all painted black and always slashed themselves with knives.

During the last of the fifties, we never had any money. It would not do you any good if you had for if you took money to the store they would just give you an order for more goods instead of the change. The Red River carts used to camp in that little grove of trees over there. We used to sell them supplies and they would give us English silver money. Once we took some to the store and they were terribly surprised to see **money.** They could not understand how we came by it. Thought we must have hoarded it, but we told them that it came from the Red River drivers.

Mrs. William J. White—1854.

My husband, Mr. White, started for Lake Addie, Minnesota Territory, in May, to join some friends and take up a claim. Mr. Hoag had named this lake in honor of his daughter. The settlement, if you could call it that, was called Grimshaw Settlement. It is now Brownton. He got up his cabin and began clearing the land. He and his friends did their cooking and only had two meals a day—breakfast at eight and dinner at three. One hot day they had just cooked a big pan of apple sauce and set it out to cool. Some Indians on their way to a war dance at Shakopee came streaking along all painted up. First one and then another plunged his fist in that apple sauce and stuck it down his throat. It must have skinned them all the way down, but not one made a sound, only looked hard when they saw the next one start in.

My husband wrote for me to come to him. I had no pilot, so could not start at once. My boy fell and broke his arm and I thought he was badly hurt inside so I wrote for father to come home. It generally took so long for a letter to go through that when two weeks later I got a chance to go with company, I started, thinking I could get there before the letter would, as they were generally much longer in going than one could travel. When I got on the Northern Belle, a fine boat, one of my children was taken with croup. Dr. N——, a Universalist minister, got off at Dubuque and bought medicine for me. This saved the child, but he was sick all the way. We were stuck in Beef Slough for several days. I never left the cabin as my child needed me, but some time during the first day a boat from St. Paul was stuck there too, so near us that passengers passed from one boat to the other all day. It was only when I got to Hastings, where I had thought to meet my husband that I found he had been on that other stranded boat. Later, I learned that he had spent some time on my boat, but of course, did not know I was there. The letter I had written him had gone straight, as a man who was going to their settlement had taken charge of it from the first. I had to wait six weeks in Hastings until he went clear to Pennsylvania and back. Evangeline wasn't in it with me.

Finally he came and we went on to our new home. I thought I had never seen such wonderful wild flowers. Mr. Grimshaw came after us with his horses. We had supper at his house the night before we got to our home, and I never tasted anything so good— pheasants browned so beautifully and everything else to match. The most wonderful welcome, too, went with that meal.

We passed fields just red with wild strawberries and in places where the land had been cultivated and the grass was sort of low, they grew away up and were large with big clusters, too. We did just revel in them. They were much more spicy than any we had ever eaten. The wild grass grew high as a man's head. When we came in sight of our home, I loved it at once and so did the children. It was in the bend of a little stream with stepping stones across. I knew at once that I had always wanted stepping stones on my place. About two feet from the floor a beam had been set in the whole length of the room. It was roped across and a rough board separated it into two sections. These were our beds and with feather beds and boughs, made a fine sleeping place. Wolves used to howl all around at night but with the stock secure and the home closed up tightly, we were happy. Our walls were plastered with mud and then papered by me with paper that was six cents a roll back east. We made a barrel chair and all kinds of homemade furniture out of packing boxes. Our rooms looked so cozy. Father was a natural furniture maker, though we never knew it before we came here.

Game was very plentiful and as we never had enough back home, we did not soon tire of it. My husband once killed a goose and eleven young ones with one shot.

The first year our garden was looking fine when the grasshoppers came in such swarms that they obscured the sun. They swooped on everything in the garden. There was no grain as the squirrels, black birds and gophers had never tasted this delicacy before and followed the sower, taking it as fast as it fell. We planted it three times and we had absolutely no crop of any kind that first year.

We bought four horses later and had them for the summer's work. They came from Illinois and were not used to the excessive cold of Minnesota. That winter it was forty degrees below zero for many successive days. It seems to me we have not had as much cold all this winter as we had in a week then. Christmas time it was very cold. We wanted our mail so one of the men rode one of the horses twelve miles to get it. When he arrived there the horse was very sick. He was dosed up and was seemingly all right. When the man wanted to start for home, he was warned that it would be fatal to take a horse which had been dosed with all kinds of hot stuff out in the terrible cold. He took the risk but the horse fell dead just as he entered the yard. We lost two others in much the same way that winter.

We then bought a yoke of young steers. They were very little broken and the strongest animals I ever saw. Their names were Bright and Bill. Once the whole family was going to a party at New Auburn, a kind of a city. My husband had made an Indian wagon. He held them in the road while we all got in. They started up with such a flourish that everything that could not hold itself on, fell off. The road was full of things we wanted with us. They ran on a keen jump for nine miles until we came to the house where we were going. It was the first house we came to. When they saw the barn, they must have thought it looked like home for they ran in there and brought up against the barn with a bang. As soon as Mr. White could, he jumped out and held them, but their fun was all gone and they stood like lambs.

I never saw anything funnier than those steers and a huge snapping turtle. They found him near the creek when they were feeding. They would come right up to him (they always did everything in concert) then look at him at close range. The turtle would thrust out his head and snap at them; then they would snort wildly and plunge all over the prairie, returning again and again to repeat the performance, which only ended when the turtle disappeared in the brook.

Wolves were very fearless and fierce that winter. They ran in packs. They would look in at our windows. Once we sent a hired boy six miles for twenty-five pounds of pork for working men. When he was near home a pack of wolves followed him, but he escaped by throwing the pork. Mr. Pollock and Mr. White were followed in the same way.

Once one of our friends killed a steer. We were all anxious for amusement so any pretext would bring on a party. All the neighbors had a piece of the meat but we thought the friends who had killed the steer should have a party and have roast beef for us all, so we sent word we were all coming. Mrs. Noble, my neighbor worked all day to make a hoop skirt. She shirred and sewed together a piece of cloth about three yards around. In these shirrings she run rattan —a good heavy piece so it would stand out well. I made a black silk basque and skirt. My finery was all ready to put on. One of the neighbor's girls was to stay with the children. The baby had been quite restless, so according to the custom, I gave her a little laudanum to make her sleep. I did not realize that it was old and so much stronger. Just before going, when I was all dressed, I went to look at the baby. I did not like her looks, so took her up to find her in a stupor. Needless to say there was no party for us that night. It took us all to awaken her and keep her awake. I naver gave laudanum after that, though I always had before.

Mrs. Paulina Starkloff—1854.

My name was Paulina Lenschke. I was twelve years old when I came to Minneapolis in 1854. We intended to stay in St. Paul but were told that this was a better place, so came here and bought an acre and a half just where the house now stands, Main Street N. E. The town then was mostly northeast. The St. Charles hotel on Marshall Street, northeast, was just below us and so were most of the stores. Morgan's foundry and Orth's brewery were just on the other side of us. We paid $600.00 in gold for the land and half of it was in my name, as my mother paid $350.00 that I had made myself. I think I was probably the only twelve year old child that came into the state with so much money earned by herself. It was this way.

OLD RAIL FENCE CORNERS

We went to Australia to dig gold in 1847. We drove an ox team into the interior with other prospectors doing the same until we came to diggings. The men would dig and then "cradle" the soil for the gold. This cradle was just like a baby's cradle only it had a sieve in the bottom. One man would have a very long handled dipper with which he would dip water from a dug well. He only dipped and the other man stirred with a stick and rocked. Most of the soil would wash out but there would always be some "dumplings" caused by the clay hardening and nothing but hard work would break them. The miners would take out the gold which was always round, and dump these hard pieces. After a day's work there would be quite a pile that was never touched by them. I would take a can and knife and go from dump to dump gathering the gold in these dumplings. One day my father went prospecting with a party of men and was never seen again. After months of fruitless search my mother took me and my little tin can of nuggets back to Germany. She sold them for me for $350.00 in gold. Then we came to Minnesota and bought this place.

The Red River carts used to be all day passing our house. They would come squeaking along one after another. Sometimes the driver would take his wife and children with him. These carts had no metal about them. One man would have charge of several.

Mrs. Anna E. Balser—1855, Ninety-four years old.

I was the only girl in our family that ever worked, but when I was ten years old I laid my plan to get myself out of my mother's tracks. She had so much to do with her big family. I could cry when I think of it now. So, when I was fourteen, my father, scared for me and holding back every minute, took me to the city to learn the trade I had chosen. I was through in six months and could do the heaviest work as well as the finest. I wish you could see the fancy bosomed shirts I used to make when I was fourteen! No one could beat me. I always had a pocketful of money for I got two and six a day. That would be 38c now. I went from house to house to work and always had the best room and lived on the fat of the land. It was a great event when the tailoress came.

I came to Lakeland in 1855. The prairies around there looked like apple orchards back home. The scrub oak grew just that way. I would bet anything I could go and pick apples if I had not known. I had thought of buying in Minneapolis, but my friends who owned Lakeland thought it was going to be **the** city of Minnesota, so I bought here. I was a tailoress and made a good living until the hard times came on. Money was plenty one day. The next you could not get a "bit" even, anywhere. Then, after that, I had to trade my work for anything I could get.

I brought a blue black silk dress with mutton leg sleeves among my things when I come. It was the best wearing thing I ever see. Cheaper to wear than calico because it would never wear out. I paid $1.00 a yard for it. It was twenty-seven inches wide. It took twelve yards to make the dress. For a wrap we wore a long shawl. I had one of white lace. We got three yards of lace webbing and trimmed it with lace on the edge. Or we would take one width of silk and finish that fancy on the edge. The ruffles on everything was fluted. When you shirred them you would hold them over the first and third finger passing under the second finger. That would make large flutings. If you had an Italian iron you could do it fast, but there wa'n't many so fortunate. An Italian iron was a tube about as big as your finger on a standard. Two rods to fit this tube come with it. You could put these heated, inside then run your silk ruffle or whatever you were making over it and there was your flute quick as a wink.

Mrs. Mary E. Dowling—1855.

As Miss Watson I came from Pennsylvania in 1855 and took a school to teach back of Marine. I got $36.00 in gold a month and so was well paid. Had from five to twenty-five children who came to learn and so behaved well.

OLD RAIL FENCE CORNERS

When I would walk through the woods I would sometimes see a bear leisurely sagging around. When I did, my movements were not like his. All kinds of wild animals were very plenty. The foxes were the cutest little animals and so tame. They would seem to be laughing at you.

A band of Indians was encamped at a lake near. One brave all dressed in his Sunday best used to come and sit in the kitchen day after day. He used to talk to the men but never said a word to us. He could speak good English. One day the chief came in and went for him. Said he had been away from his tepee for days and his squaws wanted him. Like lightning he crossed the room to where I was and said, "Me got Sioux squaw. Me got Winnebago squaw. Me want white squaw. You go?" I was very earnest in declining.

Mrs. Robert Anderson—1854.

I was the first white woman in Eden Prairie. I came in 1854 with my husband and small children and settled there in one of the first log houses built. We paid for our farm the first year, from the cranberries which grew in a bog on our land and which we sold for $1.00 a bushel.

I had never seen Indians near to, and so was very much afraid of them. One day a big hideously painted brave marched in, seated himself and looked stolidly around without making a sound. His long knife was sticking in his belt. I was overpowered with fright and for a few moments could do nothing. My children, one two years old and the other a baby, were asleep behind the curtain. Realizing that I could do nothing for them and that his anger might be aroused if he saw me run away with them, I fled precipitately in the direction where my husband was working. I had run about a quarter of a mile when my mother heart told me I might not be in time if I waited for my husband, so I turned and fled back towards the cabin. Entering, I saw my little two year old boy standing by the Indian's side playing with the things in his belt while the Indian carefully held the baby in his arms. In his belt were a tobacco pouch and pipe, two rabbits with their heads drawn through, two prairie chickens hanging from it by their necks, a knife and a tomahawk. His expression remained unchanged. I gave him bread and milk to eat and ever after he was our friend, oftentimes coming and bringing the children playthings and moccasins. When he left, he gave me the rabbits and prairie chickens and afterwards often brought me game.

One day Mr. Anderson was at work in the field, a long distance from the house. He was cutting grain with a scythe and told me he would just about get that piece done if I would bring him his supper. I had never been over on this knoll which was on the other side of a small hill from the house. I got his supper ready, taking all the dishes and food in a basket and carrying a teapot full of tea in my hand. I had to pass a small cranberry bog and could see squaws at work picking berries. As I came to a clump of trees, ten or twelve Indians with their faces as usual hideously painted, the whole upper part of their bodies bare and painted, rose from this clump of trees and looked at me. I waited for nothing, but threw my basket and teapot and made for the house. As I got to the top of the hill I looked back and could see the Indians feasting on my husband's supper. Upon his return home to supper that evening, he brought the dishes and the teapot with him.

We had been in Eden Prairie about six years and had never been to church as there was no church near enough for us to attend. We heard there was to be preaching at Bloomington, and determined to go. We had always been church-going people and had felt the loss of services very keenly. We had nothing but an ox team and thought this would not be appropriate to go to church with, so, carrying my baby, I walked the six miles to church and six miles back again. The next Sunday, however, we rode nearly to church with the ox team, then hitched them in the woods and went on foot the rest of the way.

Mr. Anderson was always a devoted friend of Mr. Pond, the missionary and attended his church for many years. One of Mr. Anderson's sons took up a claim in the northern part of the State. When Mr. Pond died, he came down to the funeral. Upon his return, he saw a tepee pitched on the edge of his farm and went over to see what it was there for and who was in it. As he neared it, he heard talking in a monotone and stood listening, wondering what it could mean. He pushed up the flap and saw Indians engaged in prayer. He asked them who taught them to pray and they replied "Grizzly Bear taught us." He told them Grizzly Bear, which was the Indian name for Mr. Pond, was dead and would be seen no more. He took from his pocketbook a little white flower which he had taken from the casket, told them what it was and each one of them held it reverently with much lamentation. This was twenty years after these people had been taught by Grizzly Bear.

Mrs. Wilder—1854.

We settled on a farm near Morristown. There was an Indian village near. We always used to play with those Sioux children and always found them very fair in their play. We used to like to go in their tepees. There was a depression in the middle for the fire. The smoke was supposed to go out of the hole in the top of the tent. An Indian always had a smoky smell. When they cooked game, they just drew it a little— never took off the feathers much or cut the head or feet off.

Some of our Indians got into a fuss with a band from Faribault and one of our Indians killed one of them. He brought a great knife that he had done the killing with and gave it to my father all uncleaned as it was. He said it was "seechy" knife, meaning bad. As they were still fighting, my father took it just as it was and stuck it up in a crack above our front door in our one room. Then he sent to Morristown for Mr.

OLD RAIL FENCE CORNERS

Morris to straighten out the fight. He had lived among the Indians for a long time and knew their language. He brought them to time. Later they came and wanted the knife but my father would not give it to them.

Geese and ducks covered the lakes. Later we had the most wonderful feather beds made from their feathers. We only used the small fluffy ones, so they were as if they were made from down. Wild rice, one of the Indians' principal articles of diet, when gathered was knocked into their canoe. It was often unhulled. I have seen the Indians hull it. They would dig a hole in the ground, line it with a buffalo skin, hair side down, then turn the rice in this, jumping up and down on it with their moccasined feet until it was hulled. I could never fancy it much after I saw this.

We had great quantities of wild plums on our own place. Two trees grew close together and were so much alike we always called them the twins. Those trees had the most wonderful plums—as large as a small peach. We used to peel them and serve them with cream. Nothing could have a finer flavor.

Just before the outbreak, an Indian runner, whom none of us had ever seen, went around to all the Sioux around there. Then with their ponies loaded, the te-pee poles dragging behind, for three days our Indians went by our place on the old trail going west. Only a few of Bishop Whipple's Christian Indians remained.

Mr. Warren Wakefield—1854.

My father came to Wayzata with his family, settling where the Sam Bowman place now is. We had lived over a year in southern Minnesota. As the hail took all our crops, we had lived on thin prairie chickens and biscuits made of sprouted wheat. It would not make bread. The biscuits were so elastic and soft that they could be stretched way out. These were the first playthings that I can remember.

A trader came with cows, into the country where we were living, just before the hail storm and as there was nothing to feed them on, my father traded

94

for some of them. He traded one of his pair of oxen for forty acres of land in Wayzata and the other for corn to winter the stock.

The first meal we had in our new home was of venison from a buck which my father shot. It was very fat and juicy and as we had not had any meat but ducks and prairie chickens in two years, it tasted very delicious. I have counted thirty-four deer in the swamps at one time near our house; they were so abundant. We lived the first winter in Wayzata on fish, venison and corn meal and I have never lived so well.

I was sixteen years old before I ever had a coat. We wore thick shirts in the winter and the colder it was, the more of them we wore. In the east, my mother had always spun her own yarn and woven great piles of blankets and woolen sheets. These were loaded in the wagon and brought to our new home. When there was nothing else, these sheets made our shirts. We never wore underclothing, but our pants were thickly lined.

My mother was a tailoress and that first year in Minnesota we could not have lived if it had not been for this. She cut out and made by hand all kinds of clothing for the settlers. My father used to buy leather and the shoemaker came to the house and made our shoes.

One spring we had a cellar full of vegetables that we could not use, so father invited all the squaws who lived near us to come and get some. They came and took them away. In the cellar also was a keg and a two gallon jug of maple vinegar. Cut Nose, one of the finest specimens of manhood I have ever seen, tall, straight and with agreeable features in spite of the small piece gone from the edge of one nostril, was their chief, and came the next day with a large bottle, asking to have it filled with whiskey. Father said he had none, but Cut Nose said he knew there was a jug and keg of it in the cellar. Father told him to go and take it if he found any. He sampled first the jug and then the keg with a most disgusted expression and up-on coming upstairs threw the bottle on the bed and stalked out. This maple vinegar was made from maple sugar and none could be better.

Cut Nose was often a visitor at our home. He was a great brag and not noted for truth telling. He was very fond of telling how he shot the renegade Inkpadutah. This was all imagination. He had an old flint lock musket with the flint gone and would illustrate his story by crawling and skulking, general-ly, to the great delight of the boys. One rainy day my mother was sick and was lying in her bed which was curtained off from the rest of the living room. As Cut Nose, who did not know this, told his oft repeated story, illustrating it as usual, he thrust his gun under the curtains and his face and shoulders after it to show how he shot the renegade chief from ambush. My mother dashed out with a shriek, but was no more frightened than Cut Nose, at the ap-parition of the white squaw.

One day my brother and I took a peck of pota-toes each and went to an Indian camp to trade for two pairs of moccasins, the usual trade. We left the pota-toes with the squaws for a moment and ran outside to see what some noise was. When we returned there were no potatoes to be seen and no moccasins to be traded. We began looking about but could see noth-ing. The fire was burned down well and was a glowing bed of coals in its depression in the center of the tepee. After a while, one of the old squaws went to the ashes and digging them with a stick, com-menced to dig out the potatoes. As the fire was about four feet in diameter, the usual width, there was plenty of room for our half bushel of potatoes. They gave us some of them which had a wonderful flavor, but we never got any moccasins.

Among the Indians living at the lake one winter was a white child about three years old. My father tried to buy her, but they would not let her go or tell who she was. They left that part of the country later, still having her in their possession.

If it had not been for ginseng in Minnesota, many of the pioneers would have gone hungry. Mr. Chilton of Virginia came early and built a small furnace and drying house in Wayzata. Everyone went to the woods and dug ginseng. For the crude product, they received five cents a pound and the amount that could be found was unlimited. It was dug with a long narrow bladed hoe and an expert could take out a young root with one stroke. If while digging, he had his eye on another plant and dug that at once, he could make a great deal of money in one day. An old root sometimes weighed a half pound. I was a poor ginseng digger for I never noticed quickly, but my father would dig all around my feet while I was hunting another chance. The tinge of green of this plant was different from any other so could be easily distinguished. When we sold it, we were always paid in gold. After ginseng is steamed and dried, it is the color of amber.

Mrs. Leroy Sampson—1854.

Six families of us came together from Rhode Island and settled on Minnewashta Lake in '54. There was only a carpenter shop in Excelsior. We spent the first few months of our stay all living together in one log shack which was already there. The first night the man who had driven us from St. Paul sat up all night with his horses and we none of us slept a wink inside that little windowless cabin on account of a noise we heard. In the morning we found it was the mournful noise of the loons on the lake that had kept us awake, instead of the wolves we had feared.

Mrs. Anna Simmons Apgar—1854.

When our six families got to the springs near Excelsior it was near dark and we struck the worst road we had found in the swampy land by it. The mosquitoes were dreadful, too. How dreadful, no one today can ever believe. One of the tiredout men said,

OLD RAIL FENCE CORNERS

"This is Hell!" "No," said another, "Not Hell, but Purgatory." The spring took its name from that.

When my father had put up his cabin he made our furniture with his own hands out of basswood. He made one of those beds with holes in the side piece for the ropes to go from side to side instead of our springs of today. They used to be very comfortable. When father got ready for the rope he had none, so he made it by twisting basswood bark. Then mother sewed two of our home spun sheets together for a tick and my uncle cut hay from the marsh and dried it, to fill it and we had a bed fit for a king. Our floor was of maple split with wedges and hewed out with a broadax. Father was a wonder at using this. A broadax was, you know, twelve or fourteen inches wide and the handle was curved a little. A man had to be a man to use one of these. It took strength and a good trained eye to hew timber flat with one of these axes.

When I was playing I tore my clothes off continually in the woods. Finally my mother said, "This has gone far enough!" and made me a blue denim with a low neck and short sleeves. Has anyone ever told you how terrible the mosquitoes were in the early days? Think of the worst experience you ever had with them and then add a million for each one and you will have some idea. My little face, neck, arms, legs and feet were so bitten, scratched and sunburned that when I was undressed I was the most checkered looking young one you ever saw. Those parts of me might have been taken from a black child and glued on my little white body.

Such huge fish as overrun the lakes you have never seen. We thought the Indians numerous and they had fished for ages in those lakes, but they only caught what they wanted for food. It took the white men with their catching for sport to see how many they could catch in one day, and write back east about it, to clean out the lakes.

Father hewed a big basswood canoe out of a log. Eight people could sit comfortably in it as long as they did not breathe, but if they did, over she went! We used to have lots of fun in that old canoe just the same and the fish got fewer after it came into commission.

When we six families first came we were all living in one little cabin waiting for our homes to be built and our furniture to come. One of the women was very sick. Dr. Ames came out to see her and cured her all right. It took a day to get him and another day for him to get home. He wanted to wash his hands and my aunt, who was used to everything, said she thought she would drop dead when she had to take him the water in a little wooden trough that father had hewed out. He made such cute little hooded cradles for babies, too, out of the forest wood.

Mrs. Newman Woods—1854, Excelsior.

When we made our tallow dips or rough candles, we took the candlewicking and wound it around from our hand to our elbow, then cut it through. We held a short stick between our knees and threw one of these wicks around it, twisting it deftly, letting it hang down. When we had filled the stick, we would lay it down and fill another until we had wicks for about ten dozen dips. My mother would then fill the washboiler two-thirds full of water and pour melted deer or other tallow on top of this. Two chairs had been placed with two long slats between them. She would dip one stick full of wicks up and down in the boiler a number of times, then place it across the slats to cool. This was continued until all the wicks were dipped. By this time, the first would have hardened and could be dipped again. We would work hard all day and make eight or ten dozen dips. Later we had candle molds made of tin. We would put a wick in the center where it was held erect and then pour these molds full of tallow and let them harden. Later the molds were dipped in hot water and then a spring at the side, pushed the candle out. This was very simple.

OLD RAIL FENCE CORNERS

We had our first kerosene lamp in '61. We were terrible frightened of it. It did smell terrible but this did not keep us from being very proud of it.

Once mother was frying pancakes for supper. A number of Indians going by came in and saw her. They were all painted or daubed. They kept reaching over and trying to get the pancakes. Finally one of them stuck out his leg acting as if it was broken. I ran madly to the back clearing where father and uncle Silas were working and told them there were Indians trying to get our pancakes and that one of them had a broken leg. They were not frightened for they knew the Indians and their customs. I just waited to see father give them a pancake apiece and that leg settle down naturally, then ran and got under the bed.

The Indians were very fond of father who had a very heavy beard. It used to be stylish to shave the upper lip. The Indians used to watch him shave with great interest. The neighborhood was full of them, generally all painted for the war dance. They used to bother father to death wanting to be shaved. One morning he did shave one of them and you never saw such a proud Indian, or more disgusted ones than those who were left out. Nearly all of the Indians who came were Sioux and fine looking.

One of the greatest pests to the pioneers around here was the thousand legged worms. They were very thick around where we were and very poisonous. My little sister nearly died from getting one in her mouth when she was lying on a quilt on the floor.

Mother used to make mince pies by soaking pumpkin in vinegar. We dried the wild grapes for raisins. My, but those pies were good. Everybody bragged on "Aunt Hannah's mince pies."

My father and brother frequently went hunting for deer. They used to run their bullets, which were round, by melting lead in a ladle in the stove. Such a looking kitchen as they would leave! Ashes from the ladle all over everything. It wasn't much of a trick to shoot deer, they were so thick and so tame. They used to come right near the house. I did not like venison for it seemed to me like eating a friend.

All six of us families used to wash at the lake in summer. We used soft soap that we made ourselves and boiled the clothes in a big kettle. They were beautifully white.

Mr. Chester L. Hopkins—1854, Hopkins.

When I was a little boy we had a grindstone in our yard which was used by us and our few scattered neighbors. One night we were awakened by hearing the grindstone going, and father went to the door to see who was using it. A party of forty Sioux braves on their ponies were standing around, while some of the braves ground their knives which each in his turn put in his belt. It was a bright moonlight night and we could see them as plainly as if it was day. The Indians were in full war paint and feathers and after their task was accomplished, rode one after the other over the hill where they stood out like black silhouettes, and finally disappeared. They were probably going to a war dance.

Miss Florinda Hopkins—Hopkins.

When I was a little girl a number of Indians came in on a rainy day, and tired from a long tramp, lay asleep on the floor of the kitchen. The party consisted of a chief and seven braves. My mother was making dried apple pies. When she had finished, she cut two of them into six pieces each and gave each Indian a piece which he ate with the greatest relish. All of them kept a watchful eye on the remaining pieces which they regarded wistfully. The chief with a noble gesture motioned them all to leave the house and remained himself. As soon as they were outside he motioned for the rest of the pie and ate it all with the greatest relish while the rest of the band looked enviously through the window. Were these not, indeed, children?

OLD RAIL FENCE CORNERS

I remember a Sioux war party of ten or more going by our house, returning from a war dance at Shakopee. They were doing their war song business as they trotted along and swinging one pitiful scalp on a pole. Their battles were generally like this. Ten was a small number to kill one Chippewa. When the Chippewa retaliated they would go in the same proportion.

One morning a party stopped here. They were very tired. Had probably trotted a long, long way for their endurance was wonderful. They just said "Chippewa?" and as soon as they knew we had seen none were flying on again.

We often traded food with the Indians as well as giving it to them, allowing them to make their own terms. They would bring a pair of fancy beaded moccasins and trade them for six doughnuts.

Mrs. J. W. Ladd—1854.

I remember seeing and hearing the Red River carts as they passed through St. Anthony. The cart was almost square with posts standing up along the sides to hold the furs which were piled high above the cart and roped down in place. There was one swarthy man to five or six ox drawn carts. He was dressed in a coonskin cap or broad brimmed hat with buckskin trousers and jumper. He had a knit bright colored sash about his waist and his hat had a bright colored band.

One day my mother was sitting sewing while I was playing about the room, when the light seemed obscured. We looked up to see a number of Indian faces in the window. They made motions to mother to trade her earrings for moccasins and failing in this, they asked for the bright colored tassels which hung from the curtain. They also very much admired my mother's delaine dress which was of triangles in blue, red, black and white. When refused they went away peaceably but afterwards often returned trying to make a trade.

OLD RAIL FENCE CORNERS

Mrs. C. H. Pettit—1854, Minneapolis.

In 1854 I attended church in the Tooth-pick church. This was a small church so called from its high, narrow tower. I had never seen Indians as we had just moved to town. I was walking along through the woods on what is now Fourth street when I was surrounded by yelling, painted Indians on ponies. Seeing that I was frightened nearly to death they continued these antics, circling round, and round me, whooping and yelling, until I reached my home. Then they rode rapidly away undoubtedly taking great pleasure in the fright they had given the Paleface.

Mrs. Anna Hennes Huston—1854.

I moved to St. Anthony in 1854. I was only a tiny tot but used to go with my brother along a path by the river to find our cow. We usually found her in the basement of the university.

The roaring of the Falls used to scare me and if the wind was in the right direction we would be all wet with the spray.

I remember that at one time in the early days, potatoes were very scarce. My mother traded a wash dish full of eggs for the same amount of potatoes.

Mr. Henry Favel—1854.

With my family I lived thirty miles from Carver. My father died and as I had no money to buy a coffin, I made it myself. I had to walk thirty miles for the nails. The boards were hand hewed and when the coffin was made, it looked so different from those we had seen, in its staring whiteness, that we took the only thing we had, a box of stove blacking, which we had brought from the east with us and stained the coffin with this.

I walked twenty miles for potatoes for seed and paid $3.00 a bushel for them. I brought them home on my back. I was three days making the journey on foot.

The wages for a carpenter at this time were $30.00 a month and found.

OLD RAIL FENCE CORNERS

Mrs. Rebecca Plummer—1854.

We came to Brooklyn Center in 1854. Mr. Plummer's father had come in '52 and had taken a claim.

We did enjoy the game, for we had never had much. Pigeons were very thick. We used to stake nets for them almost touching the ground. Under these we scattered corn. They would stoop and go in under and pick up the grain. When they held their heads erect to swallow the corn, their necks would come through the meshes of the net and they could not escape.

I saw the Winnebagoes taken to their river reservation. They camped a night on the island in the river and went through all the dances they knew and made every noise they knew how to make. The most wonderful sight though was to see that vast flotilla of canoes going on the next morning. There were hundreds of them with their Indian occupants, besides the long procession on foot.

Mrs. C. A. Burdick—1855.

We came to what is now St. Cloud settling near the junction of the Little Sauk and Mississippi. The Sauk was a beautiful little river. The strawberries were very sweet, a much nicer flavor than tame ones. The prairie was covered with them.

The Winnebagoes who had lived on Long Prairie were transferred to their new home and we went to take care of the agency buildings they had left. There were from seventy-five to a hundred of these buildings. Franklin Steele and Anton Northrup owned them. We were awfully lonesome but we braved it out. The Indians were always coming and demanding something to eat. They were always painted and had bows and arrows with them. They would everlastingly stand and look in the windows and watch us work. We were so used to them that we never noticed them, only it was troublesome to have the light obscured.

Have I ever seen the Red River carts? My! I should say I have! Seen them by the hundred. My husband had charge of a fur store for Kittson at Fort Garry, now Winnipeg and we lived there. I used to go back and forth to St. Cloud where my parents lived with this cart train for protection. The drivers were a swarthy lot of French half breeds. Likely as not their hair would be hanging way down. They wore buckskin and a fancy sash. Sometimes a skin cap and sometimes just their hair or a wide hat. A tame enough lot of men, fond of jigging at night . They **could** hold out dancing. Seemed to never tire.

Their carts had two wheels, all wood and a cross piece to rest the platform on. This platform had stakes standing way up at the sides. They were piled high with goods, furs and skins going down and supplies coming back. I can shut my eyes and see that quaint cavalcade now. Where are all those drivers?

The tracks were wide and deep and could be plainly seen ahead of us going straight through the prairie. It took twenty-one days to go from St. Cloud to Pembina. We used to go through Sauk Center, just a hotel or road house, then through what is now Alexandria. A family by the name of Wright used to keep a stopping place for travelers. I don't know just where it would be now, but I have stayed there often. We went by way of Georgetown. Swan river, too, I remember. There used to be one tree on the prairie that we could see for two days. We called it Lone Tree.

Mr. Peter Cooper—1855.

I moved to Vernon Center in the early fifties. I had never worn an overcoat in New York state, but when I came to Minnesota particularly felt the need of one. The second year I was here, I traded with an Indian, two small pigs for a brass kettle and an Indian blanket. Without any pattern whatever, my wife cut an overcoat from this blanket and sewed it by hand. This was the only overcoat I had for four years, but it was very comfortable.

When I was in the Indian war in 1862 I had no mittens and suffered greatly for this reason. In one of the abandoned Norwegian homes, I found some hand made yarn, but had no way to get it made into mittens. I carved a crochet hook out of hickory and with this crocheted myself gloves with a place for every finger, although I had never had any experience and had only watched the women knit and crochet.

Mr. Stephen Rochette—1855, St. Paul.

Indians used often to stop to get something to eat. They never stole anything and seemed satisfied with what we gave them. We were on the direct road from Fort Snelling to St. Paul. It was made on the old trail between those two places. This went right up Seventh Street. The Indians often brought ducks and game to sell.

I used to shoot pigeons and prairie chickens on what is now Summit avenue.

I used to make cushions for Father Revoux's back. He had rheumatism very badly. He used to go by our house horseback. I wanted to give him the cushions but he would never take anything he did not pay for.

I bought a number of knockdown chairs in Chicago all made by hand for $125 and sold them for much more. Those chairs would last a lifetime. The parts were separate and packed well. They could be put together easily.

Mrs. Stephen Rochette—1855.

When we first came into St. Paul in 1855 we landed on the upper levee. It was used then more than the lower one. We thought we could never get used to the narrow, crooked streets. We lived with my father, Jacob Doney, where the Milwaukee tracks now cross Seventh Street.

We soon had three cows. We never had any fence for them, just turned them out and let them run in the streets with the other cows and pigs. Sometimes we could find them easily. Again we would have a long hunt.

OLD RAIL FENCE CORNERS

Mrs. James A. Winter—1855.

We came to Faribault in 1855. My father had the first frame hotel there. The Indians had a permanent camp on the outskirts of the village. I was a small girl of sixteen with very fair skin, blue eyes and red cheeks. The squaws used to come to the house asking for food, which mother always gave them. "Old Betts" was often there. A young Indian, tall and fine looking used to come and sit watching me intently while I worked about the house, much to my discomfort. Finally one day he came close to me and motioned to me to fly with him. I showed no fear but led the way to the kitchen where there were others working and fed him, shaking my head violently all the time. He was the son of a chief and was hung at Mankato.

Mrs. George E. Fisher—1855.

Mother's name was Jane de Bow. Her father and mother were French. She came to Minnesota with the Stevens' in 1834 when she was seven years old. They were missionaries and when their own daughter died induced Jane's family to let them have her. The Indians were always sorry for her because her mother was away. They called her "Small-Crow-that-was Caught". Mrs. Stevens never could punish her for it made the squaws so angry.

The first Indian child my mother ever saw was a small boy who stood on the edge of Lake Harriet beckoning to her. She was afraid at first but finally joined him and always played with the Indian children from that time.

The Stevens' the next year had a little school near their cabin not far from where the pavilion is now. The Indian children always had to have prizes for coming. These prizes were generally turnips. Often they gave a bushel in one day.

In 1839 some Chippewa Indians ambushed a Sioux father who was hunting with his little son. The child escaped and told the story. The Sioux went on the warpath immediately and brought home forty or fifty Chippewa scalps. They had been "lucky" as they found a camp where the warriors were all away. They massacred the old men, women and children and came home to a big scalp dance. My mother had played with the Indian children so much that she was as jubilant as they when she saw these gory trophies. She learned and enjoyed the dance. She taught me the Sioux words to this scalp dance and often sang them to us. Translated they are:

> You Ojibway, you are mean,
> We will use you like a mouse.
> We have got you and
> We will strike you down.
> My dog is very hungry,
> I will give him the Ojibway scalps.

The Indian children would take a kettleful of water, make a fire under it, and throw fish or turtles from their bone hooks directly into this. When they were cooked slightly, they would take them out and eat them without salt, cracking the turtle shells on the rocks. The boys used to hunt with their bows and arrows just as they did in later years. They were always fair in their games.

My mother married Mr. Gibbs and moved to this farm on what was the territorial road near the present Agricultural college. It was on the direct Indian trail to the hunting grounds around Rice Lake.

The Indian warriors were always passing on it and always stopped to see their old playmate. By this time they had guns and they would always give them to mother to keep while they were in the house. The kitchen floor would be covered with sleeping warriors. Mother knew all their superstitions. One was that if a woman jumped over their feet they could never run again. I can well remember my gay, light hearted mother running and jumping over all their feet in succession as they lay asleep in her kitchen and the way her eyes danced with michief as she stood jollying them in Sioux. We noticed that none of them lost any time in finding out if they were bewitched.

OLD RAIL FENCE CORNERS

Our Indians when they came to see mother wanted to do as she did. They would sit up to the table and she would give them a plate and knife and fork. This pleased them much. They would start with the food on their plates but soon would have it all in their laps.

They were very dissatisfied with the way the whites were taking their lands. The big treaty at Traverse de Sioux was especially distasteful to them. They said their lands had been stolen from them. They were very angry at my father because he put a rail fence across their trail and would have killed him if it had not been for mother.

The last time these good friends came was in May, 1862. A large body of them on horseback camped on the little knoll across from our house where the dead tree now is. They were sullen and despondent. Well do I remember the dramatic gestures of their chief as he eloquently related their grievances. My mother followed every word he said for she knew how differently they were situated from their former condition. When she first knew them they owned all the country—the whites nothing. In these few years the tables had been turned. Her heart bled for them, her childhood's companions. He said his warriors could hardly be kept from the warpath against the whites. That, so far, his counsel had prevailed, but every time they had a council it was harder to control them. That their hunting and fishing grounds were gone, the buffalo disappearing and there was no food for the squaws and papooses. The Great White Father had forgotten them, he knew, for their rations were long overdue and there was hunger in the camp.

They slept that night in our kitchen, "Little beckoning boy" and the other playmates. I can still see the sad look on my mother's face as she went from one to the other giving each a big, hot breakfast and trying to cheer them. She could see how they had been wronged. She stood and watched them sadly as they mounted their ponies and vanished down the old trail.

Lieut. Governor Gilman—1855.

The winter of '55 and '56 was thirty five degrees below zero two weeks at a time and forty degrees below was usual.

I have often seen the Red River carts ford the river here. They crossed at the foot of Sixth Street between where the two warehouses are now.

Mrs. Austin W. Farnsworth—1855.

We came to Dodge County in 1855. The first year we were hailed out and we had to live on rutabagas and wild tea. We got some game too, but we were some tired of our diet before things began to grow again. When that hailstorm came we were all at a quilting bee. There was an old lady, Mrs. Maxfield there, rubbing her hundred mark pretty close. She set in a corner and was not scared though the oxen broke away and run home and we had to hold the door to keep it from blowing in. We said, "Ain't you afraid?" She answered, "No, I'm not, if I do go out, I don't want to die howling."

The first time I worked out, when I was fourteen years old, I got 50c a week. There was lots to do for there were twin babies. I used to get awful homesick. I went home Saturdays and when I came over the hill where I could see our cabin, I could have put my arms around it and kissed it, I was that glad to see home.

Mr. Theodore Curtis—1855, Minneapolis.

When I was a little boy my father was building some scows down where the Washington Avenue bridge now is at the boat landing. There were five or six small sluiceways built up above the river leading from the platform where the lumber from the mills was piled, down to where these scows were. These sluices were used to float the lumber down to the scows. A platform was built out over the river in a very early day and was, I should say, three hundred feet wide and one thousand feet long. As the lumber came from the mills it was piled in huge piles along this platform. Each mill had its sluiceway but they were all side by side.

It was very popular to drive down on this platform and look at the falls, whose roaring was a magnet to draw all to see them.

We boys used to play under this platform jumping from one support to another and then finish up by running down the steps and cavorting joyously under the falls. I used to get the drinking water for the workmen from the springs that seeped out everywhere along near where my father worked. Once he sent me to get water quickly. I had a little dog with me and we unthinkingly stepped in the spring making the water roily. Childlike, I never thought of going to another but played around waiting for it to settle, then as usual took it on top of the sluiceways. It seemed father thought I had been gone an hour and acted accordingly. I shall always remember that whipping.

Mrs. Charles M. Godley—1856.

My father, Mr. Scrimgeour, came to Minneapolis in 1855 and built a small home between First and Second Avenues North on Fourth Street. When my mother arrived she cried when she saw where her home was to be and said to her husband, as he was cutting the hazel brush from around the house, "You told me I would not have to live in a wilderness if I came here."

Mr. Morgan lived across the street. He and my father decided to dig a well together and put it in the street so that both families could use it. My father said to Mr. Morgan, "Of course, there is a street surveyed here, but the town will never grow to it, so the well will be alright here."

Mr. Morgan was a great bookworm and not at all practical. If his horse got out and was put in with other strays, he could never tell it, but had to wait until everyone took theirs and then he would take what was left.

There was a big sand hole at the corner of Second Avenue South and Fourth Street where they had dug out sand. It was the great playground for all the children, for it was thought the town would never grow there and so it was a good place for a sand hole.

When I went to school I always followed an Indian trail that led from Hoag's Lake to the government mill. It was bordered by hazel brush and once in a while a scrub oak. I was much disturbed one night on my way home, to find men digging a hole through my beloved trail. I hoped they would be gone in the morning, but to my great disappointment they were not, for they were digging the excavation for the Nicollet House. My school was in an old store building at the falls and was taught by Oliver **Gray.**

Dr. Barnard lived on the corner by our house. He was Indian agent and very kind to the Indians. One night a number of them came in the rain. Mr. Barnard tried to get them to sleep in the house. All refused. One had a very bad cough so the doctor insisted on his coming in and gave him a room with a bed. Shortly after, they heard a terrible noise with an awful yell like a warwhoop. The Indian dashed down the stairs, out of the house and away. The slats in the bed were found broken and the bed was on the floor. Later, they found that he had started for bed from the furthest side of the room, run with full force and plunged in and through.

In 1857, when the panic came, all stores in Minneapolis failed and there was not a penny in circulation. Everything was paid by order.

There was a small farmhouse where the Andrews Hotel now stands. Fourth Street North, that led to it from our house, was full of stumps. We got a quart of milk every night at this place. They never milked until very late so it was dark. I used to go for it. My mother always gave me a six quart pail so that after I had stumbled along over those stumps, the bottom of the pail at least would be covered.

No one who was used to an eastern climate had any idea how to dress out here when they first came. I wore hoops and a low necked waist just as other little girls did. I can remember the discussion that took place before a little merino sack was made for me. I don't remember whether I was supposed to be showing the white feather if I surrendered to the climate and covered my poor little bare neck or whether I would be too out of style. I must have looked like a little picked chicken with goose flesh all over me. Once before this costume was added to, by the little sack, my mother sent me for a jug of vinegar down to Helen Street and Washington Avenue South. I had on the same little hoops and only one thickness of cotton underclothing under them. It must have been twenty degrees below zero. I thought I would perish before I got there, but childlike, never peeped. When I finally reached home, they had an awful time thawing me out. The vinegar was frozen solid in the jug.

A boardwalk six blocks long was built from Bridge Square to Bassett's Hall on First Street North. It was a regular sidewalk, not just two boards laid lengthwise and held by crosspieces as the other sidewalks were. Our dress parade always took place there. We would walk back and forth untiringly, passing everybody we knew and we knew everybody in town. Instead of taking a girl out driving or to the theatre, a young man would ask, "Won't you go walking on the boardwalk?"

Lucy Morgan used to go to school with us when we first came. She had long ringlets and always wore lownecked dresses, just as the rest of us did, but her white neck never had any gooseflesh on it and she was the only one who had curls.

We went to high school where the court house now stands. It was on a little hill, so we always said we were climbing the "Hill of Knowledge."

OLD RAIL FENCE CORNERS

I can well remember the dazed look that came on my father's face when for the first time, he realized that there were horses in town that he did not know. The town had grown so that he could not keep pace with it.

Mr. Frank Slocum—1856.

When we drove from St. Paul to Cannon Falls in '56 we only saw one small piece of fence on the way. A man by the name of Baker at Rich Valley in Dakota County had this around his door yard. He had dug a trench and thrown up a ridge of dirt. On top of this he had two cross pieces and a rail on top. You call it a rail fence. We called it oftener "stake and rider." We followed the regular road from St. Paul to Dubuque.

The original Indian trail which was afterward the stage road, started at Red Wing and went through Cannon Falls, Staunton, Northfield, Dundas, Cannon City to Faribault.

My father had a store in Cannon Falls. I was only thirteen and small for my age but I used to serve. One day a big Indian came in when I was alone and asked for buckshot. They were large and it did not take many to weigh a pound. He picked a couple out and pretended to be examining them. I weighed the pound and when I saw he did not put them back, I took out two. You never saw an Indian laugh so hard in your life. You always had to be careful when weighing things for Indians, for if you got over the quantity and took some out they were always grouchy as they thought you were cheating them.

The farmers used to come through our town on their way to Hastings with their grain on their ox drawn wagons. They had a journey of two hundred miles from Owatonna to Hastings and back. They would go in companies and camp out on the way.

During the years of '56 and '57 many people could not write home as they had no money to pay postage. Our business was all in trade.

OLD RAIL FENCE CORNERS

In 1854 a man whom we all knew who lived up above Mankato took an Indian canoe and paddled down the river to St. Paul. There he sold it for enough money to pay his fare back on the boat. He was a man of considerable conscience in his dealings with white men but when a man was only "an injun" it had not caught up with him yet. Now for the sequel: The man who bought it had it under the eaves of his house to catch rain water. During a storm his window was darkened. He looked up to see an Indian with his blanket held high to darken the window so he could see in. The white man went out. The savage said, "My canoe. Want him." The man would not give it up, but the Indian and his friends went to the authorities and he had to. They had traced it all that long way.

We bought an elevated oven cook stove in St. Paul and it was in use every day for fifty years. We brought Baker knock down chairs with us and they have been in constant use for fifty-eight years—have never been repaired and look as if they were good for one hundred years more.

We made coffee from potato chips, sliced very thin and browned in the oven. Not such bad coffee, either.

Mrs. T. B. Walker—Minneapolis.

I remember going to market in the morning and seeing a wagon with all the requisites for a home, drive up to a vacant lot. On the wagon were lumber, furniture and a wife and baby. What more could be needed! When I passed in the afternoon the rough house was up, the stove pipe through the window sent out a cheery smoke and the woman sang about her household tasks.

One morning I was at church in St. Anthony. The minister had just given out the text when the squeaking of the Red River carts was faintly heard. He hastily said, "To be discoursed on next Sunday," for nothing but this noise could be heard when they were passing.

OLD RAIL FENCE CORNERS

Mrs. Virginia Jones—1856.

I lived in St. Peter in 1856. The Sioux Indians were having a scalp dance at Traverse. Their yelling could be plainly heard in St. Peter. All of that town went over to see them dance. They had a pole decorated with several scalps. These were stretched on hoops and painted red inside. The Indians danced round and round this pole, jumping stiff legged, screeching and gesticulating, while the tom-toms were pounded by the squaws. I was frightened and wanted to leave, but could not as I had been pushed near the front and the crowd was dense. Seeing my fear the Indians seized me by the hands and drew me into their circle, making me dance round and round the pole.

Some days later I started east to spend the summer with my mother. Distances were long in those days as the trip was made by steamboat and stage coach. I took one of the steamers which then ran regularly on the Minnesota river, sorrowfully parting from my husband as I did not expect to see him again until fall. That anguish was all wasted for we stuck on a sand bank just below town and my husband came over in a boat and lived on the steamer for nearly a week before we could get off the sandbar.

Mrs. Georgiana M. Way—1856.

We moved to Minnesota from Iowa. Came with a prairie schooner. The country was very wild. We settled on a farm five miles south of Blue Earth. We brought along a cow and a coop of chickens. The roads were awfully rough. We would milk the cow, put the milk in a can and the jarring that milk got as those oxen drew that wagon over the rough roads gave us good butter the next day. Our first shack was not a dugout, but the next thing to it. It was a log shed with sloping roof one way. We had two windows of glass so did not feel so much like pioneers.

The rattlesnakes were very thick. We used to watch them drink from the trough. They would lap the water with their tongues just as a dog does. Many a one I have cut in two with the ax. They always ran but I was slim in those days and could catch them.

We used prairie tea and it was good too. It grew on a little bush. For coffee we browned beets and corn meal. Corn meal coffee was fine. I'd like a cup this minute.

Once a family near us by the name of Bonetrigger lived for four days on cottonwood buds or wood browse as it was called.

We drove forty-five miles to Mankato to get our first baby clothes. When we got in our first crop of wheat, I used to stand in the door and watch it wave as the wind blew over it and think I had never seen anything so beautiful. Even the howling of the wolves around our cabin did not keep us awake at at night. We were too tired and too used to them. The years flew by. I had three children under five when my husband enlisted. I was willing, but oh, so sad! He had only three days to help us before joining his company. Our wood lot was near, so near I could hear the sound of his ax as he cut down all the wood he could and cut it into lengths for our winter fuel. You can imagine how the sound of that ax made me feel, although I was willing he should go. When he was gone, I used to put the children on the ox sled and bring a load of wood home. Pretty heavy work for a woman who had never seen an ox until she was married. I was brought up in New York City, but I did this work and didn't make any fuss about it, either. I did all kinds of farm work in those days for men's help wasn't to be had, they were all in the war.

When I needed flour, there was no man to take the wheat to mill. The only one who could, wanted to charge $1.00 a day and I did not have it, so I left my darlings with a neighbor, got him to hist the sacks aboard for me, for says I, "I'm not Dutchy enough to lift a sack of grain," and long before daylight I was beside those oxen on my way to the nearest grist mill, fifteen miles away, knitting all the way. It was tough work, but I got there. I engaged my lodging at the hotel and then went to the mill. There were a number there, but they were all men. The miller, Mr. Goodnow, said "It's take turns here, but I won't have it said that a 'soldier's widow' (as they called us) has to wait for men, so I'll grind yours first and you can start for home at sunup, so you can get home by dark; I want you to stay at our house tonight." After some demurring, for I wan't no hand to stay where I couldn't pay, I accepted his most kind invitation. In the morning, when he saw me start, after he had loaded my sacks of flour on for me, he said, "Get the man living this side of that big hill to put you down it." I said, "I came up alone, alright." He said, "Woman, you had grain then, you could have saved it if it fell off and your sacks broke, but now you have flour."

When my boy was three weeks old, I drove fourteen miles to a dance and took in every dance all night and wasn't sick afterward either. Of course, I took him along.

When I came to sell my oxen after my husband died in the army, no one wanted to give me a fair price for them, because I was a woman, but Mr. S. T. McKnight, who had a small general store in Blue Earth gave me what was right and paid me $2.50 for the yoke besides.

We had company one Sunday when we first came and all we had to eat was a batch of biscuits. They all said they was mighty good too and they never had a better meal.

We all raised our own tobacco. I remember once our Probate Judge came along and asked, "Have you any stalks I can chew?" It was hard to keep chickens for the country was so full of foxes. Seed potatoes brought $4.00 a bushel. We used to grate corn when it was in the dough grade and make bread from that. It was fine.

In 1856 and 1857 money was scarcer than teeth in a fly. We never saw a penny sometimes for a year at a time. Everything was trade.

OLD RAIL FENCE CORNERS

Mrs. Duncan Kennedy—1856.

My father moved from Canada to Minnesota. He was urged to come by friends who had gone before and wrote back that there was a wonderful piece of land on a lake, but when we got there with an ox team after a two days trip from St. Paul, our goods on a lumber wagon—we thought it was a mudhole. We were used to the clear lakes of Canada and this one was full of wild rice. It was near Nicollet Village. The road we took from St. Paul went through Shakopee, Henderson and Le Seuer. They said it was made on an old Indian trail.

The turnips grew so enormous on our virgin soil that we could hardly believe they were turnips. They looked more like small pumpkins inverted in the ground.

The wild flowers were wonderful too. In the fall, the prairies were gay with the yellow and sad with the lavender bloom.

The first party we went to was a housewarming. We went about seven miles with the ox team. I thought I would die laughing when I saw the girls go to their dressing room. They went up a ladder on the outside. There were two fiddlers and we danced all the old dances. Supper was served on a work bench from victuals out of a wash tub. We didn't have hundred dollar dresses, but we did have red cheeks from the fine clear air.

One day when I was alone at my father's, an Indian with feathers in his headband and a painted face and breast came quickly into the house, making no noise in his moccasined feet. He drew his hand across his throat rapidly saying over and over, "Tetonka-tetonka," at the same time trying to drag me out. I was terrified as I thought he was going to cut my throat. Fortunately my father happened to come in, and not fearing the Indian whom he knew to be friendly, went with him and found his best ox up to his neck in a slough. It seemed "Tetonka" meant big animal and he was trying to show us that a big animal was up to his neck in trouble.

Afterward, I married Mr. Duncan Kennedy and moved to Traverse. I papered and painted the first house we owned there until it was perfect. I did so love this, our first home, but my husband was a natural wanderer. One day he came home announcing that he had sold our pretty home. We moved into a two room log house on a section of land out near where my father lived. The house was built so that a corner stood in each quarter section and complied with the law that each owner of a quarter section should have a home on it. It was built by the four Hemmenway brothers and was always called "Connecticut" as they came from there.

My husband worked for Mr. Sibley and was gone much of the time buying furs. Then he carried mail from Traverse to Fort Lincoln. Once in a blizzard he came in all frozen up, but he had outdistanced his Indian guide—you couldn't freeze him to stay—he was too much alive. He once traveled the seventy-five miles from Traverse to St. Paul in one day He just took the Indian trot and kept it up until he got there. He always took it on his travels. He could talk Sioux French and English with equal facility. Mr. Cowen once said when my husband passed, "There goes the most accomplished man in the State."

They used to tell this story about Mr. Cowen. He had cleared a man accused of theft. Afterward he said to him, "I have cleared you this time, but don't you ever do it again."

When the outbreak came, my husband was storekeeper at Yellow Medicine. A halfbreed came running and told him to fly for his life, as the Indians were killing all the whites. Mr. Kennedy could not believe this had come, though they knew how ugly the Indians were. After seeing the smoke from the burning houses, he got his young clerk, who had consumption, out; locked the door, threw the key in the river; then carried the clerk to the edge of the river and dropped

OLD RAIL FENCE CORNERS

him down the bank where the bushes concealed him, and then followed him. The Indians came almost instantly and pounded on the door he had just locked. He heard them say in Sioux "He has gone to the barn to harness the mules." While they hunted there, he fled for his life, keeping in the bushes and tall grass. All doubled up, as he was obliged to be, he carried the clerk until they came to the plundered warehouse, where a number of refugees were hiding. That night, he started for the fort, arriving there while it was still **dark**.

A call was made for a volunteer to go to St. Peter to acquaint them with the danger. My husband had a badly swollen ankle which he got while crawling to the fort. Nevertheless, he was the first volunteer. Major Randall said, "Take my horse; you can never get there without one," but Mr. Kennedy said, "If the Indians hear the horse they will know the difference between a shod horse and an Indian pony. I will go alone." Dr. Miller tried to make him take half the brandy there was in the fort, by saying grimly, "If you get through you will need it. If you don't we won't need it." He started just before dawn taking the Indian crawl. He had only gone a short distance when the mutilated body of a white man interposed. This was so nauseating that he threw away the lunch he had been given as he left the fort for he never expected to live to eat it. He passed so near an Indian camp that he was challenged, but he answered in Sioux in their gruff way and so satisfied them. When he came near Nicollet village he crawled up a little hill and peered over. He saw two Indians on one side and three on the other. He dropped back in the grass. He looked for his ammunition and it was gone. He had only two rounds in his gun. He said, "I thought if they have seen me there will be two dead Indians and one white man." When he came to what had been Nicollet Village, the camp fires that the Indians had left were still burning. He reached St. Peter and gave the alarm.

OLD RAIL FENCE CORNERS

Major S. A. Buell—1856.

Major Buell eighty-seven years old, whose memory is remarkable says:—I came to Minnesota in 1856, settling in St. Peter and practicing law. Early in 1856, Mr. Cowen, one of the brightest lawyers and finest men Minnesota has ever known, came to Traverse de Sioux with his family, to open a store. He soon became a warm friend of Judge Flandreau who urged him to study law with him. He was made County Auditor and in his spare time studied law and was admitted to the bar. He was much beloved by all, a sparkling talker—his word as good as his bond. He had never been well and as time went on, gradually grew weaker. His house was a little more than a block from his office, but it soon became more than he could do to walk that distance. On the common, half way between the two, was the liberty pole. He had a seat made at this point and rested there. When he was no more, the eyes of his old friends would grow misty when they passed this hallowed spot.

Soon after I made the acquaintance of Judge Flandrau at Traverse de Sioux there was a young man visiting him from Washington. The judge took us both on our first prairie chicken hunt. We had no dog. On the upper prairie back of the town going along a road, we disturbed an old prairie hen that attempted to draw us away from her young. The Judge had admonished us that we must **never kill on the ground, always on the wing,** to be sportsmen. This hen scudded and skipped along a rod or two at a time. Finally, he said, "Fellows, I can't stand this, I must shoot that chicken, you won't tell if I do?" We pledged our word. He fired and missed. After we got home, we told everybody for we said we had only promised not to tell if he shot it. We never enjoyed this joke half as much as he did. We always joked him about making tatting.

Flandrau, dearest of men, true as steel, decided in character, but forgiving in heart, a warm friend— was one of the greatest men our state has ever known. He was a tall, dark man, and very active. He had often told me how he and Garvie, clerk for the Indian Trader at Traverse de Sioux used to walk the seventy-five miles to St. Paul in two days. He once walked 150 miles in three days to the land office at Winona.

In 1858 I built my own home in St. Peter and made my garden. The year before I had gone into a clump of plums when they were fruiting and tied white rags to the best. I had moved them into my garden and they were doing fine. One day I took off my vest as I was working and hung it on one of these trees. Suddenly my attention was attracted to the sky and I never saw a more beautiful sight. A horde of grasshoppers were gently alighting. Nothing more beautiful than the shimmering of the sun on their thousands of gold-bronze wings could be imagined. They took everything and then passed on leaving gardens looking as if they had been burned. When I went for that vest, they had eaten it all but the seams. It was the funniest sight—just a skeleton. Not a smitch of white rags left on the trees, either.

We people who lived in Minnesota thought there was only one kind of wild grape. A man by the name of Seeger who had been in Russia and was connected with a wine house in Moscow came to St. Peter. In the Minnesota valley were immense wild grape vines covering the tallest trees. Here he found five distinct varieties of grapes and said one kind would make a fine red wine—Burgundy. He told me how to make this wine from grapes growing wild on my own farm. I made about ten gallons. When it was a year old it was very heady.

Edward Eggleston belonged to a debating society in St. Peter and was on the successful side in a debate, "Has Love a Language not Articulate." He was a Methodist preacher here, but later had charge of a Congregational church in Brooklyn, N. Y. He said when the Methodists abolished itinerancy and mission work, he thought the most useful part of the church was gone.

In my boyhood days at home, a little boy in the

neighborhood had the misfortune to drink some lye. Fortunately the doctor was near and using a stomach pump saved his life for the time being. However, the child's stomach could retain nothing. In a short time he was a skeleton indeed. One day his father who carried him around constantly, happened to be by the cow when she was being milked. The child asked for some milk and was given it directly from the cow. Great was the father's astonishment when the little lad retained it. Milk given him two minutes after milking was at once ejected. The father had a pen made just outside his son's bedroom window and the cow kept there, and here many times a day the cow was milked and the milk instantly given. After several months the child was restored to health.

One night in Minnesota just as I was going to sit down to supper my wife told me that a man who had just passed told her that a child that lived ten miles back in the country had drank lye some days before and was expected to die, as he could retain nothing. Without waiting to eat my supper I jumped on a horse and made the trip there in record speed. This child followed the same formula and was saved.

It was easy for youngsters to get at lye for every house had a leach for the making of soap. This lye was made by letting water drip over hard wood ashes in a barrel. A cupful would be taken out and its strength tried. If it would hold up an egg it was prime for soap. It was clear as tea, if it was left in a cup it was easily mistaken for it.

During the days when New Ulm was expecting a second Indian attack and the town was full of refugees, I was ordered to destroy some buildings on the outskirts. I started with a hotel and opened all the straw ticks that had been used for refugees beds and threw the contents all around. I believed all the people had left but thought I would go in every room and make sure of this. In one room I heard a queer noise and going to the bed found a small baby that had been tomahawked. Its little head was dented in two places.

I took it with me and went out. Its grandmother who owned the place came running frantically and took it from me. Its father and mother had been killed and it had been brought in by the refugees. In the hasty departure it had been overlooked, each one supposing the other had taken it.

On the 25th day of August after the massacre of the 22nd, around New Ulm and in that vicinity, a little boy who had saved himself from the Indians by secreting himself in the grass of the swamps, came into New Ulm and said there were twelve people alive and a number of bodies to be buried sixteen miles from New Ulm. He said he had seen a man who was driving a horse and wagon, shot and scalped, but could not tell what had become of the woman and baby that were riding with him. The troops marched to the place, having the boy as a guide, buried a number of bodies and brought the twelve survivors to New Ulm. They could find no trace of the woman and baby, although the father's body was found and buried.

Later the troops marched to Mankato, stopping at an empty farm house sixteen miles from New Ulm for the night. This farm house was on a small prairie surrounded by higher land. The sentries were ordered to watch the horizon with the greatest care for fear the skulking Indians might ambush the troops. It was a night when the rain fell spasmodically alternating with moonlight. Suddenly one of the sentries saw a figure on the horizon and watched it disappear in the grass, then appear and crawl along a fence in his direction. He called, "Who goes there?" at the same time cocking his gun ready to shoot. At the answer, "Winnebago" he fired. At that moment there had been a little shower and his gun refused to fire. Later he found that the cap had become attached to the hammer and the powder must have been dampened by the shower. He dashed for the figure to find a white woman and baby and was horrified to think that if the gun had fired, she would have been blown to pieces. This was the woman for whom they had looked in the swamp thirty miles away. He aroused the troops, who took her in. She held out her baby whose hand was partly shot away, but said nothing about herself. Later they found that she had been shot through the back and the wound had had no dressing except when she laid down in the streams. Her greatest fear had been that the baby would cry, but during all those eight awful days and nights while she lay hidden in the swamps or crawled on her way at night, this baby had never made a sound. As soon as it became warm and was thoroughly fed, it cried incessantly for twelve hours. The mother said that for three days the Indians had pursued her with dogs, but she had managed to evade them by criss-crossing through the streams. She had said "Winnebago" as she thought she was approaching a Sioux camp and they were supposed to be friendly to the Winnebagoes. She would then have welcomed captivity as it seemed that the white people had left the earth and death was inevitable.

In May 1857, eggs were selling in St. Peter for 6c a dozen, butter at 5c per pound and full grown chickens at 75c a dozen as game was so plentiful.

Mrs. Jane Sutherland—1856.*

Mrs. Cowan came to Traverse in 1856 when it was almost nothing. At her home in Baltimore she had always had an afternoon at home, so decided to continue them here. She set aside Thursday and asked everyone in town, no matter what their situation in life, to come. My maiden name was Jane Donnelly and she asked me to come and "Help pass things"—"assist"—as you call it now. She had tea and biscuits. Flour and tea were both scarce so she warned me not to give anyone more than one biscuit or one cup of tea. This we rigidly adhered to. She had the only piano in our part of the country and we all took great pride in it. I could sing and play a little in the bosom of my family, but was most easily embarassed. Judge Flandrau was our great man. He dropped in, bringing his tatting shuttle, and sat and made tatting as well as

* A sister of Mrs. Duncan Kennedy.

any woman. Mrs. Cowan explained that he had learned this on purpose to rest his mind and keep it off from weighty matters. Mrs. Cowan insisted that I should sing and play while he was there. I resisted as long as I could, then was led still protesting to the piano where I let out a little thin piping, all the while covered with confusion. When I arose we both looked expectantly toward the Judge, but he never raised his eyes—just kept right on tatting.

Finally Mrs. Cowan asked, "Don't you like music, Judge?" He looked up with a far-away look in his eyes and said, "Yes, martial music in the field." Then we knew he had never heard a thing, for, as Mrs. Cowan explained to me as we were making a fresh pot of tea, "He is the kindest man in the world. If he had noticed you were singing he would have said something nice."

Shortly after this we took a claim out at Middle Lake and moved out there to live. The first time I came into town was on a load of wild hay drawn by my father's oxen. The man I later married saw me, a girl of sixteen, sitting there and said he fell in love with me then. A few days later he drove past our farm and saw me out in the corn field trying to scare away the blackbirds. I was beating on a pan and whooping and hollering. That finished him for he said he could see I had all the requisites for a good wife, "Industry and noise."

During the outbreak of 1862, after my husband went to the war, we were repeatedly warned to leave our home and flee to safety. This we were loath to do as it would jeopardize our crops and livestock. We often saw the Indian scouts on a hill overlooking the place and sometimes heard shots. One day I was with my children at a neighbors when a new alarm was given by a courier. Without waiting for us to get any clothes or tell my parents, the farmer hitched up and we fled to Fort Snelling. It was two months before I ever saw my home or parents.

There were three grasshopper years when we never got any crops at Middle Lake. When I say that, I mean just what I say; we got nothing. The first time they came the crops were looking wonderful. Wheat fields so green and corn way up. The new ploughed fields yielded marvelously and this was the first year for ours. I went out to the garden about ten o'clock to get the vegetables for dinner and picked peas, string beans, onions and lettuce that were simply luscious. The tomatoes were setting and everything was as fine as could be. I felt so proud of it. The men came home to dinner and the talk was all in praise of this new country and the crops. While we were talking it gradually darkened. The men hastily went out to see if anything should be brought in before the storm. What a sight when we opened the door! The sky darkened by myriads of grasshoppers and no green thing could be seen. Everything in that lovely garden was gone. By the middle of the afternoon, when they left, the wheat fields looked as if they had been burned, even the roots eaten. Not a leaf on the trees. My husband's coat lying outside was riddled. Back of the house where they had flown against it they were piled up four feet high. They went on after awhile leaving their eggs to hatch and ruin the crops the following year. And enough the second for the third, though we did everything. The last year the county offered a bounty of three cents a bushel for them and my little boy, four years old, caught enough with a net to buy himself a two dollar pair of boots. You can perhaps get an idea how thick they were from that. The rail fences used to look as if they were enormous and bronzed. The grasshoppers absolutely covered them.

We lived only a short distance from my father's farm. One afternoon I saw smoke coming from there and could hear explosions like that of cannon. I caught our pony, jumped on bareback, and dashed for their home. We trusted the Indians and yet we did not. They were so different from the whites. I thought they had attacked the family. I don't know how I expected to help without a weapon of any kind, but on I went. When I got there I saw my father and mother tearing a board fence down. A swamp on the place was afire and the fire coming through that long swamp grass very rapidly. The swamp had a number of large willows and when the fire would reach them they would explode with a noise like a cannon. I don't know why, but I have heard many of the old settlers tell of similar experiences. I jumped off the pony and helped tear down the fence.

Governor Swift had paid me $5.00 to make him a buffalo coat. I had put it all into "nigger blue" calico and had the dress on. When we went into the house mother said, "What a shame you have spoiled your new dress." I could see nothing wrong, but in the back there was a hole over twelve inches square burned out.

Another time my husband was a short distance from the house putting up wild hay. We had several fine stacks of it near the house in the stubble. I happened to glance out and saw our neighbor's stacks burning and the fire coming through the stubble for ours. I grabbed a blanket, wet it soaking and dragging that and a great pail of water, made for the stacks. I run that wet blanket around the stacks as fast as I could several times. My husband came driving like mad with half a load of hay on the rack and grabbed me but as the stubble was short that sopping saved the stacks.

We had a German hired man that we paid $30 a month for six months. Crops were plentiful and we hoped for a good price. No such good luck. Wheat was 25c a bushel and oats 12½. He hauled grain to market with our ox team to pay himself and was nearly all winter getting his money. That was before the war. We boarded him for nothing while he was doing it. How little those who enjoy this state now think what is cost the makers of it!

Mrs. Mary Robinson—1856.

We came to St. Anthony in 1856. Butter was

12½c a pound; potatoes 15c a bushel and turnips, 10c. I have never seen finer vegetables. We made our mince pies of potatoes soaked in vinegar instead of apples.

One of our neighbors was noted for her molasses sponge cake. If asked for the recipe, she would give it as follows: "I take some molasses and saleratus and flour and shortening, and some milk. How much? Oh, a middling good sized piece, and enough milk to make it the right thickness to bake good." Needless to say, she continued to be the only molasses sponge cake maker.

Mrs. Margaret A. Snyder—1856.

Mr. Snyder and Mr. Pettit used to batch it in a cabin in Glencoe before our marriage. In '56 we decided to move to Glencoe and live in this place. We, together with Mr. Cook and Mr. McFarland were forty-eight hours going the sixty miles. We stayed the first night at Carver and the next night got to "Eight Mile Dutchman's." When we came to the cabin we found the walls and ceiling covered with heavy cotton sheeting. My mother had woven me a Gerton rag carpet which we had with us. The stripes instead of running across, ran lengthwise. There was a wide stripe of black and then many gaily colored stripes. When it was down on the floor, it made everything cheerful. We had bought some furniture too in Minneapolis so everything looked homelike. Later, six of us neighbor women were invited into the country to spend the day. While we were gone some of the neighbors said, "The mosquitoes must be awful at the Snider's today—they have such a smudge." A little later, they saw the house was in flames. In this fire, we lost money and notes together with all our possessions. These notes were never paid, as we had no record so we were left poor indeed. We were able to get boards for the sides of our new house, but lived in it six weeks without a roof, doors or windows. We had a few boards over the bed. There was only one hard rain in all that time but the mosquitoes were awful. During this time, we lived on King Phillip's corn, a large yellow kind. We pounded it in a bag and made it into cakes and coffee. We had nothing to eat on the cakes nor in the coffee and yet we were happy. My husband always kept his gun by the bed during this time. One morning we awoke to see two prairie chickens preening their feathers on the top of our house wall. Father fired and killed both, one falling inside and the other outside.

Mrs. Colonel Stevens was our nearest neighbor. We just took a little Indian trail to her house.

We had wild plums and little wild cherries with stems just like tame cherries, on our farm. They helped out tremendously as they with cranberries were our only fruit.

One morning twelve big braves came into my kitchen when I was getting breakfast. They said nothing to me, just talked and laughed among themselves; took out pipes and all smoked. They did not ask for anything to eat. Finally they went away without trouble.

Indian Charlie, afterwards hung at Mankato, was often at the house and became a great nuisance. He would follow me all over the house. I would say, "Go sit down Charlie," at the same time looking at him determinedly. He would stand and look and then go. He once found my husband's gun and pointed it at me, but I said firmly, stamping my foot, "Put it down Charlie," and very reluctantly he finally did. Then, I took it until he left.

My husband enlisted, so in 1862 we moved to Fort Ridgely and lived in one room. One day three squaws, one of whom was old Betts, came in to sell moccasins. I asked her to make some for my baby and showed her a piece of pork and some sugar I would give her for it. She brought them later. We had eaten that piece of pork and I got another piece which was larger but not the same, of course. When she saw it was not the same, she said, "Cheatey Squaw, Cheatey Squaw," and was very angry. I then gave her the pork and two bowls of sugar instead of one and she went away. Later I saw her in the next room where another family lived and said, "Aunt Betts called me, Cheatey Squaw, Cheatey Squaw." Quick as a flash she drew a long wicked looking knife from her belt and ran for me and it was only by fleeing and locking my own door that I escaped. She was never again allowed on the reservation. Later in the year, before the massacre, I went home to Pennsylvania.

When we built on the corner of Fourth Avenue and Tenth Street, we could plainly hear the roar of St. Anthony Falls. I used to follow an Indian trail part of the way down town.

Mrs. Helen Horton—1856, Minneapolis.

When I came, things were pretty lonesome looking here. I found the young people just as gay as they could be anywhere, however. The first party I attended was a cotillion. I wore a black silk skirt, eighteen feet around the bottom, with three flounces, over hoops too. A black velvet basque pointed front and back, and cut very short on the sides gave a great deal of style to the costume. My hair was brought low in front and puffed over horsehair cushions at the sides. It stuck out five inches from the sides of my head. We danced square dances mostly. We took ten regular dancing steps forward and ten back and floated along just like a thistledown—no clumping around like they do now. Just at this time, I had a plaid silk too. It was green and brown broken plaid. The blocks were nine inches across.

One evening we were to have a sociable. It was great fun playing games and singing. They wanted me to make a cake. It was in the spring months before the boats began to run and after the teams that brought supplies had stopped. It was always a scarce time. I wanted some white sugar to make a white cake as I knew a friend who was to make a pork and dried apple cake, a dark cake, so I wanted the opposite kind. We went everywhere but could find no sugar. I was so disappointed. Finally a friend took his horse and cutter and in one of the houses we were able to find a little. My cake was delicious. Did you ever make a pork apple pie? You cut the pork so thin you can almost see through it. Cover the bottom of a pie tin with it, then cut the apples up on top of this. Put two thin crusts one on top of the other over this, then when cooked, turn upside down in a dish and serve with hard sauce. This recipe is over a hundred years old but nothing can beat it.

The first home we owned ourselves was at the corner of Ninth Street and Nicollet Avenue. There was only one house in sight, that of Mr. Welles. Our whole house was built from the proceeds of land warrants that my husband had bought.

My father had a store at the corner of Helen St., and Washington Avenue. To reach it from our home at Fourth Street and Second Avenue North, we followed an Indian trail. There was generally a big cow with a bell to turn out for somewhere on it.

Mrs. Mary Staring Smith—1856.

When we first came to live at Eden Prairie I thought I had never seen anything so beautiful as that flowering prairie. In the morning we could hear the clear call of the prairie chickens. I used to love to hear it. There were great flocks of them and millions of passenger pigeons. Their call of "pigie! pigie!" was very companionable on that lonely prairie. Sometimes when they were flying to roost they would darken the sun, there were such numbers of them. Geese and ducks were very numerous, too. Black birds were so thick they were a menace to the growing crops. I used to shoot them when I was twelve years old.

Once my father and uncle went deer hunting. They got into some poisonous wild thing, perhaps poison ivy. My uncle's face was awful and father nearly lost his sight. He was almost blind for seven years but finally Dr. Daniels of St. Peter cured him.

Once during war time we could get no one to help us harvest. I cut one hundred acres strapped to the seat, as I was too small to stay there any other way.

OLD RAIL FENCE CORNERS

We had a cow named Sarah. A lovely, gentle creature. Mr. Anderson brought her up on the boat. My dog was an imported English setter. These and an old pig were my only playmates. I used to love to dress my dog up but when I found my old pig would let me tie my sunbonnet on her I much preferred her. She looked so comical with that bonnet on lying out at full length and grunting little comfortable grunts when I would scratch her with a stick.

I never saw such a sad expression in the eye of any human being as I saw in "Otherdays" the Sioux friend of the whites. It seemed as if he could look ahead and see what was to be the fate of his people. Yes, I have seen that expression once since. After the massacre when the Indians were brought to Fort Snelling I saw a young squaw, a beauty, standing in the door of her tepee with just that same look. It used to bring the tears to my eyes to think of her.

There used to be a stone very sacred to the Indians on Alexander Gould's place near us. It was red sandstone and set down in a hollow that they had dug out. The Sioux owned it and never passed on the trail that led by it without squatting in a circle facing it, smoking their pipes. I have often stood near and watched them. I never heard them say a word. They always left tobacco, beads and pipes on it. The Indian trails could be seen worn deep like cattle paths.

At the time of the Indian outbreak the refugees came all day long on their way to the fort. Such a sad procession of hopeless, terrified women and children. Many were wounded and had seen their dear ones slain as they fled to the corn fields or tall grass of the prairies. I can never forget the expression of some of those poor creatures.

Mrs. Mary Massolt—1856.

I first lived at Taylor's Falls. I was only fourteen and spoke little English as I had just come from France. Large bands of Indians used to camp near us. They never molested anything. I took a great fancy to them and used to spend hours in their camps.

OLD RAIL FENCE CORNERS

They were always so kind and tried so hard to please me. When the braves were dressed up they always painted their faces and the more they were dressed the more hideous they made themselves. I would often stick feathers in their head bands, which pleased them very much.

The storms were so terrible. We had never seen anything like them. One crash after another and the lightning constant. Once I was sitting by a little stove when the lightning came down the chimney. It knocked me one way off the bench and moved the stove several feet without turning it over.

Mrs. Anna Todd—1856.

We came to St. Anthony in '56 and lived in one of the Hudson Bay houses on University Avenue between Fourth and Fifth Streets. They were in a very bad state of repair and had no well or any conveniences of any kind. The chimneys would not draw and that in the kitchen was so bad that Mr. Todd took out a pane of glass and ran the stovepipe through that. Everybody had a water barrel by the fence which was filled with river water by contract and in the winter they used melted snow and ice. Mr. Todd built the first piers for the booms in the river. The hauling was all done by team on the ice. The contract called for the completion of these piers by April 15. The work took much more time than they had figured on and Mr. Todd realized if the ice did not hold until the last day allowed, he was a ruined man. There were many anxious days in the "little fur house" as it was called, but the ice held and the money for the contract was at once forthcoming. I remember those winters as much colder and longer than they now are. They began in October and lasted until May.

When we were coming from St. Paul to St. Anthony, just as we came to the highest point, I looked all around and said "This is the most beautiful country I have ever seen.

Where Mrs. Richard Chute lived in Minneapolis, the view was wonderfully beautiful. Near there, was a house with the front door on the back side so that the view could be seen better. Times were very, very hard in '57 and '58. We never saw any money and to our Yankee minds this was the worst part of our new life. A friend had been staying with us for months sharing what we had. One day he said to my husband, "I'm here and I'm stranded, I can see no way to pay you anything, but I can give you an old mare which I have up in the country." He finally induced Mr. Todd to take her and almost immediately, we had a chance to swap her for an Indian pony. A short time after, there was a call for ponies at the fort and the pony was sold to the Government for $50.00 in gold. This seemed like $1,000.00 would now.

The first time I saw an apple in Minnesota was in '58. A big spaniel had come to us, probably lost by some party of homeseekers. After having him a short time, we became very tired of him. One of the teamsters was going to St. Paul, so we told him to take the dog and lose him. Better than that, he swapped him for a barrel of apples with a man who had brought them up the river as a speculation. The new owner was to take the dog back down the river that day, but that dog was back almost as soon as the teamster was. We used to joke and say we lived on that dog all winter.

The early settlers brought slips of all kinds of houseplants which they shared with all. The windows were gay with fuchias, geraniums, roses, etc. Most everyone had a heliotrope too. All started slips under an inverted tumbler to be ready for newcomers.

Mr. Edwin Clarke—1856.

On April 12, 1865, President Abraham Lincoln, two days prior to his assassination, signed my commission as United States Indian Agent for the Chippewas of the Mississippi, Pillager and Lake Winnebagosish bands, and the Indians of Red Lake and Pembina.

The Mississippi Bands, numbering about two thousand five hundred, were principally located around Mille Lac, Gull and Sandy Lakes; the Pillager and

Winnebagosish bands, about two thousand, around Leach, Winnebagosish, Cass and Ottertail Lakes; the Red Lake Bands, numbering about fifteen hundred, were located about Red Lake and the Pembina Bands about one thousand at Pembina and Turtle Mountain, Dakota.

At that time there were no white settlers in Minnesota north of Crow Wing, Long Prairie and Ottertail Lake.

The Chippewa Indians were not migratory in their habits, living in their birch-bark covered wigwams around the lakes, from which the fish and wild rice furnished a goodly portion of their sustenance and where they were convenient to wood and water. The hunting grounds, hundreds of miles in extent, covering nearly one-half of the State, furnished moose, deer and bear meat and the woods were full of rabbits, partridges, ducks, wild geese and other small game. The Indians exchanged the furs gathered each year, amounting to many thousand dollars in value, with traders for traps, guns, clothing and other goods. Some of the Indians raised good crops of corn and vegetables and they also made several thousand pounds of maple sugar annually. They also gathered large amounts of cranberries, blueberries and other wild fruit.

The Chippewa Indians had very few ponies, having no use for them, as it was more convenient to use their birch bark canoes in traveling about the lakes and rivers. At that time the Chippewas were capable of making good living without the Government annuities, which consisted of a cash payment to each man, woman and child of from $5.00 to $10.00 and about an equal amount in value of flour, pork, tobacco, blankets, shawls, linsey-woolsy, flannels, calico, gilling twine for fish nets, thread, etc.

An Indian in full dress wore leggings, moccasins and shirt, all made by the women from tanned deer skins, and trimmed with beads, over which he threw his blanket, and with his gun over his arm and his long hair braided and hanging down, and face streaked with paint, he presented quite an imposing appearance. The young men occasionally supplemented the above with a neat black frock coat.

The Indians during the time I was agent were friendly and it was only upon a few occasions when whiskey had been smuggled in by some unprincipled persons, that they had any quarrels among themselves.

The late Bishops Whipple and Knickerbocker were my traveling companions at different times thru the Indian country, as were General Mitchell of St. Cloud, Daniel Sinclair of Winona, Rev. F. A. Noble of Minneapolis, Rev. Stewart of Sauk Center, Mr. Ferris of Philadelphia, Mr. Bartling of Louisville, Doctors Barnard and Kennedy and others. The late Ennegahbow (Rev. John Johnson) was appointed by me as farmer at Mille Lac upon the request of Shawboshkung, the head chief.

Ma-dosa-go-onwind was head chief of the Red Lake Indians and Hole-in-the-day head chief of the Mississippi bands at the time I was agent.

Captain Isaac Moulton—1857, Minneapolis.

The middle of December 1857, it began to rain and rained for three days as if the heavens had opened. The river was frozen and the sleighing had been fine. After this rain there was a foot of water on the ice. I was on my way to Fond du Lac, Wis. to get insurance on my store that had burned. You can imagine what the roads leading from St. Paul to Hastings were. It took us a whole day to make that twenty mile trip, four stage loads of us.

I have often thought you dwellers in the Twin Cities nowadays give little thought to the days when the stage coach was the essence of elegance in travel. The four or six horses would start off with a flourish. The music of the horn I have always thought most stirring. The two rival companies vied with each other in stage effect. If one driver had an especial flourish, the other tried to surpass him, and so it went on. No automobile, no matter how high powered, can hold a candle to those stage coaches in picturesque effect, for those horses were alive.

On this trip, I hired a man with two yearling steers to take my trunk full of papers from the Zumbro River that we had crossed in a skiff, as the bridge was out, to Minnieski where we could again take the stage. Those steers ran and so did we eight men who were following them in water up to our knees. We reached Minnieski about as fagged as any men could be.

Mr. George A. Brackett—1857, Minneapolis.

Prior to the Indian outbreak, I had charge of the feeding of the troops, comprising Stone's Division at Poolville, Md., with beef and other supplies. In this Division were the First Minnesota, several New York (including the celebrated Tammany Regulars) and Pennsylvania troops. I continued in that service until the Sioux outbreak, when Franklin Steele and myself were requested by General Sibley to go to Fort Ridgely and aid in the commissary department, General Sibley being a brother-in-law of Franklin Steele. I remained in this position until the close of the Sibley campaign, other St. Paul and Minneapolis men being interested with me in the furnishing of supplies.

Just after the battle of Birch Coolie, when General Sibley had assembled at Fort Ridgely a large force to go up the Minnesota River against the Indians, he sent Franklin Steele and myself to St. Peter to gather up supplies for his command. We started in a spring wagon with two good horses. A number of refugees from the fort went with us in Burbank's stages and other conveyances. At that time Burbank was running a line of stages from St. Paul to Fort Ridgely, stopping at intervening points. Allen, the manager of the lines, was in Fort Ridgely. A few miles out the cry was raised, "The Indians are in sight." Immediately the whole party halted. Allen went over the bluff far enough to see down to the bottoms of the river. Soon he returned very much frightened saying, "The valley is full of Indians."

OLD RAIL FENCE CORNERS

This caused such a fright that notwithstanding our protest, the whole party returned pell-mell to Fort Ridgely, except Steele and myself. The party was so panic stricken that Allen was nearly left. He had to jump on behind. We determined to go on. A mile or so further on, we saw a man crawling through the grass. I said to Steele, "There's your Indian," and drove up to him. It proved to be a German who, in broken English said, "The Indians have stolen my cattle and I am hunting for them." Driving a few miles further, we came to what had been Lafayette, burned by the Indians days before. Some of the houses were still smoking.

We stopped at the ruins of a house belonging to a half breed, Mrs. Bush, and killed and ate two chickens with our other lunch. When the refugees got back to the fort they reported to General Sibley that we had gone on. He said we were reckless and sent George McLeod, Captain of the Mounted Rangers, with fifty men to overtake us and bring us back. However, we drove on so fast that McLeod got to St. Peter about the time we did. There we bought out a bakery and set them to baking hard tack, and purchased cattle and made other arrangements for the feeding of the troops.

One day, before this, while I was at General Sibley's camp talking to him, I saw someone coming toward the camp. I called General Sibley's attention to it and he sent an officer to investigate. It proved to be a friendly Indian who had stolen a widow and her children from the hostiles and brought them to the fort. Her husband had been killed by the Indians.

Mrs. C. A. Smith—1858.

In the spring of 1858 we came to St. Paul. We took a boat which plied regularly between St. Paul and Minnesota river points, to Chaska. There we left the boat and walked to Watertown where our new home was to be. My father carried $2,000 in gold in inside pockets of a knitted jacket which my mother had made him. With this money we paid for two quarter sections of improved land and the whole family began to farm. We lived just as we had in Sweden, as we were in a Swedish settlement. We were Lutheran, so there were no parties. Going to church was our only amusement.

The prairies were perfectly lovely with their wild flower setting. There had been a fire two years before and great thickets of blackberry vines had grown up. I never saw such blackberries. They were as large as the first joint of a man's thumb. The flavor was wild and spicy. I never ate anything so good. Cranberries by the hundreds of bushels grew in the swamps. We could not begin to pick all the hazel nuts. We used to eat turnips as we would an apple. They were so sweet, they were as good. We made sun-dials on a clear spot of ground and could tell time perfectly from them.

We children made dolls out of grass and flowers. I have never seen prettier ones. We kept sheep and mother spun and wove blankets and sheets. We had bolts and bolts of cloth that we made and brought with us from Sweden. Here, we raised flax and prepared it for spinning, making our own towels.

Nothing could be cozier than our cabin Christmas eve. We had brought solid silver knives, forks and spoons. These hung from racks. Quantities of copper and brass utensils burnished until they were like mirrors hung in rows. In Sweden mother had woven curtains and bed coverings of red, white and blue linen and these were always used on holidays. How glad we were they were the national colors here! We covered a hoop with gay colored paper and set little wooden candle holders that my father had made all around it. This was suspended from the ceiling, all aglow with dips. Then, as a last touch to the decorations, we filled our brass candle sticks with real candles and set them in the windows as a greeting to those living across the lake. A sheaf for the birds and all was done.

The vegetables grew tremendous. We used to

take turns in shelling corn and grinding it, for bread, in a coffee mill. Mother would say, "If you are hungry and want something to eat of course you will grind." We made maple sugar and fine granulated sugar from that.

My sisters used to walk from Watertown to Minneapolis in one day, thirty-seven miles, following an Indian trail and then were ready for a good time in the evening. How many girls of today could walk that many blocks?

The lake was full of the biggest fish imaginable. We used to catch them, and dry and smoke them. They made a nice variety in our somewhat same diet. We used to fish through the ice, too.

Major C. B. Heffelfinger—1858, Minneapolis.

Well I remember the St. Charles hotel as it was when I first boarded there. The beds were upstairs in one room in two rows. Stages were bringing loads of passengers to Minneapolis. They could find no accomodations so no unoccupied bed was safe for its owners. Although my roommate and I were supposed to have lodging and were paying for it, the only safe way was for one to go to bed early before the stage came in and repel all invaders until the other arrived. If the sentry slept at his post the returning scout was often obliged to sleep on the floor, or snuggle comfortably against a stranger sandwiched between them.

The strangers who arrived had made a stage coach journey from La Crosse without change and spent two nights sitting erect in the coaches, and were so tired that they went to bed with the chickens. On lucky nights for us they were detained by some accident and got in when the chickens were rising.

Nothing was ever stolen and many firm friendships were thus cemented. Our pocketbooks were light, but our hearts were also. It was a combination hard to beat.

1857 was the most stringent year in money that Minnesota has ever known. There was absolutely no money and every store in the territory failed. Everything was paid by order. Captain Isaac Moulton, now of La Crosse, had a dry goods store. A woman, a stranger, came in and asked the price of a shawl. She was told it was $15.00. It was done up for her. She had been hunting through her reticule and now put down the money in gold. The Captain looked at it as if hypnotized, but managed to stammer, "My God woman, I thought you had an order. It is only $5.00 in money."

Mrs. Martha Gilpatrick—1858, Minneapolis.

When I married, my husband had been batching it. In the winter his diet was pork! pork! pork! Mrs. Birmingham, who helped him sometimes, said she bet if all the hogs he ate were stood end to end, they would reach to Fort Snelling.

We had a flock of wild geese that we crossed with tame ones. They were the cutest, most knowing things. I kept them at the house until they were able to care for themselves, then I turned them out mornings. I would go in the pasture and say, "Is that you nice gooses?" They would act so human, be so tickled to see me and flop against me and squawk. When Mr. Fitzgerald came home they would run for him the same way as soon as they saw the horse. They were handsome birds.

I used to go to my sister's. She had a boarding house on the East Side. Her boarders were mill workers and "lathers." That is what we used to call the river drivers. They always had a pike pole in their hand. It looked like a lath from a distance, so they got the name of "lathers" from this.

Mrs. Margaret Hern—1858.

My husband enlisted in the Fall of 1861. It was not a very easy thing for him to do, for our farm was not yet very productive, our three children were very young, one a tiny baby, and we had no ready money. However, he felt that his country called him and when the recruiting officer told him that all soldier's families would be welcome at the post and that we could go there with him, he rented our farm to George Wells and went on to Fort Ridgeley. We lived forty miles from there on the Crow River, near Hutchinson.

We found that the officer had lied. We were not expected or wanted at the fort. We finally made arrangements to stay by promising to board the blacksmith in his quarters. His name was John Resoft. His rations and my husband's supported us all. Mr. Hern was very handy about the house, as he was a Maine Yankee and daily helped me with the work.

There was a great sameness about the life as there were only about a hundred men stationed at the fort. Very few of them had their families with them. The only women were Mrs. Mueller, wife of the doctor, Mrs. Sweet, wife of the chaplain and their three children, Mrs. Edson, the Captain's wife; Sargeant Jones' wife and three children; Mrs. Dunn and their three children; Mrs. Snider and three children; Mrs. Mickel and three children; Mrs. Randall, the sutler's wife, and myself and our three children.

The winter passed monotonously We used to have some fun with the squaws. Once I was writing home to mother. I wanted a little lock of Indian hair to show her how coarse an Indian's hair was. Old Betts happened to come in just then, so I took my scissors and was going to cut a little bit of her "raving locks." When she saw what I was going to do she jumped away screaming and acting like a crazy woman. She never came near that house again, but in the spring after my husband had gone to the front and Mrs. Dunn and I had joined forces and gone to living in another cabin, she stuck her head in our window to beg. I jumped and grabbed a looking glass and held it before her to let her see how she really did look. She was a sight. She had an old black silk hood I had given her and her hair was straggling all over. When she saw the reflection she was so mad she tried to break the glass.

Three weeks before the outbreak, the Sioux, our

GROUP OF CONTRIBUTORS TAKEN AT A PARTY AT THE HOME OF MRS. JAMES T. MORRIS, May 26, 1915
Upper row from left to right: Mrs. Robert Anderson, Mrs. James Pratt, Mrs. John Brown, Mrs. Mary E. Partridge, Mrs. Anna Todd, Mrs. Martha Gilpatrick, Mrs. Rufus Farnham, Mrs. Charles Godley, Mrs. Paulina Starkloff.
Second row: Mrs. Elizabeth Clifford, Mrs. Stephen Rochette.
Lower row: Mrs. Mahlon Black, Mrs. Mary Schmidt, Mrs. Margaret Hern, Mrs. Margaret A. Snyder, Miss Carrie Stratton, Mrs. Mary Weeks, Mrs. Rebecca Plummer. Eleven of these ladies are over eighty-four years old and Mrs. Weeks is ninety. All have wonderful memories.

Indians had a war dance back of the fort and claimed it was against the Chippewas. At first we believed them, but when the half-breed, Indian Charlie, came in to borrow cooking utensils, he sat down and hung his head, as if under the influence of liquor. He kept saying "Too bad! Too bad!"

Mrs. Dunn became suspicious and knowing I knew him well, as he had often stopped at our cabin, said "Ask him what is too bad." He said, "Injins kill white folks. Me like white folks. Me like Injins. Me have to fight. Me don't want to." He seemed to feel broken-hearted. I did not believe him and thought him drunk, but Mrs. Dunn said "You go over and tell Sergeant Jones what he said." I did. Sergeant Jones said, "What nonsense! They are only going to have their war dance. All of you white people go over and see that dance."

We all went. The soldiers were all there. The Indians had two tom-toms, and the squaws beat on them while the Indians, all painted hideously, jumped stiff legged, cut themselves until they were covered with blood and sweat and yowled their hideous war whoop. They were naked excepting their breech clout. Sargeant Jones had control of all the guns at the fort, and unknown to us, the cannon were all trained on the dancers. We could not understand why the soldiers were so near us, but later in the day learned that there was a soldier for everyone of us to snatch us away if it was necessary to fire on the Indians.

On Monday morning, August eighteenth, 1862, at about ten o'clock, we saw a great cloud of dust arising. Soon it resolved itself into teams, people on horseback and on foot coming pell mell for the fort. They said that Redwood Agency, twelve miles distant, had been attacked and the Indians were killing all the white settlers.

As they were flying for their lives, they passed the sutler of the Redwood store lying face downwards with a board on his back on which was written, "Feed your own squaws and papooses grass."

OLD RAIL FENCE CORNERS

He had trusted the Indians until he would do so no longer. Their annuities were long, long overdue and they were starving. They appealed to him again and again and pleaded for food for their starving families. He finally told them to "Go eat grass." The settlers had seen the consequence. They had passed seven dead, besides on the way.

This was only the beginning of a sad multitude of refugees, who, wounded in every conceivable way, and nearly dead from terror, poured into the fort.

Captain Marsh, as soon as he had heard the stories, called the soldiers out on the parade ground and called for volunteers, who would go with him to try and stop the awful carnage. Every soldier came forward. Captain Marsh told them that he thought the sight of the soldiers would cow them as it had so many times before. They at once departed, leaving about thirty men with us.

We knew nothing of what was happening to this little handful of soldiers, but as more and more refugees came in with the terribly mutilated, our fears increased. We knew a small group of the savages could finish us. Just at dusk, Jim Dunn, a soldier of nineteen who always helped us about our work, came reeling in, caked with blood and sweat. I said, "For God's sake, what is the news, Jim?" He only panted, "Give me something to eat quick." After he had swallowed a few mouthfuls, he told us that nearly all of the boys had been killed by the Indians. He said, "The devils got us in the marsh by the river. Quinn told the Captain not to go down there, but he held his sword above his head and said, 'All but cowards will follow me.' The Indians on the other side of the river were challenging us to come by throwing up their blankets way above their heads." Only three more of the boys came in that night.

All of us who were living outside, had gone into the stone barracks with the refugees. That night we were all sitting huddled together trembling with fear. We had helped feed the hungry and cared for the wounded all day long and now were so fatigued we could hardly keep awake. I had brought my little kerosene lamp with me. I lit it and brought out of the darkness the sorrowful groups of women and children. Some one called "Lights out." I turned mine down and set it behind the door. We sat in darkness. A voice called, "Up stairs." I gathered my baby in my arms, told Walter to hold on to mother's dress on one side and Minnie on the other, and up stairs we went, all pushed from behind so we could not stop. We were pushed into a large room, dark as pitch. There we all stood panting through fear and exertion. How long, I do not know. A voice in the room kept calling, "Ota! Ota!" meaning "Many! Many!" We knew there were Indians with us, but not how many. I had the butcher knife sharpened when the first refugees came and covered with a piece of an old rubber. It was now sticking in my belt. I asked Mrs. Dunn what she had to protect herself with. She said she had nothing, but found her shears in her pocket. I told her to put out their eyes with them, while they were killing us, for we expected death every minute after hearing those Indian voices. I heard Jim Dunn's voice and called him and told him where my lamp was and asked him to bring it up. He brought it to me. This was the crucial moment of my life. I sat the lamp on the floor, and with one hand on the butcher knife, slowly turned up the light. I saw only three squaws and three halfbreed boys, instead of the large number of Indians I expected. Each declared "Me good Injin! Me good Injin!"

All was confusion. William Hawley was inside guard at the door of the room we were in upstairs. He was just out of the hospital and was very weak. In spite of this he had gone with the soldiers to Redwood and had just returned after crawling out from under his dead companions and creeping through the brush and long grass those dreadful miles. He was all in. His gun had a fixed bayonet.

My eyes never left those squaws for a moment. I

147

was sure they were spies who would go to the devils outside and tell them of the weakness of the fort. Two of the squaws began to fight about a fine tooth comb. The more formidable of the two, with much vituperation, declared she would not stay where the other one was. Just at the height of the fight, a gun outside was fired. The minute it was fired, the squaw started for the door. I suspected that it was a signal for her to come outside, and tell what she knew. Hawley had left his post and come in among us. Our babies were on a field bed on the floor. Calling to Mrs. Dunn to look after them, I sprang to the door and grabbed the discarded gun. At that moment, the squaw tried to pass. I ordered her back. She called me a "Seechy doe squaw" meaning "mean squaw" and tried to push me back. I raised the bayonet saying, "Go back or I'll ram this through you." She went back growling and swearing in Sioux. Probably in half an hour I was relieved of my self-appointed task. Martin Tanner taking my place, I said to him, "Don't let that squaw get away." I sat down on a board over some chairs and made the squaw sit beside me. There we sat all that long night with my right hand hold of my knife and the other holding her blue petticoat. Didn't she talk to me and revile me? None of the others even tried to leave. At last we saw the dawn appear.

Have you ever been in great danger where all was darkness where that danger was? If so, you will know what an everlasting blessing that daylight was.

From our upper windows we could look out and see that our foes were not yet in sight. All night long among the refugees, praying, supplicating and wailing for the dead, was constant, but as the light came and we began to bestir ourselves among them, nursing the wounded and feeding the hungry, this ceased and only the crying of the hungry children was heard.

The Indians had driven away all the stock so there was no milk. My baby had just been weaned. All those ten days we stayed in the fort, I fed her hard tack and bacon; that was all we had. I chewed this for her. There were many nursing mothers, but all were sustaining more than their own.

There was no well or spring near the fort. All water had to be brought from the ravine by mule team. Early that morning, under an escort, with the cannon trained on them, the men drove the mule teams again and again for water. Busy as all the women who lived at the fort were, I never let that squaw out of my sight. I kept hold of a lock of her hair whenever I walked around. She swore volubly, but came along.

About ten o'clock in the morning Lieutenant Gere, a boy of nineteen, who was left in command when the senior officers were killed, called on me. On a hill to the northwest, a great body of Indians were assembled. He wanted me to look through the field piece and see if Little Crow was the leader. I knew him at once among the cavorting throng of challenging devils. I knew too, whose captive I would be if the fort fell, for he had offered to buy me from my husband for three ponies. He loved so to hear me sing. Mr. Gideon Pond had tried to teach him to sing. We watched them breathlessly as they sat in council knowing that if they came then we were lost. The council was long, but finally after giving the blood curdling war whoop, they rode away.

They were hardly out of sight before the soldiers who had been with us and had just left for Fort Ripley before the outbreak, filed in. Captain Marsh had sent for them just before leaving the fort for Redwood. Those noble fellows, nearly exhausted from the long march, with no sleep for thirty hours, immediately took their places with the defenders, without rest or sleep the night before. Gere had sent to St. Peter for the Renville Rangers and some of our own men. They came in the evening.

The prayers of thanksgiving that could be heard in many tongues from that mournful group of refugees, as they knew of the soldiers return, could never be forgotten. Mrs. Dunn and I had asked for guns to help fight, but there were none for us. There was little ammunition too. The blacksmith, John Resoft, made slugs by cutting iron rods into pieces. Mrs. Mueller, Mrs. Dunn and I worked a large share of that day making cartridges of these, or balls. We would take a piece of paper, give it a twist, drop in some powder and one of these, or a ball, and give it another twist. The soldiers could fire twice as fast with these as when they loaded themselves. All the women helped.

My squaw was still with me. The others made no effort to escape. Just as night came, she broke away and when she really started she could run off with me, as she was big and I only weighed one hundred and three pounds. When I found I could not stop her, I screamed to Sargeant McGrew, "This squaw is going to get away and I can't stop her." He turned his gun on her and shouted, "If you don't go back, I'll blow you to h——." That night I had to sleep and she got away.

With a hundred and sixty soldiers in the fort, all were so reassured that we all slept that night.

The next morning was a repetition of Tuesday. The care of the wounded under that great man, Doctor Mueller and his devoted wife, was our work. One woman who was my especial care had been in bed with a three day's old baby when the smoke from the burning homes of neighbors was seen and they knew the time to fly had come. A wagon with a small amount of hay on it stood near the door with part of a stack of hay by it. Her husband and the hired man placed her and the baby on this and covered them with as much hay as they could get on before the savages came, then mounted the horses and started to ride away. They were at once shot by the Indians who then began a search for her. They ran a pitch fork into the hay over and over again, wounding the woman in many places and hurting the child so that it died. They then set fire to the hay and went on to continue their devilish work elsewhere. She crawled out of the hay more dead than alive and made her way to the fort. Besides the pitchfork holes which were in her legs and back, her hair and eyebrows were gone and she was dreadfully burned.

None of the women seemed to think of their wounds. They lamented their dead and lost, but as far as they themselves were concerned were thankful they were not captives. The suffering of these women stirred me to the depths. One poor German woman had had a large family of children. They all scattered at the approach of the Indians. She thought they were all killed. She would sit looking into space, calling, "Mine schilder! Mine schilder!" enough to break your heart. I thought she had gone crazy when I saw her look up at the sound of a child's voice, then begin to climb on the table calling, "Mine schilder! Mine schilder!" In a group on the other side she had seen four of her children that had escaped and just reached the fort that Wednesday morning.

Early in the afternoon the long expected fighting began. We were all sent up stairs to stay and obliged to sit on the floor or lie prone. All the windows were shot in and the glass and spent bullets fell all around us. I picked up a wash basin heaping full of these and Mrs. Dunn as many more. By evening the savages retired, giving their awful war whoops.

Thursday there was very little fighting as the rain wet the Indians' powder. Mrs. Dunn, Mrs. Sweatt and I spent the time making cartridges in the powder room in our stocking feet. We also melted the spent bullets from the day before and ran them in molds. These helped out the supply of ammunition amazingly.

Friday was the terrific battle. A short distance from the fort was a large mule barn. The Indians swarmed in there. Sergeant Jones understood their method of warfare, so trained cannon loaded with shell on the barn. At a signal these were discharged, blowing up the barn and setting the hay on fire. The air was full of legs, arms and bodies, which fell back into the flames. We were not allowed to look out, but I stood at the window all the time and saw this. Later I saw vast numbers of the Indians with grass and flowers bound on their heads creeping like snakes up to the fort under cover of the cannon smoke. I gave the alarm, and the guns blew them in all directions. There was no further actual fighting, though eternal vigilance was the watchword. It was those hundred and sixty men who saved even Minneapolis and St. Paul, and all the towns between. If Fort Ridgely had fallen, the Sioux warriors would have come right through. General Sibley did not get there with reinforcements until the next Thursday after the last battle.

You can imagine the sanitary condition of all those people cooped up in that little fort. No words I know could describe it.

Note.—Mrs. Hern has a medal from the government for saving the fort.

Mrs. Mary Ingenhutt—1858, Minneapolis.

Mrs Ingenhutt, now one hundred years old, for ninety years has made "Apfel Kuchen," "Fist Cheese" and wine as follows:

Apfel Kuchen—Mix a rich dough using plenty of butter and rich milk. Line a pan with this, cut in squares and cover with apples sprinkled thick with sugar and cinnamon. Bake until apples are thoroughly cooked.

Fist Cheese—Take a pan of clabbered milk. Set over a slow fire. When the whey comes to the top, strain off and shape in balls. Let stand in warm place until it is ripe—that is, until it is strong.

Wine—Grape, currant, rhubarb and gooseberry wine: Mash home grown fruit with a home made potato masher, squeeze it through a coarse cloth, add sugar and place in warm spot to ferment. Draw off in kegs and allow to stand at least two years.

I used to love to go to the picnics in the early days. Everyone had such a good time, and was trying to have everyone else have one, too. Then, all were equal. Nowadays, each one is trying to be prouder than the next one.

Captain L. L. McCormack—

Georgetown on the Red River was the Hudson Bay post. After the railroad was built to St. Cloud the Red River carts crossed there on a ferry and then on the Dakota side went from point to point on the river in the timber to camp. The river is very crooked. A days journey with one of these carts was twelve miles. The first stop was at Elk River, now Dalyrimple, then to Goose River, the present site of Caledonia and then to Frog Point and from there to what is now Grand Forks. The freight was teamed to and from St. Cloud and Benson.

Mr. Charles M. Loring—1860.

On the 20th day of September 1860, I reached Minneapolis with my wife and little son, and went to the Nicollet Hotel where I made arrangements for board for the winter. The hotel was kept by Eustis & Hill. They fixed the price at $6.00 a week including fire and laundry for the family, i. e. $2.00 a week for each person. Mr Loren Fletcher occupied the rooms adjoining and paid the same price that I paid, notwithstanding there were but two in his family, but his rooms were considered to be more favorably located being on the corner of Hennepin and Washington Avenues.

The cook at the hotel was a Mrs. Tibbets from New England who was an expert in preparing the famous dishes of that section of our country, and in the many years that have elapsed since that time, I have never been in a hotel where cooking was so appetizing.

Our first winter in Minnestota was passed in the most delightful and pleasant manner.

The following spring, I rented the house on the corner of what is now Third Avenue and Sixth Street, for the sum of $6.00 a month. This house is still standing and is a comfortable two story New England house. At that time it stood alone on the prairie with not more than three or four houses south of it. One of these is still standing at the corner of Tenth Street and Park Avenue and is occupied as a "Keeley Cure."

There were few luxuries in the market, but everything that could be purchased was good and cheap. There was but one meatshop which was kept by a Mr. Hoblet. He kept his place open in the forenoon only, as his afternoons were spent in driving over the country in search of a "fat critter." The best steaks and roasts were 8c a pound and chickens 4 to 6c a pound. Eggs, we bought at 6c a dozen and butter at 8 to 10c a pound. In winter, we purchased a hind quarter of beef at 3 and 4c a pound, chickens 3c and occasionally pork could be bought at 6c a pound, but this was rarely in market. Mutton was never seen. Prairie chickens, partridges, ducks and venison was very plentiful in the season and very cheap. We used to purchase these in quantities after cold weather came, freeze them and pack them in snow. This worked well provided we had no "January thaw" and then we lost our supplies.

The only fruit we had for winter use was dried apples, wild plums, wild crab apples and cranberries. In the season, we had wild berries which were very plentiful. There was a cranberry marsh a half mile west of Lake Calhoun, on what is now Lake Street, where we used to go to gather berries. One day a party of four drove to the marsh and just as we were about to alight, we saw that a large buck had taken possession of our field. We did not dispute his claim, but silently stole away. That same autumn a bear entered the garden of W. D. Washburn, who lived on Fifth Street and Eighth Avenue and ate all of his sweet corn.

About this time the settlers on Lake Minnetonka were clearing their claims in the "Big Woods" burning most of the timber, but some of the hard maple was cut as cordwood and hauled to Minneapolis and sold for from $2.00 to $2.50 a cord.

The winters were cold but clear and bright. The few neighbors were hospitable and kind and I doubt if there has been a time in the history of Minneapolis when its citizens were happier than they were in the pioneer days of the early sixties.

There were few public entertainments, but they enjoyed gathering at the houses of their neighbors for a game of euchre and occasionally for a dance in Woodmans' Hall which was situated on the corner of Helen Street, now Second Avenue, and Washington Avenue. One violinist furnished the music. Sleighing, horse racing on the river and skating were the out-of-doors amusements for the winter. A favorite place for skating was in a lot situated on Nicollet Avenue between Fourth and Fifth Streets. Nicollet Avenue had been raised above the grade of this lot, causing a depression which filled with water in the fall. There was a small white house in the center of the lot and the skaters went around and around it, and no skating park was more greatly enjoyed.

At the time the war broke out, the town began to show signs of recovering from the effects of the panic of 1857 and its wonderfully beautiful surroundings attracted new settlers and the foundation of the great commercial city was laid.

Dr. Stewart of Sauk Center.

I was government physician for many years and so was back and forth all the time. I used to meet old man Berganeck, an old German, who carried supplies for the government. He always walked and knit stockings all the way. This was very common among the German settlers. The government paid such an enormous price for its freighting that one could almost pay for an outfit for supplies in one trip. Berganeck became very wealthy.

I often passed the night near the bivouac of the Red River drivers. They knew me and were very glad to have me near. I never saw a more rugged race. They always had money even in the panic times of '57. If I treated them for any little ailment, I could have my choice of money or furs. The mosquitoes did not seem to bother them, though they would drive a white man nearly crazy.

I started for Fort Wadsworth, a four company post, in January '68. The winters, always severe, had been doubly so in '67 and '68. I went by team, leaving Sauk Center with the mercury at forty below zero. It never got above forty five below in the morning, while we were on the trip. The snow was three feet on a level and we broke the roads. It took us twelve days to make this three day's trip. My driver was drunk most of the time. There were no trees from Glenwood to Big Stone Lake on the trail. When I drove up to Brown's station, a big log house with a family of about forty people, Nellie met me. To my inquiry as to whether I could stay over night, she answered, "Yes, but there is no food in the house. We have had none for three days. My father is somewhere between here and Henderson with supplies. He knows we are destitute, so will hurry through." About three o'clock, we heard an Indian noise outside. It was Joe with his Indian companions. All he had on that big sled was half a hog, a case of champagne and half a dozen guns. These men were always improvident and never seemed to think ahead.

His daughters, Amanda and Emily, twins, had a peculiarity I never knew before in twins. One day, one would be gay, the other sad. The next day, it would be reversed.

Mrs. J. M. Paine, Minneapolis.

During the early days of the war my husband raised a company of cavalry and wanted me to inspect them as they drilled. I was only a girl of seventeen, but had instructions enough how to behave when they were drilling, for a regiment. I was mounted on one of the cavalry horses and was to sit sedately, my eye on every maneuver and a pleased smile on my face.

I was ready with the goods, but unfortunately

when I was ready, my steed was not. At the first
bugle call he started on a fierce gallop, squeezing himself in where he had belonged, while a terrified bride
clung to his neck with both arms. The only reason
that I did not cling with more was that I did not have
them.

I went once on a buffalo hunt with my husband.
It does not seem possible that all those animals can be
gone. The plains were covered with them. The
steaks from a young male buffalo were the most delicious I have ever tasted.

Miss Minnesota Neill.

My father, the Reverend Mr. J. D. Neill, first came
to St. Paul in April '49, then returned east to get my
mother. In July, when they arrived at Buffalo on
their way west, at the hotel, they met Governor and
Mrs. Ramsey who were on their way to Minnesota to
take up their duties there. They were delighted to
meet my father as he was the first man they had ever
met who had seen St. Paul. When they arrived, they
were much surprised at the smallness of the place.
My mother was not easily consoled over the size of
their metropolis. Among other supplies she had
brought a broom as she had heard how difficult it was
to get them. Mr. H. M. Rice, who came down to
meet them, chided her for being disappointed and putting the broom over his shoulder with pure military
effect, led her along the little footpath which led over
the bluff to the town, and to the American House. Although this was a hotel par excellence for the times,
the floor was made of splintered, unplaned boards.
My mother was abliged to keep her shoes on until she
had got into bed and put them on before arising, to
escape the slivers. The furniture of the bedroom consisted of a bed and wash stand on which last piece,
the minister wrote powerful sermons. My mother
wished to put down a carpet and bring in some of her
own furniture, but the landlady would not allow this,
saying, "There was no knowing where it would stop,
if one was allowed to do the like."

OLD RAIL FENCE CORNERS

They early began the construction of a small chapel and a large brick house which later became the stopping place of all ministers entering the state. In the fall of '49 the house was not completed, but the chapel was. They felt that the Scotts, where they then lived, needed their room, so moved into the chapel and putting up their bed on one side of the pulpit and stove on the other, kept house there for six weeks. The only drawback was that the bed had to be taken down every Sunday. In all the six weeks it never rained once on Sunday.

My mother used often to go alone through a ravine at night to see the Ramsey's. She carried a lantern but was never molested or afraid although it was often very dark. Their storeroom, in those days everyone had one, was stocked in the fall with everything for the winter. My father would buy a side of beef and then cut it up according to the directions his wife would read from a diagram in a cook book. This was frozen and placed in an outside storeroom.

One Sunday my father announced from the pulpit that if anyone was in need they always stood ready to **help. That night everything was taken from the** storehouse. It was thought the act was done by someone who respected my father's wishes as expressed in his sermon.

Their first Christmas here, the doorbell rang. When it was answered, no one was there, but a great bag containing supplies of all kinds hung from the latch. A large pincushion outlined in black was among the things. It was years before the donor was known.

Once some eastern people came to see us and we took them for a long drive. The bridges were not built, so we had to cross the Mississippi on a ferry. We went first to Fort Snelling which seemed to be abandoned. In one of the rooms we found some peculiar high caps which had belonged to the soldiers. My father took one and amused the children much when he went under Minnehaha Falls by leaving his own hat and wearing that funny cap.

Mr. L. L. Lapham.

When we were coming to Houston County, if we couldn't get game we breakfasted on codfish. I think it was the biggest slab of codfish I ever saw when we started. It made us thirsty. The fish called for water and many's the time mother and I knelt down and drank from stagnant pools that would furnish fever germs enough to kill a whole city now-a-days, but I suppose we had so much fresh air that the germs couldn't thrive in our systems.

Speaking of codfish, reminds me that one day we met a man and his family making their way to the river. I halted him and asked him what he was going back for. You see we met few "turnouts" on the road for all were going the same way.

"Well," said he, "I'm homesick—homesick as a dog and I'm going back east if I live to get there." "Why what's the matter with the west?" I asked. "Oh nothing, only it's too blamed fur from God's country and I got to hankering fer codfish—and I'm agoin' where it is. Go lang!" and he moved on. I guess he **was** homesick. He looked, and he talked it and the whole outfit said it plain enough. You can't argue with homesickness—never.

Arnold Stone and his good wife lived up there on the hill. One day in the early 60's an Indian appeared in Mrs. Stone's kitchen and asked for something to eat. They were just sitting down to dinner and he was invited to join the family. The butter was passed to him, and he said, "Me no butter knife." "I told Arnold," said Mrs. Stone, "that when it gets so the Injuns ask for butter knives it's high time we had **one.**"

ANTHONY WAYNE CHAPTER
Mankato

LILLIAN BUTLER MOREHART
(Mrs. William J. Morehart)

Mrs. Margaret Rathbun Funk—1853.

I came to Mankato in the year 1853 on the Steamer Clarion from St. Paul. I was eleven years old. My father, Hoxey Rathbun, had left us at St. Paul while he looked for a place to locate. He went first to Stillwater and St. Anthony, but finally decided to locate at the Great Bend of the Minnesota River. We landed about four o'clock in the morning, and father took us to a little shack he had built on the brow of the hill west of Front Street near the place where the old Tourtelotte Hospital used to be. Back of this shack, at a distance of a couple of blocks were twenty Indian tepees, which were known as Wauqaucauthah's Band. As nearly as I can remember there were nine families here at that time and their names were as follows: Maxfield, Hanna, Van Brunt, Warren, Howe, Mills, Jackson and Johnson, our own family being the ninth.

The first winter here I attended school. The school house was built by popular subscription and was on the site of the present Union School on Broad Street. It was a log structure of one room, and in the middle of this room was a large, square, iron stove. The pupils sat around the room facing the four walls, the desks being wide boards, projecting out from the walls. Miss Sarah Jane Hanna was my first teacher. I came from my home across the prairie, through the snow in the bitter cold of the winter. Oftentimes I broke through the crust of the snow and had a hard time getting out. One of the incidents I remember well while going to school, was about a young Indian whom we called Josh, who pretended he was very anx-

ious to learn English. Most every day he would
come to the school, peer in at the windows, shade his
eyes with his hand and mutter "A" "B" "C", which
would frighten us very much. The education the children received in those days had to be paid for either
by their parents or by someone else who picked out a
child and paid for his or her tuition. That was how I
received my education. My parents were too poor to
pay for mine, and a man in town, who had no children
volunteered to pay for same. I went to school for a
few years on this man's subscription.

The first winter was a very cold one and although
we were not bothered much by the Indians as yet,
they often came begging for something to eat.

Although the Indians had never harmed us we
were afraid of them. When we came to this country we brought a dog, and when these Indians
came begging we took the dog into the house with us
and placed him beside the door, where his barking
and growling soon frightened them away. They
seemed afraid of dogs, as there were very few in this
country at that time. One time when father was on
his way home he saw an Indian boy who had been
thrown from his horse. He picked him up and put
him back on his horse and took him to his tepee.
Later this same Indian remembered my father's kindness to him by warning us that the Indians were planning an uprising and telling us to leave the country.

My father was the first mail carrier through
this part of the country. John Marsh and his brother,
George Marsh contracted with him to carry the mail,
they having previously contracted with the government. He was to carry the mail from Mankato to
Sioux City and return. He made his first trip in the
summer of 1856. The trip took about three weeks.
He made several trips during the summer. His last
trip was in the fall of 1856, when he started from here
to Sioux City. The government was supposed to have
built shacks along his route at regular intervals of
about twenty miles, where he could rest and seek

shelter during cold weather and storms, but this had been neglected. He often slept under hay stacks, and wherever shelter was afforded.

On his way to Sioux City he encountered some very severe weather, and froze one of his sides. The lady where he stopped in Sioux City wanted him to stay there for a while before returning home, and until his side had been treated and he had recovered, but he would not have it so, and started on his return trip during exceedingly cold weather. He did not return on schedule time from Sioux City on this trip, and mother became very much worried about him. She went to the men who had contracted with father to carry the mail and asked them to send out men to look for him. They promised to send out a Frenchman, and a dog team. This contented mother for awhile, but as father did not return she again went to these men and this time they sent out three men with a horse and cutter to look for him.

After traveling over the route for some time they came to a shack on the Des Moines river, near where Jackson, this state, now is and in this shack they found my father, badly frozen and barely alive. He lived but a few moments after shaking hands with the men who found him. They brought the body back to Mankato and he was buried out near our place of residence, at the foot of the hill. The weather was so extremely cold at that time that the family could not go out to the burial.

Later, after I was married, myself and husband came down to what is now the central part of town for the purpose of buying a lot for building a home, and we selected the lot where I now live, at the corner of Walnut and Broad streets. We purchased the same for $487. We could have had any lot above this one for $200, but selected this for the reason that it was high. The country around us was all timber and we had no sidewalks or streets laid out at that time.

At the time of the Indian outbreak I lived on what is now Washington street, directly across from where the German Lutheran school now stands. The Indians started their out-breaks during the Civil war. They started their massacres in this neighborhood in July and August of 1862. I can distinctly remember seeing, while standing in the doorway of my home, a band of Indians coming over the hill. This was Little Priest and his band of Winnebagoes. These Winnebagoes professed to be friendly to the white people and hostile to the Sioux. They claimed that a Sioux had married a Winnebago maiden, and for that reason they were enemies to the Sioux. To prove that they were their enemies they stalked the Sioux who had married a maid of one of their tribes and murdered him, bringing back to show us his tongue, heart, and scalp, and also dipped their hands in the Sioux's life blood and painted their naked bodies with it.

Mrs. Mary Pitcher—1853.

The old Nominee with a cabin full of passengers and decks and hold loaded with freight bound for St. Paul was the first boat to get through Lake Pepin in the spring of 1853. The journey from Dubuque up was full of interest, but although on either side of the Mississippi the Indians were the chief inhabitants, nothing of exciting nature occurred until Pigseye Bar on which was Kaposia, the village of the never-to-be-forgotten Little Crow was reached. Then as the engines were slowed down to make the landing a sight met our gaze that startled even the captain. The whole village of several hundred Indians was in sight and a most frightful sight it was. Everyone young and old was running about crying, wailing, with faces painted black and white. They did not seem even to see the big steamer. It was such an appalling spectacle that the captain deemed it best not to land, but there were two men on board, residents of St. Paul returning from St. Louis who got into a boat and went ashore.

They learned that there had been a fight in St. Paul the day before between this band of Sioux and a party of Chippewas in which one of the Sioux was killed and several wounded. It was not a very pleasant thing to contemplate, for these people on board the boat were going to St. Paul with their families to make homes in this far away west.

There were also on board some Sisters of Charity from St. Louis, one of them Sister Victorine, a sister of Mrs. Louis Robert. They all fell on their knees and prayed and wept and they were not the only ones who wept either. There were many white faces and no one seemed at ease.

I remember my mother saying to my father, "Oh Thomas, why did we bring these children into this wild place where there can be an Indian fight in the biggest town and only ten miles from a fort at that."

The excitement had not subsided when St. Paul was reached, but the first man that came on board as the boat touched the landing was my mother's brother, Mr. W. W. Paddock. The sight of him seemed to drive away some of the fear, as he was smiling and made light of the incident of the day before. He took us up to the Old Merchants' Hotel, then a large rambling log house and as soon as we had deposited some of our luggage, he said, "Well, we will go out and see the battlefield." It was in the back yard of our hotel, an immense yard of a whole block, filled with huge logs drawn there through the winter for the year's fuel.

The morning of the fight, a party of Chippewas coming into St. Paul from the bluffs saw the Sioux in canoes rounding the bend below and knowing they would come up Third Street from their landing place, just below Forbes' Store and exactly opposite the hotel, the Chippewas made haste to hide behind the logs, and wait the coming of the Sioux.

The landlady, Mrs. Kate Wells, was standing on one of the logs, hanging up some clothes on a line. Frightened almost to death at the sight of the Indians running into the yard and hiding behind the logs, she jumped down and started to run into the house. Instantly she was made to understand she could not go inside. The Indians pointed their guns at her, and motioned her to get down behind the logs out of sight, which she did and none too soon, as just then the Sioux came in sight and were met by a most deadly fusilade that killed Old Peg Leg Jim and wounded many others. Some of the Sioux took refuge in Forbes store and opened fire on any Chippewa who left his hiding place. Pretty soon the inhabitants began to come into hailing distance and the Chippewas concluded to beat a hasty retreat but not before they had taken Old Jim's scalp. When the Sioux ran into Forbes store, the clerk, thinking his time had come, raised a window and taking hold of the sill, let himself drop down to the river's edge, a distance of over fifty feet.

Between the Sioux and Chippewas ran a feud further back than the white man knew of and no opportunity was ever lost to take the scalp of a fallen foe.

The Indians mourn for the dead but doubly so if they have lost their scalps, as scalpless Sioux cannot enter the Happy Hunting Grounds.

One of the things about this same trip of the old Nominee was the fact that almost every citizen of St. Paul came down to see this welcome messenger of spring.

Provisions had become very scarce and barrels of eggs and boxes of crackers and barrels of hams, in fact almost everything eatable was rolled out on the land and sold at once. It didn't take long to empty a barrel of eggs or a box of crackers and everyone went home laden.

Mrs. J. R. Beatty—1853.

I landed in Mankato on my twelfth birthday, May 26, 1853. We came from Ohio. My father, George Maxfield and his family and my uncle, James Hanna and family and friend, Basil Moreland, from Quincy, Ill. We took the Ohio River steam boat at Cincinnati. Somewhere along the river we bought a cow. This cow started very much against her better judgment and after several days on the boat decided she wouldn't go west after all and in some way jumped off the boat and made for the shore. We did not discover her retreat until she had reached the high bank along the river and amid great excitement the boat was turned around and everybody landed to capture the cow. She was rebellious all along the way, especially when we had to transfer to a Mississippi boat at St. Louis, and when we transferred to a boat on the Minnesota river at St. Paul, but she was well worth all the trouble for she was the only cow in the settlement that first summer. She went dry during the winter and not a drop of milk could be had for love or money in the town.

The want of salt bothered the pioneers more than anything else. Game abounded. Buffalo herds sometimes came near and deer often came through the settlement on the way to the river to drink. The streams were full of fish, but we could not enjoy any of these things without salt. However, our family did not suffer as much inconvenience as some others did. One family we knew had nothing to eat but potatoes and maple syrup. They poured the syrup over the potatoes and managed to get through the winter. Sometimes flour would be as high as $24 a barrel. During the summer when the water was low and in the winter when the river was frozen and the boats could not come down from St. Paul, the storekeepers could charge any price they could get.

Our family had a year's supply of groceries that father had bought at St. Louis on the way up. We had plenty of bedding and about sixty yards of ingrain carpet that was used as a partition in our house for a long time. There was very little to be bought in St. Paul at that time. Father bought the only set of dishes to be had in St. Paul and the only clock.

There were only a few houses in Mankato and the only thing we could find to live in was the frame of a warehouse that Minard Mills had just begun to build on the south end of the levee, where Otto's grocery store now stands. My uncle purchased the building and we put a roof on and moved in. We were a family of twenty-one and I remember to this day the awful stack of dishes we had to wash after each meal. A frame addition was put along side of the building and in July my cousin, Sarah J. Hanna (later Mrs. John Q. A. Marsh) started a day school with twenty-four scholars. It was the first school ever held in Mankato.

In 1855, a tract of land twenty four miles long and twelve miles wide was withdrawn from civilization and given as a reservation to two thousand Winnebago Indians who took possession in June of that year against the vigorous protest of the people. Everyone in the town was down to see them come in. The river was full of their canoes for two or three days. As soon as they landed, the Indians began the erection of a rude shelter on the levee of poles and bark, perhaps twenty feet long and twelve feet wide. The squaws were all busy cooking some kind of meat and a cake something like a pancake. We soon discovered that they were preparing a feast for the Sioux who had come down in large numbers from Fort Ridgely which was near New Ulm to meet them. After the shelter was finished the feast began. Blankets were spread on the ground and rows of wooden bowls were placed before the Indians, one bowl to about three Indians. The cakes were broken up and placed near the bowls. After the feast was over, the peace-pipe was passed and the speaking began. The first speaker was a Sioux chief, evidently delivering an address of welcome. He was followed by several others all very dignified and impressive.

We had heard that the Sioux would give a return feast on the next day and when we got tired of watching the speakers, we went down to the Sioux wigwams to see what was going on there and found an old Indian squatting before the fire. Dog meat seemed to be the main article of food. Evidently it was to be a ceremonial feast for he had a large supply of dog beside him on the ground and was holding one over the fire to singe the hair off. When we came near, he deftly cut off an ear and offered it to me with a very fierce look. When I refused it, he laughed very heartily at his little joke.

The Winnebagoes were sent to the agency four miles from town soon after. The agency buildings were where St. Clair is now located.

One day at noon the school children heard that the Indians were having a squaw dance across the river. It was in the spring, just as the snow was beginning to melt. We found about twenty-five squaws dancing around in a circle and making a fearful noise in their high squealing voices. They danced in the same way that the Indians did, and I had never seen any other form of dancing among them. They were wearing moccasins and were tramping around in the water. The Indians were sitting on logs watching them. One was pounding on a tom-tom.

One day when we were eating dinner, about twenty-five Indians came to the house and looked in the window. They always did that and then would walk in without knocking. They squatted down on the floor until dinner was over and then motioned for the table to be pushed back to the wall. Then they began to dance the begging dance. In their dances they pushed their feet, held close together over the floor and came down very heavily on their heels. There were so many of them that the house fairly rocked. Each Indian keeps up a hideous noise and that with the beating of the tom-tom makes a din hard to describe. The tom-tom is a dried skin drawn tightly over a hoop and they beat on this with a stick. After they were through dancing they asked for a pail of sweetened water and some bread which they passed around and ate. This bread and sweetened water was all they asked for. It is a part of the ceremony, although they would take anything they could get.

The Sioux were the hereditary foes of the Chippewas who lived near the head waters of the Mississippi and during this summer about three hundred Sioux on their way to Fort Ridgely where they were to receive their annuity, pitched their wigwams near our house. They had been on the war path and had taken a lot of Chippewa scalps and around these bloody trophies they held a savage scalp dance. We children were not allowed to go near as the howling, hooting and yelling frightened everybody. It continued for three nights and the whole settlement was relieved when they went away.

Mrs. A. M. Pfeffer—1858.

My father, Miner Porter had been closely connected with the early history of Fox Lake, Wis. He had conducted the leading hotel and store for years, was Postmaster, and did much by his enterprise and liberality for the town. He went to bed a wealthy man and awoke one morning to find everything but a small stock of merchandise swept away by the State Bank failures of that state. Selling that, he came to Mankato in 1857 and pre-empted a tract of land near Minneopa Falls, now our State Park. It was one half mile from South Bend, located on the big bend of the Minnesota River.

The following year, 1858 father started to build on our claim. There were sawmills in our vicinity where black walnut and butternut for the inside finishing could be bought, but the pine that was needed for the other part of the building had to be hauled from St. Paul by team. It took all summer to get the lumber down.

After our house was finished it came to be the stopping place for lodging and breakfast for settlers traveling over the territorial road towards Winnebago and Blue Earth City.

Pigeon Hill, a mile beyond our house was used as a camping ground for the Sioux all of that winter. We could see the smoke from their campfires curling up over the hill, although they were supposed to stay on their reservation at Fort Ridgely they were constantly coming and going and they and the Winnebagoes roved at will over the entire country.

One night mother was awakened by an unusual noise. She called father, who got up and opened the bedroom door. The sight that met their eyes was enough to strike terror to the heart of any settler of those days. The room was packed with Indians—Winnebagoes—men, women and children, but they were more frightened than we were. They had had some encounter with the Sioux and had fled in terror to our house. After much persuasion, father induced them to leave the house and go down to a small pond where the timber was very heavy and they remained in hiding for two days. We were in constant terror of the Sioux. All the settlers knew they were a blood thirsty lot and often an alarm would be sent around that the Sioux were surrounding the settlement. Mother would take us children and hurry to the old stone mill at South Bend, where we would spend the night.

They became more and more troublesome until father thought it unsafe to remain any longer and took us back to our old home in Wisconsin.

Mr. I. A. Pelton—1858.

I came into the State of Minnesota in April, 1858 and to Mankato May 1, 1858 from the State of New York, where I was born and raised. This was a pretty poverty stricken country then. The panic they had in November 1857 had struck this country a very hard blow. It stopped immigration. Previous to this panic they had good times and had gone into debt heavily, expecting to have good times right along. Everyone was badly in debt and money was hard to get. Currency consisted of old guns, town lots, basswood lumber, etc. These things were traded for goods and groceries. Money was loaned at three to five per cent per month, or thirty-six to sixty per cent per year. I knew of people who paid sixty per cent a year for a short time. Three per cent a month was a common interest. I hired money at that myself.

The farmers had not developed their farms much at that time. A farmer who had twenty to twenty-five acres under plow was considered a big farmer in those days. The summer of 1858 was a very disastrous, unprofitable one. It commenced very wet and kept raining during the summer until North Mankato was all under water and the river in places was a mile wide. The river was the highest about the first of August. The grain at the time of this heavy rain was ripening causing it to blight, ruining the crop. Wheat at this time was worth from $2 to $3 per bushel. A great many of the farmers did not cut their grain because there was nothnig in it for them. The man where I boarded cut his grain but he had little or nothing, and that which he did get was soft and smutty. He took the same to be ground into flour and the bread the flour made was almost black, as they did not at that time have mills to take out the smut.

The people in the best condition financially were mighty glad if they had Johnny cake, pork and potatoes and milk and when they had these they thought they were on the "top shelf."

At this time too, they had to watch their fields with guns, or protect them with scarecrows and have the children watch them to keep them clear from the blackbirds, which were an awful pest. There were millions of these birds and there was not a time of day when they were not hovering over the fields. These birds would alight in the corn fields, tear the husks from the corn and absolutely ruin the ears of corn; also feed on the oats and wheat when it was not quite ripe and in a milky condition.

During the winter they would go south, but come back in the spring when they would be considerable bother again, by alighting on fields that had just been sown and taking the seed from the ground. Farmers finally threw poisoned grain in the fields. This was made by soaking wheat and oats in a solution of strychnine. It was ten years before these birds were exterminated enough to make farming a profitable occupation.

Farming was more successful after that, for the reason that these birds did not need watching. During the summer of 1858 and all durnig the summer of 1859 the river was navigable. St. Paul boats came up often and sometimes a Mississippi boat from St. Louis. We had no railroads in the state at that time.

During the year of 1859 State Banks were put into the state but these did not last long. I know at that time my brother sent out $150 that I had borrowed of Harry Lamberton. He sent this money by a man named David Lyon from New York. He came to where I was boarding and left State Bank money. The people where I was staying gave me the money that night when I came home and told me about what it was for. I started for St. Peter the next day to pay the debt and during the time the money was left and when I arrived at St. Peter it had depreciated in value ten per cent and it kept on going down until it was entirely valueless. Money was very scarce at that time and times were hard. We had some gold and a little silver.

In the year of 1859 we had the latest spring I ever experienced. We did not do any farming of any kind until the first week in May and this made it very late for small grain. We had a short season, but the wheat was very good. We had an early frost that year about the third of September and it killed everything. I saw killdeers frozen to death the third day of that month. Corn was not ripe yet and was ruined. It would have been quite a crop. It was dried up afterwards and shrunk, but was not good. Oats and wheat however were good and it made better times.

The country was gradually developing. In the spring of 1860 we had an early spring. The bees flew and made honey the seventeenth of March. We commenced plowing on the sixteenth of March. I brought down potatoes that spring and put them in an open shed and they did not freeze. This summer was a very productive one. Wheat went as high as forty bushels to the acre, No. 1. All crops were good.

The fall of 1860 was the time they held president-ial election and Lincoln was elected that fall. We had very many speakers here at Mankato and excitement ran high. General Baker, Governor Ramsey, Wm. Windom, afterwards Secretary of the Treasury and other prominent men spoke.

After the war commenced and the volunteers were called out, most of the able bodied men joined the army. These men sent their pay home and after-ward business began to get better and conditions im-proved. Early in August of 1862 Lincoln called for five hundred thousand men and those men in this im-mediate vicinity who had not already joined, went to war, leaving only those not able to join to protect their homes and property.

Mr. John A. Jones.

We were among the very earliest settlers in the vicinity of Mankato and came from Wisconsin. I had come in April and pre-empted a claim at the top of what is known as Pigeon Hill. Two other families came with us.

Traveling across country, we and our teams and live stock made quite a procession. We had five yoke of oxen, several span of horses, and about forty head of cattle, among them a number of milch cows. The wagons, in which we rode and in which we carried our household goods were the real "prairie schooner" of early days. We found our way by compass and made our own road west, traveling over the soft earth in which deep ruts were made by our wheels. The fol-lowing teams were compelled to proceed with care in order not to get stalled in the ruts made by the first wagons.

We made the trip in four weeks, fording all rivers and streams on the way. At La Crosse we hired both ferries and took all day to cross. During the difficult journey we averaged about twenty-two miles, some of us walking all the time driving the large drove of cattle. No Indian villages were passed although we met a number of friendly redskins. At night we slept in the wagons and cooked our meals as all emigrants did. We brought a large store of provisions and on Saturdays would set a small stove up in the open and do our weekly bread baking. We passed through eighteen miles of heavy timber beyond what is now Kasota, coming out from the forest about three miles this side onto a very nice road.

We finally arrived at the homestead. We set our stove up in the yard by a tree and lived in the shanty until our new log house was completed. The shanty was covered with seven loads of hay to make it warm inside and a quilt was hung over the door. Here we lived for two months, suffering at times from rain penetrating. At one time a heavy cloud burst nearly drowned us out.

The first winter in our new home was a severe one. For three weeks the cold was very intense, and what was known as three "dog moons" at night and three "dog suns" during the day heralded the cold weather, the moon and sun being circled with these halos for the entire three weeks. Provisions began to run low. The prices were very high and Mr. Jones went to St. Paul to lay in a stock of provisions. Among other things he brought home sixty barrels of flour and eight barrels of salt. The superfine flour was $16 a barrel and the second grade $13. The provisions were brought by boat to Kasota, where they were stranded in the sand and were brought the rest of the way by team. There was also a barrel of sugar and one of apples. Sugar in those days sold at the rate of six pounds for $1.00.

The families used this flour until they raised their own wheat and after that they used graham flour. The Jones' planted five acres to wheat the following spring.

OLD RAIL FENCE CORNERS

Mrs. Clark Keysor.

After my husband had enlisted and went to Fort Snelling, I was quite timid about staying alone and got a neighbor girl to stay with me. The third night I thought I might as well stay alone. That night a rap came at the door. A neighbor was there and wanted to know if Mr. Keysor had a gun. He said the Indians had broken out and they wanted to get all the guns they could. Of course we were paralyzed with fear. From that on the trouble began.

As soon as the rumor reached Fort Snelling my husband's company was sent back. On the day they arrived I got a good dinner for them. I knew they would be tired and when he arrived he looked worn and haggard, having marched all the way from Fort Snelling to Mankato. We could not eat much dinner, we were so excited. He left right away for the frontier. The last thing he told me before he went away was, "Fight 'til you die, never be taken prisoner."

The bluest day of all was one Sunday. Everyone who could get away was packing up. Women and children were walking the streets and crying. They expected the Sioux to start from Fort Ridgely to kill all the whites, but when they got to Birch Coolie where the Winnebagoes were to join them, the Indians found a barrel of whiskey there. They became intoxicated and had a big fight, so they did not come to Mankato. That was one time when whiskey served a good purpose.

One night not very long after the Indians broke out, there were four of our neighbors' families came into our house, as they felt safer together. There were twelve children in the house. About midnight we heard the town bell begin to ring and one of the women got up and went to the door to see what the trouble was. When she opened the door, she saw a fire, which was Seward's Mill, but she cried out, "The Indians have come, the town is all on fire." The children began screaming and we were all nearly frightened to death but it proved it wasn't Indians at all. Someone had set the mill on fire.

A few of the men who were left thought that we had better pack a few of our best things and go to Leeche's old stone building for protection. What few men there were could protect us better there than at different homes. This old building was three stories high. Some women were sick, some screaming. It was a scene of trouble and distress. It was the worst bedlam I ever got into.

Mr. Hoatling was then our best friend and helped me get my things over to this store building. We stayed one night. The cries of women in pain and fright were unbearable, so the next day I went back home thinking I would risk my chances there.

Judge Lorin Cray—1859.

While at St. Peter and in the early part of December, 1862 a few of us learned, by grapevine telegraph, late one afternoon, that an effort was to be made the following evening, by the citizens of Mankato, New Ulm and vicinity, to kill the Indian prisoners, three hundred and more then in camp at Mankato near the present site of Sibley Park. As no admission fee was to be charged the select few determined to be present at the entertainment. The headquarters of the blood-thirsty citizens was the old Mankato House located where the National Citizens Bank now stands, where liquid refreshments were being served liberally, without money and without price.

I have never seen a correct history of this fiasco in print. A very large crowd congregated there, and there seemed to be no great haste to march on the Indian camp. Several times starts were made by a squad of fifty or one hundred persons, who would proceed for a few hundred feet, and then halt and return for more refreshments.

Finally at nearly midnight the supply of refreshments must have been exhausted for the army moved. Several hundred citizens started south along Front Street for the Indian camp, straggling for a distance of several blocks. When the head of the column reached West Mankato it halted until the rear came up, and while a rambling discussion was going on as to what they should do and how they should do it, Capt. (since governor) Austin with his company of cavalry, surrounded the whole squad and ordered them to move on towards Colonel (since governor) Miller's headquarters, right at the Indian camp. They seemed reluctant to go, and refused to move. Capt. Austin ordered his men to close in, which they did—crowding the citizens and yet they refused to move. Finally Capt. Austin gave the command to "draw sabers" and when a hundred sabers came out in one movement, the army again moved on Colonel Miller's headquarters at the Indian camp.

The scene here was supremely ridiculous. Colonel Miller came out from his tent and spoke kindly to the citizens and asked why they were congregated in such large numbers. He finally ordered their release and suggested that they go home which they hastened to do.

The next morning these Indians were removed, under guard of all the troops in the city, to log barracks, which had been built for them on Front Street diagonally across the street from where the Saulpaugh now stands. The Indians remained in these barracks only about two weeks. They had been there but a short time when the officer of the day, making his morning inspection, which was very formal, thought that he saw a hatchet or knife under the blanket of one of the Indians. Without a change of countenance or a suspicious movement he proceeded with the inspection until it was completed, and retired from the barracks, and at once caused to be mustered around the barracks every soldier in the city with loaded guns and fixed bayonets. Then with a squad of soldiers he entered the barracks and searching every Indian, he secured a large number of hatchets, knives, clubs and other weapons. These weapons, it was learned had been gotten at the Winnebago agency about twelve miles away by several squaws, who prepared food for these Indians and who were allowed to go to the woods to gather wood for their fires. Immediately after this discovery the Indians who were under sentence of death were removed to a stone building near by where they were kept under heavy guard. A few days after this incident, Dec. 26, 1862, my company came from St. Peter to act as guard on one side of the scaffold at the execution of the thirty-eight Indians who were then hanged on what is now the southerly end of the grounds of the Chicago and Northwestern freight depot, in Mankato. A granite monument now marks the place.

Captain Clark Keysor.

I served as first Lieutenant, Co. E, 9th Minnesota of the frontier extending from Fort Ridgely through the settlement at Hutchinson, Long Lake and Pipe Lake. At the latter place we built a sod fort and I was in charge. Mounted couriers, usually three in number, travelling together, reported daily at these forts. I was stationed along the frontier for more than a year and we had many encounters with the Indians, and I soon learned that a white man with the best rifle to be bought in those days had a poor chance for his life when he had to contend with an Indian with a double barrel shot gun.

The Indian, with one lightning like movement throws a hand full of mixed powder and shot into his gun, loading both barrels at once and takes a shot at his enemy before the white man can turn around, and when the Indian is running to escape, he jumps first to this side and then to that, never in a straight line, and it is an expert marksman, indeed, who can hit him.

I worked on the Winnebago agency as carpenter and mill-wright and learned to know the habits of the Indians very well. I learned to follow a trail and later during the Indian trouble that knowledge came in very handy.

It is very easy for a white man to fall into the habits of the Indian, but almost impossible to raise the

Indian to the standard of the white man. The head chief of the Winnebagoes was well known to me, and we became fast friends. He was a friendly man to all the settlers, but I knew the characteristics of the Indian well enough to trust none of them. He never overcomes the cunning and trickery in his nature and I learned to know that when he seemed most amiable and ingratiating was the time to look out for some deviltry. The Indians were great gamblers, the squaws especially. They would gamble away everything they owned, stopping only at the short cotton skirt they wore.

"Crazy Jane" was an educated squaw and could talk as good English as any of us. She was very peculiar and one of the funny things she did was to ride her Indian pony, muffled up in a heavy wool blanket carrying a parasol over her head. She had the habit of dropping in to visit the wives of the settlers and would frequently, on these visits, wash her stockings and put them on again without drying. One day when we were living at the agency I came home and found my wife in a great fright. Our little three year old girl was missing. She had looked everywhere but could not find her. I ran to the agency buildings nearby, but no one had seen her. They were digging a deep well near our house and I had not dared to look there before, but now I must and after peering down into the depths of the muddy water and not finding her, I looked up and saw Crazy Jane coming towards me with a strange looking papoose on her back. When she came nearer I found it was my child. I snatched the little girl away from her. She said she was passing by and saw the child playing outside the door and had carried her away on her back to her teepee, where she had kept her for several hours but had meant no harm.

We were ordered to New Ulm after the outbreak. We found the place deserted. The doors had been left unlocked and everyone had fled for their lives. The desk and stamps from the postoffice were in the street and all the stores were open. I put out scouting parties from there and we stood guard all night. After two or three days a few came back to claim their property. They had to prove their claim before I would allow them to take charge again. Uncle "Tommy" Ireland came to us a few days after we arrived there. He was the most distressed looking man I ever saw in my life. He had been hiding in the swamps for seven days and nights. He had lain in water in the deep grass. When we examined him, we found seventeen bullet holes where he had been shot by the Indians. He told me about falling in with Mrs. Eastlake and her three children.

They had all come from Lake Shetek. The settlement there comprised about forty-five people. They had been attacked by the Indians under Lean Bear and eight of his band, and the bands of White Lodge and Sleepy Eye, although Sleepy Eye himself died before the massacre.

Many of the settlers knew the Indians quite well and had treated them with great kindness. Mr. Ireland and his family were with the rest of the settlers when they were overtaken by the Indians. Mrs. Ireland, Mr. Eastlake and two of his children, were among the killed. Mrs. Eastlake was severely wounded, and wandered for three days and nights on the prairie searching for her two children, hoping they might have escaped from the slough where the others met their death. Finally on the way to New Ulm she overtook her old neighbor, Mr. Ireland, whom she supposed killed, as she had last seen him in the slough pierced with bullets, but he had revived and managed to crawl thus far, though in a sorry plight. From him she received the first tidings from her two missing children. Later on when she found her children, they were so worn by their suffering she could hardly recognize them. The eldest boy, eleven years old had carried his little brother, fifteen months old on his back for fifty miles. All the baby had to eat was a little piece of cheese which the older boy happened to have in his pocket. When within thirty miles from New Ulm they found the deserted cabin of J. F. Brown in Brown County, where Mrs. Eastlake and children, a Mrs. Hurd and her two children, and Mr. Ireland lived for two weeks on raw corn, the only food they could find. They dared not make a fire for fear the Indians would see the smoke. Mr. Ireland had been so badly injured that he had not been able to leave the cabin to get help, but finally was forced by the extreme need of the women and children to start for New Ulm. He fell in with a priest on the way, and together they came to our headquarters and told their story. We started at four o'clock next morning, with a company of soldiers and a wagon with a bed for the injured women. When we reached the cabin the women were terribly frightened and thought it was the Indians after them again. On our return to New Ulm we took a different turn in the road. It was just as near and much safer. One of our men, Joe Gilfillan had not had his horse saddled when the rest started and when he came to the fork in the road, he took the one he had come by and was killed by the Indians. Undoubtedly we would have met the same fate had we taken that road as the Indians were on our trail and were in ambush waiting for our return. However, we got safely back to New Ulm and later Mrs. Eastlake and her children and Mr. Ireland came to Mankato where they were cared for with the other refugees. The sufferings and hardships endured by the older Eastlake boy soon carried him to an untimely grave.

OLD RAIL FENCE CORNERS

COLONIAL CHAPTER
Minneapolis

CARRIE SECOMBE CHATFIELD
(Mrs. E. C. Chatfield)

RUTH HALL VAN SANT
(Mrs. S. R. Van Sant)

Miss Carrie Stratton—1852.

My father was Levi W. Stratton who was born in Bradford, N. H., who came to St. Croix valley in 1838, taking up a claim where Marine now stands.

He helped to build the old mill there, the ruins of which are still to be found there. After two or three years he removed to Alton, Ill., where he remained for ten or twelve years marrying my mother there in 1842.

In 1852 he returned to Minnesota, coming up the river in the old "War Eagle." His family consisted of my mother, myself and my four brothers and sisters, the youngest an infant of six months.

We arrived at St. Paul on June 8. Being a child of but seven years, my memory of the appearance of the town at that time, is very indistinct. In fact the only clear remembrance of anything there, is of a large sign upon a building directly across the street from the little inn or tavern where we stopped for the night. It was "Minnesota Outfitting Company." On account of our large family of little children, I had been put into school when I was between two and three years of age and so was able to read, write and spell, and I have a very vivid recollection of the three long words of that sign.

We came from St. Paul to St. Anthony in the stage of the Willoughby Company, which was the first stage line in Minnesota. The driver stopped to water his horses at the famous old Des Noyer "Half Way House."

OLD RAIL FENCE CORNERS

We stopped at the old St. Charles Hotel while the house my father had engaged was made ready for us. It was the Calvin Tuttle home, which was on the river bank at the foot of the University hill.

My father's previous residence in Minnesota had taught him to understand and speak the Indian language and so the Indians were frequent visitors at our house on one errand or another, generally, however to get something to eat. The first time they came, my father was absent, and my mother, never having seen any Indians before, was very much frightened. Not being able to understand what they wanted, she imagined with a mother's solicitude, that they wanted the baby, and being actually too terrified to stand any longer, she took the baby and went into her room and laid down upon the bed. After a while, either from intuition, or from the motions the Indians made, it occurred to her to give them something to eat, which was what they wanted and they then went peaceably away. The rest of the children, like myself, did not appear to be at all frightened, but instead, were very much entertained by the novel sight of the Indians in their gay blankets and feathered head dress. After that they were frequent visitors but always peaceable ones, never committing any misdemeanor.

One of the earliest diversions I can remember was going up University hill to the old Cheever tower and climbing to the top, in accordance to the mandate at the bottom, to "Pay your Dime and Climb," to get the magnificent view of the surrounding country, which included that of the great falls in their pristine glory. I can remember too, like all the others here who were children at that time, the stupendous roar of the falls, which was constantly in our ears especially if we were awake at night, when every other noise was stilled.

In the fall of that first year, I entered school, which was an academy in a building on University Avenue opposite the present East High School. This school was the nucleus of the State University and was presided over by Mr. E. W. Merrill, who was afterward a Congregational minister and home missionary.

After two or three years we moved into the home of the Rev. Mr. Seth Barnes above Central Avenue, and between Main and Second streets. Here my father cultivated a fine garden which included, besides corn, beans and other usual vegetables, some fine sweet potatoes, which were quite a novelty in the town at that time.

Mr. Irving A. Dunsmoor—1853.

In 1852 on account of poor health, my father resolved to come to Minnesota and become a farmer, and in the fall of that year, he set out with his family, consisting of my mother, myself and my three brothers.

We arrived at Galena, Ills., only to find that the last boat of the season had gone up the river the day before. So my father left us there for the winter and came up by the stage.

The end of his journey found him in the little town of Harmony, which was afterwards changed to Richfield, and is now within the city limits of Minneapolis.

Here he was able to buy for $100 a claim of two hundred and sixty acres, with a house upon it, which was only partly finished, being, however entirely enclosed. This particular claim attracted his attention on account of the house, as his family was so soon to follow. It began at what is now Fiftieth street and Lyndale Avenue and continued out Lyndale three quarters of a mile. The house (with some addition) is still standing on Lyndale Avenue between Fifty Third and Fifty Fourth streets. Minnehaha creek ran through the farm and the land on the north side of the creek (part of which is now in Washburn Park) was fine wooded land.

When the first boat came up the river in the spring it brought my mother and us boys. My father had sent us word to come up to Fort Snelling on the boat, but we had not received the message and so got off at St. Paul and came up to St. Anthony by stage and got a team to take us to our new home. We found it empty, as my father and an uncle who was also here, had gone to the fort to meet us. As we went into one of the back rooms, a very strange sight met our eyes. My father and uncle had set a fish trap in the creek the night before and had poured the results of their catch in a heap on the floor and there was such a quantity of fish that it looked like a small haycock. This was done for a surprise for us, and as such, was a great success, as we were only accustomed to the very small fish that lived in the creek that ran through our home town in Maine, and these long pickerel and large suckers were certainly a novelty.

We salted them down and packed them in barrels and for a long time had plenty of fish to eat, to sell and to give away.

Our house soon took on the character of a public building, as my father was made Postmaster, Town Treasurer and Justice of the Peace, and all the town meetings were held there, as well as church and Sunday school. My father gave five acres down at the creek to a company who erected a grist mill and the settlers from fifty or sixty miles away would come to have grain ground and would all stop at our house to board and sleep while there. Then the house would be so full that we boys would have to sleep on the floor, or out in the barn or anywhere else we could find a place.

During our first winter, a party of about fifty Sioux Indians came and camped in our woods just west of where the Washburn Park water tower now stands. They put up about twenty tepees, made partly of skins and partly of canvas. We boys would often go in the evening to visit them and watch them make moccasins, which we would buy of them. They would often come to our house to beg for food, but in all the time they remained there (nearly the whole winter) they committed no depredations, except that they cut down a great deal of our fine timber, and killed a great quantity of game, so that when they wanted to come back the next winter, father would not allow it.

Once after they had gone away, they came back through the farm and went off somewhere north of us, where they had a battle with the Chippewas. When they returned, they brought two scalps and held a "pow-wow" on the side of our hill.

We had a great deal of small game in our woods, and great quantities of fish in the creek. We used to spear the fish and sometimes would get two upon our spears at once.

My mother was very fond of dandelion greens, and missed them very much, as she could find none growing about our place. So she sent back to Maine for seed and planted them. But I hardly think that the great quantities we have now are the result of that one importation.

After a few years we had a school at Wood Lake, which is down Lyndale avenue two or three miles.

Mrs. Mary Pribble—1854.

My father, Hiram Smith arrived in Minnesota Apr. 21, 1854 settling first in Brooklyn, Hennepin County. My mother followed in July of the same year, with the family of three children, myself, aged seven, and two brothers aged two and five years. We arrived in St. Paul July ninth and my mother, with her usual forethought and thrift, (realizing that before long navigation would close for the winter and shut off all source of supplies) laid in a supply of provisions while we were in St. Paul. Among other things she bought a bag of rice flour which was all the flour in our colony until April of the next year.

We came by stage to Anoka and were to cross the Mississippi river in a canoe, to the trading post of Mr. Miles, which was on a high point of land in what is now Champlin. It was where Elm creek empties into the Mississippi. But the canoe was too small to carry us all at once and so I was left on the east shore sitting upon our baggage, to wait for a return trip. When I finally arrived across the river, there were Indians gathered at the landing and they touched me on the cheek and called me "heap pale face."

There was great joy in our little colony when that same autumn my father discovered a fine cranberry marsh. Much picnicking and picking followed. My parents secured seven bushel and alloted very much on the winter supplies that these cranberries would buy when they could send them to St. Paul, our only market.

Soon one of the neighbors prepared to set out on a trip by ox-team to St. Paul. The only road at that time was by the Indian trail, which for several miles was where the county road now leads from Robbinsdale to Champlin. Then to the ferry at St. Anthony Falls, and so on down the east side of the river to St. Paul.

My mother had made out a careful list of the real necessities to be purchased, putting them in the order of the need for them, in case he would not be able to buy them all.

She knew very well that there would be no possible way to purchase any new clothing all winter and so the first items on the list were: new cloth for patches and thread to sew them with. This latter came in "hanks" then, instead of on spools.

After that came the list of provisions, as seven bushels of cranberries were expected to buy a great many supplies. How well I remember the joy upon my mother's face, when those precious cranberries were loaded on the neighbor's already full wagon and the oxen slowly disappeared down the old trail! It was a long tedious journey to be made in that way, and they had many days to wait before they would receive the fruits of that wonderful wagon load.

Finally the neighbor was back, and came to my mother and said: "Thee will be disappointed when I tell thee that the last boat left for St. Louis the day before I arrived in St. Paul. There is not a yard of cloth or a hank of thread in the town, and I could only get thee **three brooms** for thy fine cranberries."

The next spring my father made maple sugar and was able to buy a cow and six hens from a man who came overland from southern Illinois, driving several cows and bringing a box of hens, and so we began to live more comfortably.

In 1856 many people came, and by that time we had school, church and Sunday school and a lyceum, the pleasures of which I can never forget. We also had a portable saw-mill.

I think it was in the winter of 1855 that an agent, a real live agent, appeared in our midst to tell us of the remarkable qualities of a new oil called **kerosene.** He said if he could be sure of the sale of a barrel, it would be brought to St. Paul and delivered to any address on or before Aug. 15. I have the lamp now, in which part of that first barrel was burned.

Mrs. Edmund Kimball—1855.

My father, Freeman James, left his home in New York state and came to Hasson, Minn., in 1854. The next year he decided to go after his family and so wrote my mother to be ready to start in August. My mother got everything in readiness to start, but for some reason my father was delayed in getting back home, and my mother, thinking that she had misunderstood his plans in some way, decided to start anyway, and so she loaded our belongings on the wagon and we started alone. I was only eleven years old, and well I remember how great an undertaking it seemed to me to leave our pleasant home and all my playmates and start without father on such a long trip. But when we arrived at Dunkirk, where we took boat to cross Lake Erie, we found father, and so made our journey without mishap. We arrived by boat in St. Paul in August '55 and started at once for Hasson, stopping that first night at the home of Mr. Longfellow, at a place called Long Prairie. We were most cordially received and found other settlers stopping there for the night too, which made the house so crowded that they were obliged to make beds on the sitting room floor for all the children. After we were put in bed, still another traveler arrived, a man who was expecting his family and had come part way to meet them. Just for fun the family told him that his family had arrived and pointed to us children on the floor. He was overjoyed, and came and turned the covers down to see us. Only for a moment was he fooled but shook his head and said we were none of his.

I shall never forget the shock I felt at the first view I had of our new home. It was so different from what we had left behind, that to a child of my age, it seemed that it was more than I could possibly endure. It was growing dark and the little log cabin stood in the deep woods, and the grass was so long in the front yard, it seemed the most lonely place in the world. And dark as it was, and as long as I knew the way back to be, I was strongly tempted and half inclined to start right off to my dear old home. This was all going through my mind while I stopped outside to look around after the rest had gone in. When they had lighted one or two candles and I followed them in, the homesick feeling was increased by the new prospect. My father had evidently left in a great hurry for every dish in the house was piled dirty upon the table, and they were all heavy yellow ware, the like of which I had never seen before. The house had been closed so long that it was full of mice, and they ran scurrying over everything.

But there was much work to do before we could get the place in order to go to bed, and it fell to my lot to wash all those dishes, no small task for an eleven year old girl.

In the morning, when the house was in order and the sun was shining in, and we could see what father had done to make us comfortable, the place took on a very different aspect and soon became another dear home.

OLD RAIL FENCE CORNERS

He had made every piece of the furniture himself. The bed was made of poles, with strips of bark in place of bedcords, the mattress was of husks and the pillows of cat-tail down. There were three straight chairs and a rocking chair with splint bottoms. The splints were made by peeling small ash poles and then pounding them for some time with some heavy instrument, when the wood would come off in thin layers. The floor was of split logs. Father had made some good cupboards for the kitchen things.

That first year mother was not well and young as I was, I was obliged to do a great deal of housework. I did the washing and made salt-rising bread. And one time I surprised the doctor who came to see mother by making him a very good mustard poultice.

Mr. Frank G. O'Brien—1856.

The Reason I did not Graduate.

In the winter of 1856-57 I worked for my board at the home of "Bill" Stevens, whose wife was a milliner —the shop, or store, was located a short distance below where the Pillsbury mill stands, on Main Street.

My duty while there this particular winter, was to take care of the house and chaperone Lola Stevens, the young daughter to the private school which was called the "Academy"—the same being the stepping stone to our great State University.

There were two departments up stairs and two below—hallway in the center and stairs leading from this hallway to the upper rooms. I do not recall who were the teachers in the primary department on the lower floor, but I do remember those on the floor above. Miss Stanton (later on the wife of D. S. B. Johnston) taught the girls in the east room and "Daddy" Roe the boys.

I was a pupil of Mr. Roe and Lola of Miss Stanton and were it not that I was wrongfully accused of making charcoal sketches on the wall of the hall, I might have been numbered among the charter mem-

bers of the first graduating class of the Academy—
the forerunner of the State University.

"Daddy" Roe informed the boys at recess time
that he was going to flog the perpetrator of the act—
yet, if they would own up, and take a basin of water
and scrub same from the walls, he would spare the
rod. The guilty one, no doubt, held his hand up and
gained the attention of Mr. Roe, and stated that
Frank O'Brien did it. I denied it, but it did not go—
yet I being innocent, was determined I would not take
the basin from the teacher's hand; but he forced same
upon me and said if it was not washed off within half
an hour, he would give me a severe flogging.

The threat did not prove effective, because I was
so worked up over the affair that when I closed the
door to enter the hall, I gave the basin and its contents
a fling down stairs, the sound of which aroused all
four of the departments, while I double quicked it for
home—leaving Lola to reach home as best she could.

I explained matters to Mr. Stevens and had it not
been for Mrs. Stevens and her sister, Miss Jackman,
he would have proceeded at once to the school room
and meted out the punishment on "Daddy" Roe which
he intended for me.

Something to Crowe Over.

The little village of St. Anthony had good reason
to become elated when the news spread up and down
Main street and was heralded to St. Paul, that three
"Crowes" had perched on the banner of our village
during the early morning of June 26th, 1859, when
Mrs. Isaac Crowe gave birth to three white Crowes,
two girls and one boy. The father of these three
birds—wingless, though fairest of the fair, was a
prominent attorney of St. Anthony and one of its
aldermen.

Bridge of Size (900 feet long.)

It was while our family resided on the picturesque spot overlooking St. Anthony's Falls in the year
1857, the "Howe Truss" passenger bridge was com-

pleted from the east to the west side of the Mississippi river, a short distance down the hill from the State University at a cost of $52,000.

All went well as a means of traffic and many a dollar was taken in for toll, but an evil time came to disturb conditions, owing to an over abundance of rain which came in torrents, which caused the river to rise to that extent that the logs which followed in the wake of the flood, acted as a battering ram and proved too much for the structure and great was the fall thereof. I among others of our family were witnesses of this event, which took place at eight o'clock on the morning of June first, 1859.

Mr. Michael Teeter—1857.

Tom and Bill were the first horses which came into Lyle township. They were fine powerful fellows and created much comment throughout that section of the country.

Some of my neighbors envied me my prize while others thought that a fool and his money had easily parted, for I had paid three hundred and forty dollars for them, and the best yoke of oxen in the country side could be bought for seventy. But I was well satisfied, for I was able to do my work and get about quickly. When haste was necessary, Bill and Tom were pressed into service.

I recall very well one dark rainy night when I was taking a neighbor to nurse a settler who lived at some distance to the west. So thick was the darkness that we could never have kept the trail had it not been for the flashes of vivid lightning. The horses showed so much intelligence through it all that I finally gave them the lines and they brought us safely to our destination.

New Year's day, '58 we took the ladies of Otranto village for a sleigh-ride—not on the snow, for the ground was bare—but on the Red Cedar river, which was frozen clear and smooth as glass. We fairly flew over the ice and the home-made sleigh swerved from side to side, as Bill and Tom took it upon themselves to show off their speed to friends who were in the habit of riding behind deliberate and stubborn oxen. Suddenly, without warning, the sleigh tipped and we found ourselves in a heap, and although there was much shouting and crying, no damage was done, and the little shaking up tended to make the day memorable.

Another incident that stands out vividly in my mind after all these years, has no amusing aspect. Late in the fall of '57 I found it necessary to make a trip to Decorah, Iowa, for supplies of various kinds. My absence from home was to be shorter than usual on such trips, for Bill and Tom had endurance as well as speed. All went well during the journey, and on my return I halted for supper at Little Cedar and hoped to reach home that evening. When I was ready to start, the tavern keeper told me that I had better stay the night, for a prairie fire was sweeping from the northwest. This was unwelcome news— but sure enough, the red light was very bright and growing more so all the time. I calculated the distance and decided to hasten on across the path of the fire before it reached the road, so I started. I had miscomputed both time and distance, so before I was aware of it, I found myself on a small knoll, with the fire directly in front and coming on at a great rate through the tall dry weeds and grasses. The horses snorted and shook their heads, but I urged them on. They plunged forward and in a very short time (although it seemed hours) we found ourselves out of the flames. We paused but a moment to rest, for the ground was very hot. The horses shook with fright and their bodies were badly singed. We reached home in safety, and I think Bill and Tom were no less thankful than was I, to be out of the danger and discomfort of the situation.

In 1857 I moved from Decorah, Iowa, to Otranto on the state line. There I found a number of families living in rude houses which were a poor protection against the hard winters we had those early years.

OLD RAIL FENCE CORNERS

There was plenty of good timber along the Red Cedar river, but the settlers were farmers who had little or no experience in cutting and dressing logs and for that reason handled their few small tools to poor advantage. They were anxious, too, to be "breaking" the prairie so that a crop could be harvested that first year. So after all, these first houses were rather poor specimens of the joiner's craft. I was a carpenter and put up a rather more substantial house than the others, but none too comfortable during the winters that were to follow. The unbroken stretch of prairie to the north and west of Otranto gave those old "northwesters" a splendid sweep before they struck our frail little homes.

Fortunately there was plenty of fine wood, but the cracks were so numerous and large in our houses that we veritably warmed the outdoors in keeping ourselves warm. We chopped and sawed wood every spare moment in winter and summer in order to keep the booming fires which were necessary all winter long. We used to talk and think much of the settlers who were on the prairie who were so unsheltered and far from standing timber.

This "yarn" about one of them went the rounds and was enjoyed by all, for the "victim" was a merry fellow and always ready for a joke, no matter how great the privations and anxieties. The story runs thus: Jim sat before a fine fire washing his feet. Soothed by the warmth of the room and the water, he fell asleep to awaken suddenly toward morning with his feet nearly to his knees embedded in a solid cake of ice! We laughed at our hardships, for there was no escaping them, and we learned to turn them, as well as everything else we possessed, to some useful purpose.

Robes, buffalo coats, all available garments, were used during those first winters for bed-clothing. There was one flock of chickens in Otranto, but not until much later were flocks of ducks and geese raised so that feather pillows and beds could be used. Floor covering at first was uncommon, but finally rag carpets added to the comfort of the home during the winter.

Had food been abundant, or even sufficient, we would have felt less anxious, but with the winter hanging on far into the spring months, we had good reason to watch our stores carefully. Buckwheat ground in a coffee mill kept one family for two months in the winter of '57. Another neighbor's family subsisted upon musty corn meal, ground by revolving a cannon ball in the scooped out trunk of a tree. So long drawn out was the winter, that the amount of meal for each member of the family was carefully measured out each day. One family living near the river could get plenty of fish through the ice, but having no fat in which to fry them, were obliged to use them boiled. When their salt was exhausted, they ate the fish unflavored.

I possessed a good team of horses and made trips to Decorah for supplies. I went only when it was really necessary, for the journey was beset with many dangers and discomforts. Flour and salt pork were the foods purchased, which I sold to the other settlers in small quantities. Prairie chickens were abundant, and some of the pioneers tried drying the breasts and found that one way to provide meat for the winter.

In the winter of '56, there was a thick coating of ice over the snow, sufficiently strong to hold a man's weight, but the deers' legs cut through the crust. My neighbors told of how easily they were able to get plenty of venison without venturing far from home. Never did a settler dare to go far away to hunt during those first winters, for the dangers of being lost and frozen were very great. I have often heard the wish expressed that fresh meat could be had every winter, with as few risks as in that year before I moved to Otranto.

We all felt the lack of fruit, for all of us had come from districts where fruit was grown, so on festive days such as Thanksgiving and Christmas, we had dried wild crab-apples boiled up in soda water, then sweetened with molasses. We were all used to better than this, but we never complained and felt that better times were coming.

Mrs. W. L. Niemann.

My mother was Sophia Oakes. She was born in Sault Ste. Marie in 1823. She was the daughter of Charles Oakes who had charge of a trading post for the American Fur Company. Her mother died when she was a very small child and her father removed with his two children, my mother and her sister two years younger, to La Pointe, where he had charge of another post of the same company.

The winters there were very long and severely cold and many times they would be shut in by the depth of the snow for weeks at a time. One time in particular the snow was so deep and the cold so intense that they had been snowbound so long that their supplies were almost exhausted, and my grandfather sent the men off to get a fresh supply. They were gone much longer than usual and the little family began to suffer for want of food and were obliged to go out and scrape away the snow to find acorns. They also ate the bark of trees.

Finally my grandfather concluded that he, too, must start out to try and get some food. The windows of the cabin were covered in place of glass, with deerskins. In getting ready to leave the children, grandfather took down these skins and replaced them with blankets to keep out the cold and boiled the skins to provide a soup for the children to drink while he was gone. My mother was twelve and her sister was ten.

Grandfather had not gone far when his feet were both frozen and he lay disabled in the snow. Some men chanced along, and carried him to a house which was about a mile further along. When they reached the house he refused to be carried in, for he knew he would surely lose his feet if he went in where it was warm. He asked for an awl and punctured his feet full of holes and had the men pour them full of brandy. This, while it was excruciatingly painful, both at the time and afterwards, saved him his feet.

When he and his men returned to the cabin, he had been gone all day and all night and into the next afternoon, and they found the little girls locked in each other's arms fast asleep, having cried themselves to sleep the night before.

Soon after the little girls were sent to school back in New York and my mother stayed until her education was completed, graduating from a seminary in Fredonia.

On her return to her home, she was married to my father, Jeremiah Russell, who had come in 1837 to Fort Snelling on an exploring trip. He settled first at Edina Mills, but soon went to Marine, where with Franklin Steele and Levi Stratton he built a saw-mill, (1838) the ruins of which can still be seen.

In '49 he went to take charge of a trading post for the American Fur Company which was located two miles above Sauk Rapids. After a few years he purchased the land where Sauk Rapids stands, laid out the town and moved down there, building a large hotel which was called the Hyperborean Hotel, which took a prominent part in the history of the town as it was the scene of many large gatherings. It served to shelter the townspeople when they were driven from home through fear of the Indian uprisings. Later it was remodeled by new owners and rechristened the Russell House in honor of my father.

One time, before I was born and while my parents still lived at the post, a band of warlike Indians, each armed with a gun came to the house and completely filled the kitchen. My brother, who was a very small child was attracted by the fire arms and went up to one of the Indians and put his hand on the gun. This angered the Indian and with a terrible scowl he put his finger on the trigger as if to shoot my brother. My father sprung up before him and with a very fierce voice (which was the only way to deal with them when they were unruly) ordered him to put down his gun. This he did but with bad grace. My father then spoke to the chief and told him to keep order, which he did, and they soon went away. But my father was sorry he did not keep them a little longer and give them up to the authorities, for he found, soon after, that they had killed and scalped three white men, just a short time before they came into our house.

At another time after we were living in Sauk Rapids, a Chippewa came and begged for shelter for the night. My father knew that there was a band of Sioux camped just across the river, in plain view of our house. So father surmised that this was a spy from the Chippewas. But he gave him permission to stay in the house, providing that he would not show himself outside, for it would enrage the Sioux against us if they knew we were harboring a Chippewa. The Indian promised, but very soon my sister who was playing outside, saw him raise the window and aim his gun across the river. She told my father, who went in and made him desist and nailed up the window. When we went to bed that night father did not take pains to lock the Indian in. After we were asleep he crept out and slipped away, and before morning, the Chippewas descended upon the sleeping Sioux and killed every one of them.

Christmas in those hard times did not mean to us little pioneer children what it does now. There was no spare money with which to buy presents. We always hung up our stockings, but got nothing in them but a little cheap candy, and perhaps a few raisins. But one year, father determined to give us and the other children of the village a little better Christmas than usual. So he went out to his woods and cut enough fire wood to exchange in St. Cloud for a barrel of apples. Then he divided off one end of our sitting room with a sheet and arranged a puppet show behind it. And with the village children in one end of the room eating apples, and father in the other managing the puppets, we celebrated the day in a very happy way.

Mrs. F. Hoefer of Mound was an old settler of Watertown, and gives some interesting information of the prices of food-stuffs after the war, as follows:

"Flour was $15 a barrel, wheat was $5 a bushel, potatoes were $2.50 a bushel and calico was thirty-five cents a yard. My husband's salary for that summer season was $5. During the winter months we had barley coffee and pancakes, no bed clothes and no clothes for the children. Our bed quilt was a bear skin. When my first child was six weeks old, I went out washing, walking twelve miles to my work, washing all day and then walking the twelve miles back home again."

Ex-Governor Samuel R. Van Sant—1857.

My father with his family moved to Illinois in 1837, coming on the "Adventure," on the Ohio and Mississippi rivers. Like most of the early pioneers he was poor and had to work. Tickets were sold at a less price if the passenger would help to wood the boat; my father took advantage of this proposition. On board as a passenger, was the old Indian Chief, Black Hawk. He was much interested in my little sister and gave her a very fine string of beads. The beads, or a part of them, are still in our family.

My father took up a claim near Rock Island on the banks of the Rock River. While there, the family suffered all the privations of early settlers in a new country. Farming was new to him and he did not make a great success of it. He was a ship builder by trade.

Once he took a load of pumpkins to town, some twelve or fourteen miles, getting fifty cents for them. On his return he broke his wagon, costing a dollar to repair it. He often said he never felt so poor in all his life, although he lived to be ninety-two years of age. On another occasion we were out of provisions. He made a trip to the old water mill, a few miles distant, to get 50c worth of cornmeal, but the proprietor would not trust him so he had to return home to get a half dollar that had been laid by for a rainy day. He was thus forced to make another trip to secure the purchase; by this time we children were good and hungry.

On another occasion, after killing his hogs, he drove with them one hundred miles to the lead mines at Galena, but the market was over stocked so he proceeded to Platteville, Wisconsin, twenty or more miles further, where he sold the pork for two and one-half cents per pound, taking one half in store pay and the other half in a note. The note is still unpaid. It required a week or more to make the trip.

I have always had a great fondness for the Mississippi River. I was born on its banks and for more than forty years navigated its water. My first dollar was spent to buy a small skiff. As soon as I was old enough, I commenced running on the river. My first trip to St. Paul was in 1857. I was a boy of thirteen. What progress since that time in our state!

The steamboat was a mighty factor in the settlement growth and development of Minnesota. I feel safe in saying that during the palmy days of steamboating, more than one thousand different steamers brought emigrants, their household goods and stock to this commonwealth.

While there were regular lines of steamers, there were also many outside boats which were termed "wild" boats. These boats would often secure a full cargo on the Ohio River, or at St. Louis and come to St. Paul. If water was at a good stage, large profits would result.

A story is told of the steamer, "Fire Canoe." (I will not mention the captain's name.) The water was low and the boat got aground a good many times causing much delay. For a meal or two, the passengers were without meat but soon there seemed to be a plentiful supply of nice fresh veal—one of the passengers who, with his family and stock of young calves, was moving to Minnesota, complimented the captain highly upon securing such fine meat, but after going to the lower deck and finding some of his fine young stock missing, hunted up the Captain and said, "Captain, if it is all the same to you, I would prefer to dispense with meat for the rest of the trip for I will need that young stock when I reach my claim."

There was always great strife to be the first boat to arrive at St. Paul and many risks were taken by steamers to get through Lake Pepin before the ice had really left the lake. Many steamers were crushed by the ice in so doing. One advantage to the first boat was free wharfage the balance of the season in every town and city along the river.

Two steamers hardly ever came in sight of each other without a race. We owned and operated a good many boats. We had a fast one named the "Mc-Donald." I remember on one occasion my partner, Mr. Musser, a well known lumberman of Muscatine, and wife were making a trip with us. We had a very spirited race with another swift boat; after a long, hard chase we passed her, but we had to trim boat and carry big steam to do it. After it was over, Mr. Musser said to me, "If I were you, I would not race any more. It is expensive, dangerous and hard on the boat." I agreed that he was right and that we would not do so again. We had not been in our berths long before another boat was overtaken and a race was on. Mr. Musser arose, forgot his advice of a few hours previous, and said, "Pass that boat and I will pay for the extra fuel." The boat was passed, but no bill was presented for the extra fuel.

OLD RAIL FENCE CORNERS

REBECCA PRESCOTT SHERMAN CHAPTER
Minneapolis

MISS RITA KELLEY
MISS BEATRICE LONGFELLOW

Mrs. Delilah Maxwell—1855.

We were married in Illinois, April 12, 1855 and in three days we started. We went one hundred miles by team to the Mississippi river, put our wagon and mules on a steamer, and came up. Every business place on the west side of the river in Minneapolis was a rough boarding house and a little ten-by-twelve grocery store. We camped there, cooked our breakfast, and came on out to Maxwell's bay at Minnetonka. The bay was named for my husband and his two brothers who came up the year before and took claims.

It was the roughest trip you ever saw. The road was an Indian trail with enough trees cut out on either side to let a wagon through and the stumps were sticking up a foot or two high and first you were up and then you were down over those stumps. It was the trail through Wayzata and Long Lake, known as the Watertown road.

We built an elm shack, a log house with the logs standing up so the Indians couldn't climb over them, and stripped bark off elm trees for a roof. The mosquitoes were terrible bad—and deer flies too. The men had to wear mosquito bar over their hats down to their waists when at work.

Mrs. Martha French lived on the Bestor place on Crystal Bay, the Burdon claim. She and Mr. French had come the fall before in '54. We had a short cut through the woods, a path about a mile long. They were our nearest neighbors. They came over to our house one Sunday. The men were going to Minneapolis on business, to see about their land and Mr.

Maxwell was to start, Tuesday. Mrs. French said "Why can't us women go too, on a pleasure trip? I've been here pretty near two years and Mrs. Maxwell has been here over a year. I think it's about time we went on a pleasure trip."

Mr. French was a slow talking man and he drawled, "Well, you can go, but it won't be much of a pleasure trip."

"I don't see why it wouldn't. You jest want to discourage us," Mrs. French said and he said, "Oh, no-o! I don't want to discourage you."

I didn't want to go very bad. I had a kid five months old and the mosquitoes were so bad. It was June and awfully hot. But Mrs. French hadn't any children and insisted that we ought to go for a pleasure trip. So I fixed up on Tuesday night and went over and stayed all night so we could get an early start. My husband went on ahead and we were to meet him Wednesday noon in Minneapolis, or St. Anthony.

Mr. French lined up old Bob and Jerry, their team of oxen and we got started about sunrise. A mile from the house we came to a terrible steep hill. We got up it all right and just as we started down Mrs. French said, "Old Bob hasn't any tail, but Jerry has a lovely tail. He'll keep the mosquitoes off all right."

Just then Jerry switched his tail around a young sapling and it came off. It was wet with dew and it lapped tight, and we were going down hill so fast something had to give way. It was the tail! Well we had an awful time with that tail. There was only a stump left, less than a foot long, and the ox like to bled to death. Mrs. French was afraid the wolves would get Jerry's tail and kept worrying, and when we had gone about a mile she made Mr. French go back and get it.

We started on again and went about a mile and a half till we came to Tepee hill where the Long Lake cemetery is. It's a steep hill now, but then it hadn't been worked any and it was just straight up and down. We had boards across the wagon to sit on, and they slid off. Mr. and Mrs. French got out, they wouldn't ride. But I had just got the baby to sleep—she was awful hard to get to sleep and didn't sleep much—so I said I'd ride. I sat down in the bottom of the wagon with her in my arms and we started up. We got clear to the top and the tongue came out of the wagon and down we went! I crouched over the baby and just thought my time had come. Before we got clear to the bottom the wagon veered and stopped on two wheels.

Mr. French came down and got us fixed up and we went on to where the Parrish place is now and camped, ate our lunch and built a smudge. We stayed about an hour and hooked up and started on again. Mr. Maxwell had gone on expecting us at Minneapolis by this time and here we were about three miles from home.

Mr. French was an awfully sleepy man. He could go to sleep any place. He didn't have to lead the oxen. They couldn't get out of the road. We were in the big woods all this way with just a road of stumps to go through. Mr. French went to sleep and we hit a stump. He pitched forward, and I raised up and caught him right by the pants. Busted a button or two—but he'd broken his neck if he'd gone out. Mrs. French just sat there and never offered to grab him.

Finally we got to Wayzata. We bought a pound of flour and got some rags and bound up Jerry's tail. We stayed all night at Clay's and got up at 4 o'clock and started on.

It was awfully hot. We went on till we came to the big marsh the other side of Wayzata. The lake came up farther then, and the marsh was filled with water, and all covered round the edges with logs and tree stumps. The oxen saw the water and made one lunge for it. They made down the side of the hill over stumps and logs and never stopped till they were in the water. Mr. French got out and took the ox chain and tied the tongue on the back of the wagon and hauled us up again. I remarked to Mrs. French, "I guess we will be killed yet!" "Oh," Mr. French said, "This is just a pleasure trip."

Mrs. French wouldn't crack a smile, but I thought I'd die laughing. We stopped at the six-mile house Thursday night. We had started at 4 o'clock in the morning and traveled till eight at night and gone about seven miles.

We got up at four and started on again. We chugged along till towards noon and we camped and ate our lunch and met my husband. He'd been to Minneapolis, looked after his business and was on his way home.

"Why, what's the matter?" he said. "Oh, not much. Jerry pulled his tail off," we said. "Oh," Mr. French said, "it's only a pleasure trip."

My husband was for going home, but I said, "Oh no, you won't go back. I'm all wore out now with the baby. This is a pleasure trip and we want you to have all the pleasure there is."

We got to St. Anthony at eight thirty, tired—oh, dear! We did some shopping and came back with a big load; made six miles in the afternoon and stopped at the six-mile house for the night.

Across Bassett's creek was a narrow, tamarack pole bridge. We might have known there would be trouble but we never thought of it. Old Jerry seen the water and made one lunge for it. One ox went over the edge of the bridge and one went through, and there they hung across the beam. We skedaddled out the backside of the wagon. "Well, Martha, I guess we will be killed yet," I said. But Mrs. French never smiled. She took her pleasures sadly.

The men took the pin out of the ox yokes and let the oxen down into the water and they grazed while the men went on a half a mile to borrow an ax and cut tamarack poles to fix the bridge. We stayed all night again at Mr. Clay's and got up Sunday morning and started. When we got to Tepee hill I said, "I'll walk down this hill. I rode up it."

The rest of them rode. I walked on through the woods to Mr. Barnes' beyond Long Lake and got there just as supper was ready. They wanted me to eat supper, but I said, "No, they are coming on in a few minutes. I'll just take a cup of tea." I waited—and waited—and waited—for an hour or so; and they didn't come. Finally I ate my supper and they came.

"Well, what in the world," I said, "is the matter?"

Well old Jerry had got in the creek at the bottom of Tepee hill, the outlet of Long Lake into Minnetonka and they couldn't get him out. Mrs. French was in the wagon and the mosquitoes like to ate her up.

We got to our place that night. It was Sunday night and we'd been gone since Wednesday morning. We wanted the French's to stay all night, but they said they couldn't think of it; they had to go. Their mother had a girl staying with her and expected them back Thursday night and would be scared to death wondering what had happened to them. So they left the oxen and took the path through the woods. I started in to get supper for my husband and I heard them hollering. I said, "They're lost. Go out and yell as loud as you can and build a big fire." They got back to our place all right and had to stay all night. Mrs. French followed me out to the barn. "Don't it make you mad to hear of that pleasure trip?" she said. The men couldn't get through talking about it. "Well, it makes me mad," I said, " but I can't help laughing."

"Well," Mr. French yawned, "I believe this winds up the pleasure trip."

Mr. B. F. Shaver—1853.

My parents came from Lucerne Co., Pa., father in the fall of 1850 and mother just two years later. She came to Rockford, Ill., by rail, then to Galena by stage and up the Mississippi by boat. One of her traveling companions was Miss Mary Miller, sister of Mrs. John H. Stevens. Mother spent the first night in Minneapolis in the old Stevens house, at that time the only residence on the west side of the river, about where the Union Station was.

Two years before this father had learned of Lake Minnetonka and had taken some pork and flour and a frying pan and started west to find the lake, over somewhat the route of the Great Northern railroad track to where Wayzata now is. He reached the site of Minnetonka Mills and located a claim about where Groveland park on the Deephaven trolley line is. This was some time before the government survey. He blazed out a claim. Like the old lady in the Hoosier Schoolmaster, he believed "While ye're gittin,' git a plenty" for after the survey he found he had blazed out seven hundred acres where he could pre-empt only a hundred and sixty. He had been up the creek several times to the lake where there was a beautiful pebbly beach. Once, while wandering back, he had come upon this spot, he said, "Beautiful as a poet's dream." A forty acre prairie right in the midst of dense woods covered with wild flowers and prairie grass. He blazed out his claim right there.

On November 8, 1852, father and mother traveled from St. Anthony to Minnetonka Mills with an ox team and sled on eight or ten inches of snow. They kept boarders at Minnetonka Mills that winter and in March moved to their claim. The house was not completed. There were no windows, no outside door and no floor. The following August were born twin boys, the first white children born in Hennepin county outside the city limits of Minneapolis. Mother was the first pioneer woman of Minnetonka township.

When we were about three weeks old mother's nearest neighbor, Mrs. Robinson, who lived on a claim near the present site of Wayzata, came over to assist her with the twins, as she was all worn out. It was a hot, sultry night early in September and Mrs. Robinson made a bed on the ground beside mother's and put us into it. She became very drowsy towards morning and lay down on the ground beside us. She was aroused by my brother stirring about and complaining and reaching over was surprised to feel something like a paw of a large dog thrust through a crack between the logs and pulling the baby towards the crack by its hand. She got up quietly and moving aside the blanket that hung for a door, stepped out around the corner of the house. At the crack was a large wolf. It was frightened off at seeing her and ran into the woods.

Before mother came, in August, 1850, father and three others took a boat at Minnetonka Mills with provisions and went up to Gray's Bay and westward on Lake Minnetonka to explore the lake and get a definite idea of its area and characteristics. They went through Hull's narrows and explored the upper lake several days, landed at a point about at Zumbra Heights and decided to carry their boat across to the Minnesota river and row down to Fort Snelling. After wandering in the woods several days they abandoned the boat and subsisted for days on basswood sprouts and raspberries. They reached the Minnesota river directly north of Shakopee, descended a bluff and found the shanty of a squaw man. The squaw gave them some fat pork with gravy over it and mixed up dough which she baked on a griddle. Father said he had been to many a fine banquet but that was the best he ever had tasted.

Father, mother and some of the men from the sawmill were eating supper one night by candle light, when there came a loud knocking at the door. Father opened the door and an Indian in hunting regalia staggered into the house, holding his sides and evidently in great pain. Mother did the best she could for him, gave him pain killer and hot drinks and made him a bed on the floor beside the kitchen stove, where after a time he fell into deep sleep. About daylight several members of the tribe, including his squaw, came in search of him and learned from the crew at the mill that he had been cared for during the night. His squaw came into the house, talked with him for a while and then with the other Indians started east.

They were gone about two hours, returning with the carcass of a very fine deer. The Indian had started hunting the day before and pursued a deer till almost night, finally bringing it down. Having had nothing to eat since early morning he was ravenous and cut a piece of steak from the deer and ate it raw. This made him desperately sick and on his way back he had to stop at the mill. His squaw and the other Indians proceeded to skin the deer at the house and the squaw brought in the deer's kidneys to mother. This she thought very odd but a few days later was informed by Martin McCloud, an interpreter, that the gift of a deer's kidneys was one of the highest tokens of esteem that an Indian could bestow. Afterwards the Indian and his squaw were very kind, sending her fish and venison and the squaw presented her with some beautiful bead work.

The cruelty of the male Indians always astounded mother. Once she sold an Indian a sack of flour. He was to come for it the next day. At the time appointed he came, bringing with him his squaw who had with her a little papoose, and his mother, an aged woman. He brought an empty sack along. Mother presumed he would empty a small portion of the flour into this for his wife and mother to carry and he would shoulder the remainder in the sack which contained the flour. He emptied about one third of the flour into the sack which he had brought. This he put down by the side of his mother. He took the papoose out of a broad strap around the squaw's head hanging in a loop in the back and taking up the remaining flour, put it in the strap on his wife's back, she stooping over to receive the load. It was so heavy he had to help her straighten up; she could not rise alone. Then he took the papoose and set it atop the sack of flour. He then assisted his mother about getting her portion of flour in her strap. His conduct provoked mother greatly and she told him in decided terms that he should be ashamed of himself. At her remarks he grinned and folding his arms complacently around his gun, strutted off after the women muttering. "Me big Injun."

A curious trait about the Indians was that they wanted you to trust them and have no suspicions about their honesty. When going away from the house it was better not to lock it, but take a stick and lean it up against the house outside, intimating to them that you were away; and nothing would be molested. If the house was locked they were likely to break in and steal something.

Not far from our house at Spirit Knob, now Breezy Point, Lake Minnetonka, on a bold hill projecting out into the water was a stone idol, a smoothly polished stone a little larger than a wooden water pail. The Indians came regularly to worship this idol and make offerings to their god. In very early times, probably not later than 1853, a doctor from St. Louis, Mo., is said to have stolen this image and taken it to St. Louis and put it in a museum. The Indians were very much enraged at this and some people have assigned to this deed a motive for many of the atrocities committed in 1862.

One winter day father was away teaming and was not expected home till late in the evening. As night drew on mother and her little boys were busy about the chores. In cold winter weather we did not use the woodshed and kitchen, but the two large rooms only, having to come through the two unused rooms to the main part of the house. We boys had finished our work, hung up our caps and put away our mittens for the night and mother was bringing in her last arm load of wood. She had passed through three doors and turned around to shut the last one and there, right behind her, stood a giant of an Indian. He seemed a foot taller than **her** and she was two inches less than six feet. So quietly had he followed her that she had no intimation of his presence. As she confronted him he said, "Ho" in deep, guttural tones, and then laughed at her fright.

OLD RAIL FENCE CORNERS

He evidently wanted something, but could speak little or no English. He peered about the house, looked in every corner and finally in order to make us understand what he wanted, he took the ramrod out of his gun, set it up on end on the table, put the index finger of his left hand on top of the ramrod and made counter motions up and down the rod with his right hand. Mother divined it was pole beans that he had seen growing and she got him some and he went away satisfied.

One cold winter day four Indians were in the kitchen. Mother was preparing beans for dinner. Like all good housewives she first parboiled them with pork before baking. She stepped into the pantry for something, when one of the braves slipped his hand into the kettle and stole the pork. He was just tucking it under his blanket when she, suspecting something, whirled around, caught up the teakettle of boiling water and poured some on the Indian's hands. He roared with pain and mortification, but the other braves thought it very amusing. One of them slipped up, and patting her on the back said, "Tonka squaw! Tonka squaw!" Tonka meaning big or brave. The Indians reversed their words, like Minnetonka—water-big—Minne meaning water.

That Indian never came into the house again. The men at the mill were a little afraid. They thought it unwise of her and kept close watch. The Indians would come in from hunting and sit around on our floor. Mother would give them a good kick if they got in the way. This made her more popular than ever. They considered her a very fine lady because she was not afraid of them, but cudgelled them about. There were always three or four of them sitting around on the kitchen floor.

The Indians' sense of humor was very keen. Mrs. Maxwell's little girl was tow-headed. The Indians always stroked her head and laughed. My older brother had beautiful curly hair. The Indians called it "Ha-ha hair"—curling or laughing. He was very fond of the Indians and used to tumble about them examining their powder horns, until one day an Indian pulled up his top curl and ran around it with the back of his knife as if to say what a fine scalp that would be. The frightened boy never would go near them again.

"Washta Doc" pronounced gutturally and meaning North Bay is the original of Wayzata, pronounced, Waytzete.

Colonel A. P. Connolly—1857.

By rail and boat we reached St. Paul on Friday, in May '57. A party of us who had become acquainted on the steamer, chartered a small four-wheel craft, two-horse affair and headed toward St. Anthony. We came up to the old government road passing the "Half Way House" and the well known Larpenteur and Des Noyer farms. It had been raining and the roads were bad. Four times we had to get out, put our shoulders to the wheels and get our little craft on the terra firma.

The palatial Winslow house built at this time was largely patronized in summer by the slave-holding aristocracy of the South. I remember one southerner, Colonel Slaybeck, by name, who used to come each year with his family and servants. He would always say to his slaves, "Now you are in the north where they do not own slaves, and if you wish to escape, this is your chance to run away." Not one of his servants ever took the opportunity.

My first unpleasant experience was in connection with this house. I was one of its builders for I put on lath at 4 cents a yard. By working early and late, I made $4 a day. I was very economical and trusted my employer to hold my hard earned money. So far as I know, he is holding it yet, for he "skipped" in the night, leaving his boarding mistress to weep with me, for we had both been too confiding.

Somewhat cast down by the loss of my first earnings, but not totally discouraged, I shipped with six others on board a prairie schooner, well supplied with provisions and three good horses and headed for the north and fortune. After thirteen days of frontier hardships, we landed at the mouth of the Chien River where it empties into the Red River of the North. Here we erected two or three good log houses, surveyed and platted our town, and planted common vegetables. They grew wonderfully well. We caught fish and shot ducks and geese. On paper our town could not be excelled, with its streets and boulevards, its parks and drives, its churches and schools and public buildings. It was so inspiring to look at, that we each took one hundred and sixty acres adjoining the town, intending them as an addition to plat and sell to the on-rushers when the boom should commence.

We also built a boat here, or rather made a dugout, so we could explore the river. We had amusements in plenty, for wolves, Indians, mosquitoes and grasshoppers were in great abundance. The wolves were hungry and told us so, congregating in great numbers for their nightly concerts. We had to barricade our doors to keep them out and burn smudges on the inside to keep mosquitoes out as well. Sixty-five Indians paid us a visit one day and they were not at all pleasant. We had a French half breed with us and he influenced them to leave. They only intended to take our yoke of cattle, but finally, after much parleying they moved on, and we breathed easier.

All things come to an end, and so did this wild goose chase after riches and in time we got back to God's country and St. Anthony. I will not worry you by reciting our experiences in getting back, but they were vexatious and amusing.

To sum up my reward for this five months of hard work, privation and danger, I had one red flannel shirt, one pair of boots, one pair of white duck pants and $13 worth of groceries. Wasn't this a jolt?

It was late in the fall, with a long cold winter ahead and things looked rather blue. Judge Isaac Atwater was the owner of "The St. Anthony Express," a good looking weekly paper of Whig politics. I went to work in this office at four dollars a week and as I advanced in efficiency, my salary was increased to twelve dollars. About this time an important thing happened. I married the daughter of Alonzo Leaming, who had come here in 1853. My wife was the first teacher of a private school in Minneapolis. The school being located near Minnehaha, she boarded with the Prescott family who lived on a farm not far from the Falls. After the Indian outbreak in August 1862, as we were marching up to the Lower Agency, we found Mr. Prescott's body about twelve miles out from the fort, and I helped bury him. His wife and children were prisoners at that time, held by the hostile Sioux.

I think it was in 1858, the people got clamorous for railroads and voted the State credit for Five Million Dollars. The pamphlet exploiting the celebrated "Five Million Dollar Loan Bill," was printed in the "St. Anthony Express" office and I pulled the issue off on a very antiquated hand press, known as the "Foster". It was too early for railroads Times were too hard. But half the issue was made, and a foundation laid for some of our great railroad systems. The St. Paul and Pacific was built and operated for a few miles and was the pioneer of the Great Northern system. The first locomotive landed in St. Paul was the "William Crooks," named in honor of the Civil Engineer of the road, Col. William Crooks, who was the Commander of the "Sixth Minnesota," in which I served. Colonel Crooks is buried in Oakland, St. Paul and the locomotive is on the retired list.

As I said, one half of these bonds were issued and after several legislatures had bandied them about and pigeonholed them, the debt was wiped out at fifty cents on the dollar with interest, which gave the holders par, and the credit of the state was saved. The bonds were thrown about as worthless and I had an opportunity to get some of them at $1 each.

I erected the first street light in St. Paul. You could not see it a block away. All the rest of the town was in darkness. Minneapolis had one of these lights also, located on Bridge square. Burning fluid for lamps was one dollar a gallon. Candles were mostly used. Matches, hand made, were sold for five cents a bunch—five cents being worth twenty-five cents now.

In 1858 Minnesota was over-run with "Wild Cat" money. Perhaps I had better explain this. It had no value outside the state and was not a sure thing in it. You took money at night, not knowing whether it would be worth anything in the morning. However, it looked well and we all took chances. Any county could issue money by giving some sort of a bond, so we had among others "Glencoe County," "Freeborn County", "Fillmore County," "Chisago County," "La Crosse and La Crescent," and many others. Daily bulletins were issued telling what money was good. In the final round up, the only money redeemed at face value was "La Crosse and La Crescent." I printed a directory with a Mr. Chamberlain of Boston. I sold my book and took "Wild Cat" in payment and, after paying the printer, had quite a bunch of it on hand, but merchants would not take it at its face value. We had no bank of exchange then. Orin Curtis had a little place he called a bank, but I never saw money go in or out of it.

I found what was termed a bank on the west side of the river—a two room affair, up one pair of stairs, and presided over by J. K. Sidle, who afterwards was president of the First National Bank. He was at that time loaning money at three per cent a month. The nearest bank of Exchange was that of Borup & Oakes of St. Paul, and the only way to get there was to walk or pay Allen & Chase one dollar and a half for the round trip. I preferred to walk, and so did, to receive an offer of eighty five cents on the dollar for my "Wild Cat." "No, sir," I said, "I'll go back home first," and walked back. I made three other trips and finally took twenty-five cents on the dollar and was glad to get it, for in a short time, it was worthless. Merchants issued their own individual scrip and payed many local bills that way. For instance: "David Edwards will pay five dollars in goods at his store upon presentation of this paper, etc." Times were hard, but pioneers never desert. They are always on deck. Hence our Minneapolis of today.

While on this subject of three and five per cent, I will relate an incident. There was a great revival in the First Methodist Church on the East Side, J. F. Chaffee, pastor. We all got religion, and I thought I had a call to preach, so with a dozen others, took on theological studies. We were very studious and zealous with a prospective D. D. ahead; but, I "flunked," got disgusted, side tracked the call, and in time enlisted for the war and went fighting rather than preaching. But, during the same revival and while it was at white heat, old Squire Geo. E. H. Day was in the fore front. Now brother Day was very zealous and at times thought he got at the very foot of the throne; but, he loaned money at five per cent a month. I really think he was in dead earnest, especially in the per cent business. On this particular night he was on his knees and was calling very loudly on the Lord, in his extremity, he said, "Oh, Lord give us more interest in Heaven." The crowd was so great they were in the door and at the windows. A wag, Al Stone, was among the outside crowd, and heard this urgent appeal of old Squire Day, and he cried out: "For God's sake, isn't five per cent enough?"

Among the enterprising men of the Falls was Z. E. B. Nash, or "Zeb" as we called him. He operated a line of steamers from Fewer's Landing, on the East Side above the present bridge, to St. Cloud. There were only two small boats, but they served the purpose well.

Colonel Levi Longfellow—1851.

One day back in my old home in Machais, Maine, when I was six years old and my sister Mary nine, my father said to her, "I will give you ten cents for your little tin trunk." This trunk was one of her most treasured possessions, and she asked him what he

MRS. MARGARET KING HERN
(ST. PAUL)

Medal presented to Margaret King Hern by the State in 1896.
(See page 143.)

Late type Red River Cart, taken in the Fifties. Earlier Carts had
tires eight inches wide. (See pages 14-22-218)

wanted it for. He answered, "I am going to save money to take you all out to Minnesota and I want the trunk to hold the pennies and dimes we shall save for that purpose." She was so delighted with the idea that she readily gave up the trunk and contributed a dime to start the famous fund. Many times we emptied the contents of that little trunk and counted to see how much we had, though we all knew that not more than one or two dimes had been added since we last counted. It took us three long years to save enough for the eventful trip. In those days, instead of a run of two or three days, it took a month to make the journey.

One bright day in June, an ox team drove to our door and took us, a family consisting of my father, mother, two boys and two girls with our luggage to the Boston boat. From Boston, a train carried us to Albany, New York, and from there by canal boat we went to Buffalo. Here we boarded a lake steamer for Chicago. This place I remember as the muddiest hole I had ever seen. A plank road led from the boat landing to the hotel. One railroad ran west out of Chicago for a distance of about ten miles. Beyond this lay the unexplored country we were to enter. We hired a man with a team and a covered farm wagon to drive us across the prairies to Galena. One week was occupied in this part of the journey. This same man three months later drove a herd of cattle from his home to St. Anthony Falls. From Galena we took a steamboat to St. Paul where we were met by my grandfather, Washington Getchell, who had come west with his family three years previous. He brought us to St. Anthony Falls with his ox team. Among our luggage was a red chest. Every family in those days owned one, and I remember in unloading our things from the boat, the bottom came out of the chest scattering the contents about. Men, women and children scrambled to pick up the things but mother always said one half of them were lost.

OLD RAIL FENCE CORNERS

On the second of July, 1851 we arrived, receiving a hearty welcome from our relatives. My grandfather had built the second frame house erected in the town.

Early in the winter of 1854 at nine at night I was crossing the unfinished bridge one evening with a schoolmate named Russell Pease. We had been over to see his father who lived on the west side of the river. When we had reached the middle, Russell slipped and fell through onto the ice beneath. I ran back and down the bank to where he was lying, but he was unconscious and I could not lift him, so I ran back for help, found some men and they carried him home.

One day, before there was a bridge of any kind across the river, my father carried two calves over on the ferry, to pasture on the west shore. Several days later as he stood on the river bank, he noticed something moving on Spirit Island, the small island below the falls. Going out in a boat he found the two calves running about seeking a way to reach the east bank. They had evidently become homesick and started to swim across above the falls, and in some miraculous manner had been carried over the falls and landed safely on the island. Father rescued them, bringing them to shore in a boat.

I remember the greatest excitement each summer was the arrival of the caravans of carts from the Red River of the North. They would come down to disperse their loads of furs, go into camp in St. Anthony and remain three or four weeks while selling their furs and purchasing supplies. The journey and return required three months.

In the spring of 1853 our family moved from St. Anthony to a farm in Brooklyn Center, about nine miles out from town. Roving bands of Indians often used to camp near our home. We never enjoyed these visits, but neither did we wish them to think we were afraid, so we never locked our doors or refused them anything they demanded in the way of food. Often my mother has fed a troop of those hideously painted fellows.

OLD RAIL FENCE CORNERS

In those days the only means of communication between the settlers was a messenger, going from house to house. The people of our community wished to have some way of signaling each other in case of danger. So a number of tin horns were purchased, each family being given one, with the understanding that if a blast was heard from one of these horns, the men would ride as fast as possible to the home giving the signal for help. Among the settlers was an old German who was given his horn along with the rest. After a few days, this old fellow became curious to know what sort of a sound the horn would make. Not wishing to give any alarm, he went into his cellar, thinking to be out of hearing, and blew a tremendous blast to test the power of the horn. The effect was far from what he had anticipated. The neighbors hearing the signal came from all directions, expecting to find serious trouble. My brother, Nathan, with his friend Will Fisher, mounted their horses as quickly as they could and rushed to the scene. In about an hour the boys came back disgusted, and what the settlers said and did to the old German, I leave to your imagination.

This same German figured in another amusing incident. When my father was building one of the roads in Brooklyn, he hired this man to work for him. One Sunday morning the old fellow reported for duty. My father informed him they did not work on Sunday. The man threw up his hands and exclaimed "Mine Gott! is this Sunday? My ole woman is at home washing; she tinks it is Monday too!"

I enlisted in '62 expecting our regiment would be ordered immediately to the Army of the Potomac, but within a week after the formation of the regiment, news was received of the Sioux outbreak on the frontier. We were ordered to report at once to St. Peter where we arrived August 24. Four days later we were hurried across country forty miles to Fort Ridgely which was then in a state of siege. After a sharp skirmish with the Indians, we drove them off on the second of September. We were ordered to Birch Cooley, sixteen miles away. Capt. Grant, with his command had been sent out to bury the victims of the Indian massacre, including twenty-seven men of Capt. Marsh's Fifth Minnesota troops. He had gone into camp at Birch Cooley when the Indians attacked him. The firing was heard across the plain at Fort Ridgely and we were sent to his relief. We arrived early in the morning and the command was halted to wait for daylight. With the break of day the Indians opened fire, but after a hard fight we drove them off and made our way into the camp. It was a sickening sight. Twenty-three men lay dead with fifty or sixty wounded. In the camp was a woman lying in a wagon. She had been picked up on the prairie where the Indians had left her for dead. After the Indians had gone she had managed to crawl to a rock which had a cleft in it, and there had fainted. One of our boys jumped up on this rock and noticing what seemed to be a bundle of rags lying in the opening, poked his gun into it. To his horror he found it was a woman's body. He called and another of the boys, Comrade Richardson, now living in Champlin, Minn., sprang up beside him and together they lifted her out and she was placed in a wagon. When the Indians attacked the camp, the wagons were drawn around in a circle with the camp inside and this poor woman laid there for thirty-six hours all through the fight. The wagon was riddled with bullets and she herself had been hit in the arm, though she was scarcely conscious of what was going on, having not yet rallied from her terrible experience in the massacre. I understand she afterwards recovered and lived in Minnesota.

At Wood Lake, I also helped to bury the dead, among them sixteen Indians killed in the fight there. At Camp Release situated on the west side of the Mississippi river opposite where Montevideo is now located, we surrounded an Indian camp and compelled them to give up over one hundred captive women and children. We were also sent out with a small squad and surrounded and captured another camp of hostile Indians, bringing them in to our camp. Col. Crooks, of our regiment, was appointed Judge Advocate and I was present at the trial of over one hundred of these Indians. All were found guilty and sentenced to be hung. President Lincoln commuted the sentence of all but thirty-nine, the rest being sent to the government prison at Rock Island where they were kept as prisoners of war. At that time my wife who was then Olive Branch, was attending High School in Moline, and she went with some friends to see these Indians in the Rock Island prison. She recalls distinctly the interest the people felt in seeing the savages who had been the authors of such atrocities.

In February of 1863, our regiment was sent to Forest City to build a stockade for the protection of the settlers. From there we marched across country to Camp Pope, where the main forces were being assembled, preparatory to our expedition across the plains to the Missouri river a few miles below where Bismarck now stands. We had no fresh water on this trip and were also on half rations for two months. When we finally reached the river we rushed in to fill our canteens, when the Indians suddenly opened fire on us from the opposite bank. Fortunately they fired over our heads with but few casualties. While we were halted at the river, Gen. Sibley, who had remained at his headquarters, two miles in our rear, sent a message to Col. Crooks, carried by an officer with his orderly. Col. Crooks received the message, wrote his answer leaning on his saddle, and the messengers started back to Gen. Sibley with the reply. On our return trip we found the bodies of this officer and his orderly horribly mutilated. The Indians had come up in our rear and encountered them as they rode back to camp.

OLD RAIL FENCE CORNERS

MINNEAPOLIS CHAPTER

CAROLINE ROGERS SHEPLEY
(Mrs. O. H. Shepley)

FLORENCE SHEPHERD LITTLE
(Mrs. F. W. Little)

MARY SHERRARD PHILLIPS
(Mrs. Alonzo Phillips)

Mrs. Helen Godfrey Berry—1849.

My part in the history of the Godfrey house is the first chapter. My idea of geography in 1847—at the age of eight years—was that Maine was the only state and that Bangor was not far from Boston in size and importance. "Out West" was a wonderland in my child mind. I did not realize when or how my father, Ard Godfrey, went so far from home as to St. Anthony Falls, but I did realize his return to take my mother and us children west. My father was obliged to leave us with our relatives, Alex. Gordon's family. We stayed in Beloit, Wisconsin for the winter. He, with Capt. John Rollins and some others went through on ponies, or as best they could travel. Cold weather had stopped the boats from running. That trip was one they did not forget and often told of it.

In the spring of '49 we took a stage coach from Beloit, with our baggage strapped on behind. I remember well the black mucky mud we rode through, the wheels sinking in to the hubs first on one side then the other. Father met us in St. Paul and we children at once got on the calico covered settee of the Bass House, too sleepy to eat. My next idea of being anywhere was in a room given up, very kindly, by Mrs. Calvin Church to my mother, in what was called the "messhouse," Main St. S. E. It was the most comfortable place to be had. We were hungry for

222

mother's cooking. Our first meal was of biscuits, salt and tea with strawberry jam, mother had found in the blue chest. This was in April. If the work had not been already begun on our house, it must have been hurried as in May my sister was born in the house.

There was considerable concern because there was no doctor nearer than St. Paul to call on in case of need, but a few days before my sister, Harriet was born, someone said there was an old gentleman living on the lower island, a Doctor Kingsley, so he was called in. There was no foot-bridge and but one way to get to the island, that of fording the river.

The house was built before the time of baloon frames. The principal workmen were Chas. Merceau and James Brisette, who must have worked faithfully and well. Doors and window-sash were done by hand, the lumber having to be seasoned after it was hauled to the spot. I was so interested in the many kinds of planks and tools used by these carpenters, every floor board being tongued and groved by them. The cellar under the whole house was dug after the house was partly built. I have a faint recollection that a lime-kiln was built near the old landing and lime burnt before the walls and plastering could be done. A brick oven was built, which did good service while we lived there.

When it came to the painting of the outside of the house, father and mother wondered if the natural color of Minnesota pine was not a shade or two different from that of the old state of Maine. They were so impressed they concluded to paint the house as near the shade of this new pine as possible, but were hardly satisfied because not a perfect imitation.

My mother was favored with much-needed help most of the time. The house was often a hospital. Two years after we built, the brother of the young woman who was helping my mother, came with a bad attack of cholera. He was brought in, cared for and sent away comfortable. Many families came from the far east with sickness from the long journey, many of them cases of typhoid fever. My mother was not behind in extending a welcome and assistance to these sufferers.

I would not omit my recollection of our first Fourth of July. It was either in '49 or '50 and carried out with all patriotism. I went early in the morning with my new friend, Emma J. Tyler, to touch the Liberty pole set up on the hill not far from the mills and near where was afterward built the Winslow Hotel. It was a genuine celebration. In my mind, somehow, like a dream of a birthday in spring, comes a faint picture of a number of pioneer mothers, in my mother's partly furnished parlor. I rushed in after school and stood upon the threshold. I saw bright colors in stripes, and stars of blue that they seemed to be in a quandary how to place and how many to use. Was this the first flag made in St. Anthony? Was it made in the old Godfrey House, or was I only dreaming? Anyway, it was a real celebration that came after. The Declaration of Independence was read, I think by J. W. North, a volunteer choir of our best singers—Mrs. Caleb Dorr, Mrs. North and others—sang the patriotic hymns, Isaac Atwater, Capt. John Rollins and others sat upon the platform and my father was marshall of the day.

I probably took the first music lesson on the piano given to a learner in St. Anthony, my teacher being Mrs. J. W. North, living at First on Hennepin Island in the house afterward known as the Tapper House, where Capt. John Tapper lived while running the ferry-boat, before the bridge was built from our side to the island. It was not a very safe or easy trip for me to skip over on the logs, but I got to be quite an expert. My piano came later than Mrs. North's, but was the first new piano brought and bargained for to be sent to St. Anthony.

By this time the house was comfortably furnished. At first a few articles were brought from the Slaymakers who had been one of the families who had lived in the building I have spoken of—father's shop.

OLD RAIL FENCE CORNERS

This family became discontented enough to return to their old home so from them we got our large six-legged dining table, the cradle, both of black walnut, and a few other pieces of furniture.

If such a thing could be done after fifty years, I could replace any piece of furniture as my mother had then. The parlor with its warm colored red and green carpet, the piano in its corner, the round mahogany table of my mother's with its red and black table spread and always the three worsted lamp mats I had made when seven years old. Mother's hair-cloth rocker, the parlor stove and the round back chairs, also in the sitting room were mother's small two-leaved tea-table and the settee like four chairs in a row, a-stove, etc., all so comfortable. We never lived in a house in Minnesota in which we felt the cold so little in winter. From an item in my old scrap-book concerning the moving of the house, it said it had three thicknesses of floor boards, and the same for the outside, so it was built for comfort. My little room over the parlor —my first own room—had in it the bureau made by my grandfather Burr. My bedstead, a posted one, was corded with bed cords, had one good straw bed and a fluffy feather bed on top of that, with patch work quilts. In that little room I made many beginnings. I learned to wash the floor on my knees for I had no carpet.

At the time when the Mill Company's property was partly owned by a bachelor named A. W. Taylor, the other owners were very anxious to buy out his share so were making great effort to persuade him to sell. My mother was given the money, all in gold, or probably father put it in her care, ready to make the payment if he came to terms which he finally did. My knowledge of this fact came from mother being all alone at night. She told me that in one corner of the blue chest were bags of gold amounting to $10,000. Afterward I could understand that she felt too anxious to sleep and that in case of any foul deed, I could answer for her. In those days, however, men were honest and money plentiful. Many times has my father ridden to or from St. Paul with a sack of money in the buggy seat beside him.

About this time it was getting to be the custom in Washington and other large cities for ladies to receive gentlemen callers on New Year's Day, so the first year St. Anthony followed that custom, by Mrs. Camp's suggestions and help, I was the first to receive callers, with Mrs. Camp as chaperone. I am not quite sure who were our callers, probably Mr. Camp, T. E. B. North, J. B. Shaw and others. Pound and fruit cake with fragrant coffee and rich cream were served.

In our house was organized the first Masonic Lodge. I remember it perfectly well. My mother had arranged the house in such perfect order we children felt something unusual was to happen. Mother first was elected Tyler. I couldn't understand why we couldn't even peep through the key-hole. I saw Mr. John H. Stevens and Mr. Isaac Atwater pass into the parlor where they spent the evening with my father. Mother proved a faithful Tyler and all the satisfaction we got was that they had "Ridden the goat."

Father had told brother Abner wonderful stories about the country he was intending to take us to and one was that "sleds grow on trees" and he should have one when we got there. He did not forget. Maybe he was reminded, but some time before one Christmas day daddy brought home two strips of wood that he said could be bent into the shape he wanted it. It took some time and I do not know whether brother suspected what was coming until his own frame sled was brought to him, all completed but the steels— they came later. So he can claim having had the first real coaster, for the other boys had only board runners or barrel staves.

The mills (now burned) new then, with two upright saws, the people were as proud of as they are now proud of all the fine mills in Minneapolis. Ard Godfrey had reason for feeling proud. He had the management of the building of the first mill dam across the Mississippi River, had stood waist deep in its waters, half days at a time with his men to accomplish this work. He was owner to not over one-seventh and not less than one-tenth interest in the Mill Co. business—was agent for Franklin Steele, of whom he always spoke with the greatest respect. I can realize that he was a very busy man during the time he served there and that he needed the rest and quiet he found afterward in his Minnehaha home.

Our first nearest neighbors were Mrs. Marshall with her two sons, Wm. R. and Joseph, and her daughter, Rebecca. Their store was the first started in our neighborhood until John G. Lennon built his a little later. Mrs. Marshall impressed me when she said to my mother that "If one of her sons was foolish enough to get into a fight and get whipped she would whip him again when he came home." I thought of her in after years when I heard people speak of Wm. R. Marshall while he was Governor of Minnesota. Once on our first acquaintance, my mother sent my brother, then about six years of age, to Mrs. Marshall for an article from the store. She gave it to him with the change. The child was so interested in his play with some boys, he hurried home, gave mother the package and was hurrying off when she asked him for the change. He said he hadn't any and from his eagerness to get away she feared he had spent the money without leave, to treat the boys. I heard her say something about "Not letting this pass a first time, if it is an act of dishonesty now is my time," etc. So to sift the matter to the bottom, she took the reluctant boy to Mrs. Marshall, who said, "Don't you see, Mrs. Godfrey, he has done nothing wrong; he has the money; look again." Sure enough, under the wonderful things, balls and strings in his pocket, was the money just where Mrs. Marshall had put it herself and he was the most surprised one to see it. The tears were dried and Mrs. Marshall had saved him from punishment only that he had lost his noon hour for play.

OLD RAIL FENCE CORNERS

One last rememberance is that of the great flood which came and spoiled so much of the work done in the beginning; I have still in my mind the grandest picture of Almighty God I ever saw. Man seemed but an atom against Him, when the waters rushed and roared in their strong surges over the ledges that made the Falls of St. Anthony; the long logs that had been, but a few months before, proud monarchs of the pine forests, sailed along toward this brink like sticks, then with their long ends balancing out over the rushing fall would tilt over and down into the rushing, curling, foaming torrent out of sight. But little else was thought of just then for we who were near were watching, watching the grandeur but dreading the effect. One thing I realized that drew my attention from this mighty picture, that was the anxious face of my father. Had he not foreseen the future possibilties of this great water-power? I am sure now that he had, and soon had the first stroke come and waived aside all that had been partly accomplished. A set-back because the work had been begun with rough tools and lack of material. I think he realized what might be—what has been. What we all can see now, power harnessed by inventions into monstrous manufactories, costing mints of gold, paying out mints of gold in return, costing more than half a century of time and labor.

Why do I think he foresaw all this? For several reasons. At that time he secured title to a small island outside the others just at the brink of the Falls, although by some re-survey, I think it was afterward considered a part of Nicollet Island, causing him to leave it, if I am right. Another reason seems indirect, but it was from what he said in regard to San Pedro Harbor in his first visit to California, that Los Angeles might become a city, but not what San Pedro could be with a harbor, a nucleous or center for business for all the surrounding country. It may take years enough to see all this, to make up its half century too, but when I see what is already the beginning I know he was right and knew what he was talking about. So as I now often sit and listen to the breakers of the grand old Pacific Ocean, I am given an old home-feeling, I am listening, in memory, to the roar of that might water-fall, the Falls of St. Anthony, as they sounded fifty years ago.

Abner Crossman Godfrey—1849.

In the early days, before we had street cars, or any of the present day improvements, the country was all new. New families and interests were pouring in from the East. We had to travel by stage coach and very often the roads were so muddy that the wheels of the coach would sink in to the hub. I remember the year so well that the first State Capitol was dedicated. That was the time of the pleasure trip that I am going to tell you about. They got a four horse lumber wagon and put in long seats on either side, and piled in heavy robes. This was to convey the people from Minneapolis to St. Paul for the very important services. There were three boys—Stillman Foster, Oat Whitney, Sam Tyler of the neighborhood and myself that chummed together. The rig started off from the old mill office, Main Street. That was the starting place for everything in those days, and is now Second Avenue Southeast. We boys decided that it would be a great lark to get in the wagon and hide under the robes and ride around to the St. Charles Hotel, where the passengers were waiting. Much to our surprise, we were not ordered to get out when we were discovered. We soon arrived at the old Des Noyer place half way to St. Paul. It was bitter cold, about forty-five degrees below zero. In St. Paul, I left the rig and wandered over to the old American House. My hands were frozen and I soon began to cry with the pain. My fingers were white to the first joint. A Frenchman who was standing near by, seeing my distress, took compassion on me, took me inside and put my hands into hot whiskey. That saved them.

OLD RAIL FENCE CORNERS

Major Benjamin Randall—1849.

In 1860, to prevent conflict between the Indians and white settlers, a military post called Fort Ridgely was built one hundred and eighty mile northwest of Winona on the Minnesota River. Major Woods arrived soon after navigation on the river was demonstrated to be practicable by that veteran, Smith Harris and steamboats from the Ohio river were not infrequent visitors. Ridgely was in no sense a fort, but by general acceptation. It was not designed or constructer as a place of defense. It was built on a plain forty rods from the edge of a steep bluff of the river on the south and a gradual sloping bluff, less abrupt, to a creek running at right angles on the east about the same distance. A deep wooded ravine extended up through the river bluff to about one hundred yards of the southwest corner, while a considerable depression was continued some distance farther. The St. Peter road led up the creek bluff ravine along the north side of the fort, with a level stretch of prairie to the north. It was such a place as the Indians would have selected for the building, if they had contemplated its capture.

The Indians were frequent visitors at the fort and watched the Light Battery drill with wonder and surprise. The horses flying across the prairie like an Egyptian chariot race, the sudden changes of front and position, and the rapid firing, awed the savage. In the spring of 1861, all this was changed. The artillery were ordered south. One and sometimes two companies of volunteers were stationed for a short time, and others succeeded them. The Indians knew the country was claiming its able bodied and best men in its support, and watched with interest the departure of volunteers for its defence, and believed, as they talked, that only women and old men were left. The soldiers they respected and feared had gone from our frontier.

The anxiety to rush everybody to the front had left our posts without garrison, and people without protection, and protests to officials were unheeded or disregarded. The Indians felt that the time and opportunity was present when they could win back without resistance the inheritance they had lost. In furtherance of this scheme, on Monday morning, the 18th of August, 1862, an attack was made on the citizens at the lower agency, twelve miles above the fort. Those that could, tried to escape. J. C. Dickinson, who kept a boarding-house, with his family and others, in a two-horse wagon, was the first to cross the ferry, notifying the settlers as he made his way toward the fort. A little before nine o'clock in the morning, I was out about two miles from the agency in a buggy and met him. His team was jaded and I reached Capt. Marsh's quarters sometime in advance of him. A courier was sent after Lieut Shehan, who with fifty men, was on his return to Fort Ripley. Capt. Marsh and forty-six men, started for the scene of the uprising, and were ambuscaded by the Indians, twenty-eight of the men being killed and Capt. Marsh drowned.

That night small parties of Indians that were raiding the settlements, were drawn together and celebrated their victory by dance and song, which gave us valuable time at the fort, saving hundreds of lives by the delay.

The fort was left under the command of Lieut. Gere, a young man of less than twenty years, without military or frontier experience. The situation would have appalled the most experienced frontier officer. Fortunately the advice and experience of Sergeant Jones was available. The four Reike brothers, who had the contract for furnishing hay to the post, notified settlers, and hauled water, filling all the barrels that could be found. All the water used at the post was hauled from a spring at the foot of the river bluff, nearly half a mile distant, and near the ravine which the Indians went up two days later to make their attack.

After a day of preparation and suspense, Lieut. Shehan returned with his fifty men, who were welcomed with joy by those holding the post, and later, about forty-six men arrived from St. Peter, the Renville Rangers. There were enough men to post sentinels, to guard the salient points. I visited some of these posts with an officer and a lantern later in the night, and no one was sleeping on them; they were deserted. We followed to where they had taken shelter in the barracks among the refugees, and they were ordered from under bedsteads, to resume their guns and duties.

The ravine was between my house and the garrison, where my family had taken shelter. About twelve o'clock I was at the house, with a horse and buggy, when guns were discharged and sentinels shouting "Indians." Seeing them running, I was not long in reaching the fort, and had been there but a short time, when flames shot up from my dwelling and the ravine I had just crossed swarmed with painted savages.

Miss Sara Faribault.

My father, Oliver Faribault, built a house which was his home and trading post near "Little Six" or Shakopee's village in 1844. It was a fine point for a trading post, as three Indian villages were near; Good Roads, Black Dog's and Shakopee's. He was a very successful trader. I can well remember the great packs of furs. We used to play all around the country near. I could shoot an arrow as well as a boy. The hunting was fine.

We used often to go to the sacred stone of the Indians and I have often seen the Sioux warriors around it. It was on the prairie below town. There was room for one to lie down by it and the rest would dance or sit in council around it. They always went to it before going into battle. They left gifts which the white people stole. I can remember taking some little thing from it myself. I passed a party of Indians with it in my hand. One of the squaws saw what I had and became very angry. She made me take it back. She seemed to feel as we would if our church had been violated. This stone was stolen by a man from the east and taken there. This loss made the Indians very angry.

Little Crow was often at our house and was much loved by us children. He used to bring us candy and maple sugar. My father was fond of him too, and said he was always honest.

The Indians did not understand the white man's ways. When the white man had a big store-house full of goods belonging to the Indians and the Indian was cold and hungry, he could not see why he could not have what was there, belonging to him, if it would keep him warm and feed him. He could not see why he should wait until the government told him it was time for him to eat and be warm, when the time they had told him before was long past. It was the deferred payments that caused the outbreak, I have often heard from the Indians.

One morning in the summer of '58 we heard firing on the river. Most of the Sioux had gone to get their annuities but a few who were late were camped near Murphy's. These had been attacked by a large band of the Chippewa. The fighting went on for hours, but the Chippewa were repulsed. That was the last battle between the Sioux and the Chippewa near here.

I have often seen Indians buried on platforms elevated about eight feet on slender poles. They used to put offerings in the trees to the Great Spirit and to keep the evil spirits away. I remember that one of these looked like a gaily colored umbrella at a distance. I never dared go near.

Mary Sherrard Phillips—1854.

At the time of the Indian massacre in Minnesota, August, 1862, John Otherday, who was married to a white woman, sent word to the agent's wife to leave the Agency within an hour. This was at half past nine at night. The trouble began at a small store a short distance from the agent's house. The shooting and fighting could be heard from the house.

Otherday, with a party of sixty-two refugees, instead of taking them to the fort, had them ford the Minnesota River and pass through the wild country, avoiding the main traveled roads. He was never with them, would be seen in the distance on a hill to the right, and then in the opposite direction. They came to the river at Carver, where they re-crossed, then to Shakopee, their old home, where I saw them.

When Major Galbraith was given the office of Indian Agent at Yellow Medicine, most of his employees went with him. Mrs. Galbraith and her three children, and Miss Charles, a teacher, went in a one-horse buggy. They took this at the time of the outbreak and were in Otherday's party. Part of the time they walked and let others ride to rest them. This little band of fugitives could make only a few miles in twenty-four hours. The Indians did not follow them, as they thought they would go to the fort, and then they would attack them as they neared the fort. Mrs. Galbraith and children came to father's house. They were a sorrowful looking band. Dr. Wakefield and Maj. Galbraith were at the fort.

The women told us this story. The day before the outbreak, Mrs. Wakefield and her two children, with George Gleason, started for Fort Ridgely. They saw some Indians coming. Mrs. Wakefield said: "I am afraid," but Gleason said, "They are our own Shakopee Indians, they will not hurt us." Then as soon as they passed, they shot Gleason in the back, and he fell out of the buggy, dead. They took Mrs. Wakefield and the children captives. She was saved by one Indian taking her as his squaw. For two days, he had them hid in a straw stack.

Mother asked Mrs. Galbraith if she saved any of her silver. She replied; "When life is at stake, that is all you think of."

When Col. Sibley and his men came to Shakopee, they came mostly by boat. They pressed into service all the horses and wagons in town to transport them to the seat of the Indian war. There was only one old white horse left, that belonged to Dr. Weiser. The Little Antelope that passed down the Minnesota did not have room for one more. The town was packed with refugees, every house had all it could shelter. The women did what they could to help the ones that had come there for shelter and safety, and carried them provisions and clothes. We had refugees from Henderson, Belle Plaine, St. Peter, Glencoe, and all through the country, fleeing from the Indians.

The Faribault House, covered with siding, is still standing.

Shah-kpa-dan. or Shakopee in English, was named after Shakopee Indian Chief, (Little Six), who with his band, had a village just across the river. He died and was buried there in the fifties. I saw the dead body in the winter, which they had elevated on a platform, held up by four slender poles, about eight feet high. In the trees near the camp, they had something that looked like a closed umbrella. They had a number of these to drive away the evil spirits.

The Sioux counted their money by dimes, which they called Coshpoppy. Then they counted up to ten; One-cha, No-pah, Yam-any, To-pa, Zo-ta, Shakopee, Sha-ko, Sha.kan-do, Nep-chunk, Wix-chiminey. Then these numerals would be used as One-cha Cosh-poppy, No-pa Cosh-poppy, up to Wix-chimneyi Cosh-poppy, which would be $1.

I saw some squaws the day after a battle, mourning. They had lost relatives. They sat on the ground and were moaning and rocking their bodies back and forth. The squaws always carried a butcher knife in their belts. They took the point of the knife and cut the skin of their legs from the knees down to the foot, just enough so it would bleed and a few drops trickle down these gashes. There were three or four of these squaws.

In 1854 fifteen hundred Winnebago Indians came up the Minnesota River to Shakopee, in their birch bark and dugout canoes, which lined the shore. They were on the way to their new agency. Their agent was to meet them at Shakopee with their government money and rations. He failed to come on the day appointed. They waited several days for him and were angry at the delay. The citizens found the Indians were being supplied with fire water and for their own safety, they hunted for it. They found three barrels of it in the kitchen of a dwelling. They took it and broke in the barrel-heads and flooded the kitchen. The agent came that evening, gave the Indians their money and rations, so they went on in their canoes early the next morning. I saw them off, I was in the canoes with some of them. They gave me beads and the little tin earrings, which they used by the dozens, as ornaments. The river was filled with their canoes, but their ponies and other heavy baggage went on land.

The Winnebagoes gave a money dance in front of the hotel. Their tom-tom music was on the porch. They formed in a semi-circle. They were clad in breech-clouts with their naked bodies painted in all the colors of the rainbow, put on in the most grotesque figures imaginable. They would sing and dance to their music, pick up the money that had been thrown them, give their Indian war-whoops and yells, then fall back to form the semi-circle and dance up again. This was an exciting scene with the side and back scenery made up of hundreds of live and almost naked red-skins.

I saw one scalp-dance by the Sioux. They had a fresh scalp, said to be off a Chippewa chief. It was stretched on a sort of hoop, formed by a green twig, or limb. It was all very weird. This was in '54.

The Indians enjoyed frightening the white women. They often found them alone in their homes. They were always hungry, would demand something to eat, and would take anything that pleased their fancy. My mother, Mrs. Sherrard, was very much afraid of the Indians. Once one of the braves shook his tomahawk at her through a window.

I have seen a dog train in St. Paul, loaded with furs from the Hudson Bay Fur Company.

OLD RAIL FENCE CORNERS

WENONAH CHAPTER
Winona

JEANETTE THOMPSON MAXWELL
(Mrs. Guy Maxwell)

Mr. H. L. Buck—1854.

In the spring of '54 Cornelius F. Buck and his young wife, located a claim and built a log cabin on the present highway just before it enters the village of Homer in Winona County. Homer at that time seemed a much more promising place than Winona. The few incidents I give are those I heard from my mother's and father's lips during my childhood. The country had been opened for settlement a year or two before, but few settlers had arrived at this time and everything that went to make a frontier was present, even to native Indians. They were peaceable enough but inclined to be curious and somewhat of a nuisance. One spring morning shortly after the cabin had been built, my mother was dressing, when, without warning of any kind, the door was opened and in stalked a great Indian brave. My father had already gone out and my mother was greatly frightened, but her indignation at having her privacy thus disturbed exceeded her fright and she proceeded to scold that Indian and tell him what she thought of such conduct, finally "shooing" him out. He took the matter good naturedly, grinning in a sheepish sort of way, but my mother had evidently impressed him as being pretty fierce, for among all the Indians of the neighborhood she became known as the "Little Hornet."

The second spring my father and another settler securing some brass kettles, went to a maple grove a mile below their homes on the river bank and commenced gathering sap for sugar. During the night their kettles were stolen and suspecting some Indians who were encamped on the Wisconsin side of the river, they armed themselves to the teeth with guns, revolvers and bowie knives and taking a canoe, crossed the river, entered the Indian camp and demanded to see the chief.

He was told that some of his cowardly "braves" had stolen the paleface's kettles. The chief denied the theft. My father, allowing all his weapons to be plainly seen, again demanded the return of his kettles, and said if they were not returned by the next morning he would make war on the chief's whole tribe and annihilate them. This was too much for the natives and the next morning the kettles were returned.

My mother, who had spent her childhood and youth in the prairie country, had never seen any hills worth mentioning. She told me that when she landed from the steamboat on which she had traveled from Galena and took up her abode under the overtopping bluffs that lined the banks of the river and the boat disappeared in the distance, she had an overpowering feeling that she had been imprisoned far from the world, that she was shut out from civilization and would never be able to get out of these "mountains" and for several years that feeling stayed with her. The river was the only highway over which came human beings. In the winter the river still was the main traveled road, but with sleighs instead of boats. It was a rare treat for her to go as far as La Crosse. In the winter this trip was often accompanied with danger, from the uncertainty of the strength of the ice. I recall one trip she and my father made going to La Crosse one day upon the ice in the month of February. They had planned to stay over night in the latter place and return in the morning. In the morning they hitched up the horse and drove to the river bank, but the ice had entirely disappeared during the night and the steamboating was again good.

In '62 when the Indian outbreak occurred in the west, while Winona was far removed from the danger zone, much excitement prevailed here. My father organized a company of men of which he became captain and the Winona Rangers marched west to help in driving back the Indian forces. They met thousands of settlers fleeing to the east. Assisting them in such ways as they might they continued westward until they reached Lake Shetek where they were stationed for several months. They met no Indians but were of assistance in restoring confidence in the returning settlers.

Mrs. Harriet Gleason—1854.

I was twenty-seven years old when I came to Minnesota, landing at a townsite on the Mississippi River then known as Manton, but now known as La Crescent. My brother, Samuel Spalding had come the year preceeding and had taken a claim near that place and at his request I came and took a claim there also and kept house for him.

The country at that time was one almost unbroken wilderness. There were no roads of any kind, only "blazed trails" through the timber from one place to another.

There were wild animals in those days, and still wilder Indians, though there were some "Good Indians." One morning a "Good Indian" came to our place and wanted a needle and some thread, which I gave him. He said he was going away hunting and thanked me. In the evening he came back and I lost confidence in the "Good Indian" pretty quick. He had been drinking and wanted me to give him more whiskey. I told him that I had none, but that did not satisfy him. He kept asking for whiskey. I thought, "What must I do?" I gave him the camphor bottle which he threw away; also water, with which he did the same, repeating his request for whiskey and flourishing his tomahawk over my head. I was now thoroughly frightened but tried not to let him see that I was. I then gave him a loaf of bread, which he took and then he wanted me to go with him to his wigwam. I opened the door and told him to "Get out quick," which he did with a whoop and a run. From that time on the Indians did not trouble us.

Mrs. Bradley—1854.

When our family, the Grants, came to Winona, there were more Indians here than whites and to one who had never seen the Red Skins, a vivid impression which can never be forgotten was left. There were very few houses and the inhabitants were limited to a dozen families.

Mr. Oliver K. Jones—1857.

In the summer of '62 I enlisted in Company G of the Eighth Minnesota Infantry. Before the six regiments required of Minnesota were fully organized the Sioux Indian massacre occurred. As fast as a company was organized it was rushed off somewhere on the frontier to protect the white settlers and drive back the Indians. My company and Company D of the 7th Regiment were sent on a forced march to Fort Abercrombie, two hundred and fifty miles northwest of St. Paul on the Red River, twelve miles down the river from Breckenridge. This garrison was besieged by Indians. All the white people in that vicinity who had not been killed or captured had fled there for protection. There was but one company of soldiers there at this time under command of Captain Vanderhorck, who had himself been wounded. This fort was nothing but a few buildings located on the open prairie on the Dakota side of the river. Earthen breasworks had been hastily thrown up for the better protection of the people within. It required constant vigilance on the part of all the soldiers to hold the garrison for the three or four weeks before our arrival. The only water supply they had was the river, some rods outside of the fort embankment. Their supply of rations had become nearly exhausted, so that on our arrival about the middle of September, we found a very hungry and badly scared lot of people. There were some unburied dead, some badly wounded and some sick. One woman who had been wounded by the Indians at Breckenridge a few days before and left for dead, had regained consciousness and crawled on her hands and knees the entire twelve miles to the fort where she was taken care of and finally recovered. Two mornings some Indians concealed themselves among the willows which grew on the Minnesota side of the river and fired upon some teamsters who were watering their horses. One teamster died the next day; the other, although wounded, recovered after several weeks treatment at the fort hospital. These teamsters were citizen farmers who had been pressed into service to help haul the supplies of grain and provisions to the starving people and animals at the fort.

On our way to the fort, Sauk Center was the last place at which we found any settlers. Many from the surrounding country had assembled here for safety. A station with soldiers to guard it was established there and one also at Alexandria, some miles beyond.

We did not see any Indians until the day before our arrival when a few were seen by our scouts. A mile or so from the fort, before we came to the river, we found in the woods the mutilated remains of two soldiers who had been killed the day before by some Indians who attacked the escort of eight soldiers who were returning to the fort after taking a messenger through the woods on his way to Fort Snelling to officially notify the officers in charge there, of the conditions at Abercrombie. Other messengers had been sent but it was not known whether or not they had gotten through, communication having been entirely cut off between that garrison and the settlements below. The messenger, having met our expedition, returned with us to the fort.

Immediately after our arrival, details of men were set to work cutting logs to put a twelve foot stockade around the fort to provide better protection against the Indians. Scouting parties were sent out every few days to scour the country round about from ten to fifty miles in all directions. Our company remained at Abercrombie until the spring of '64. We never saw another Indian except the few captured by the scouting parties and brought to the fort for safe keeping.

About the middle of October when we had been at the fort about a month, a call for volunteers was made to form a guard to some thirty Indian prisoners and take some cattle to Sauk Center. I was one of the four from our company; not that I was more brave or reckless than many others, but I preferred almost anything to doing irksome guard and fatigue duties at a fort. So a little train of wagons in which to carry our camping outfit, our provisions and the few squaws and children, was made up. The guards, cattlemen and Indian men had to walk. While on this trip we did not suppose there was an Indian in the whole outfit who knew or could understand a word of English, so we were not at all backward about speaking our minds as to Indians in general and some of those whom we were guarding in particular. On the second or third day out I was walking along behind the wagons near one of the big buck Indians who was filling up his pipe preparatory to having a smoke. When ready for a light he walked up alongside of me and said, "Jones, have you got any matches?" Before this, no matter what we said to him or any of the others, all we could get from them would be a grunt or a sullen look. We arrived at our destination without seeing any Indians. We turned ours over to the officer in charge of Sauk Center post. Here we had to wait a long time for a train of supplies which was being made up at St. Cloud to be taken to Abercrombie. By this time winter had set in and there was no need for guards, so each man of our squad was assigned a six mule team to drive up to the fort. If anyone thinks it is all pleasure driving and caring for a six mule team from St. Cloud to Fort Abercrombie, one hundred and seventy miles, in midwinter, with nothing to protect him from the cold but an ordinary army uniform, including an unlined tight blue overcoat, let him try it once.

OLD RAIL FENCE CORNERS

That spring our company was ordered to go to Fort Ripley, nobody ever knew what for. We stayed there until sometime in May when we were ordered to Fort Ridgely, to get ready for an expedition across the plains after the Indians who were somewhere between Minnesota and the Bad Lands of Dakota and Montana.

In the June battle of Killdeer Mountain '64, a cavalry boy sixteen years old, as soon as the Indians were in sight, put spurs to his horse. He rode in among the Indians, killing two with his sword, picked up the lariat ropes of their ponies and returned to our firing line leading the ponies, and never received a scratch of injury to himself. The boy hero said the Indians had killed his father and mother and he enlisted on purpose to avenge their death.

On August 8, 1864, General Sully was sick and turned the entire command over to Colonel Thomas. Before noon Indians were reported all around us. Colonel Thomas put strong guards in front, rear and on the flanks. Firing soon commenced on all sides, the soldiers having orders to fire at an Indian whenever one was in sight. The Indians always appeared singly or in small bands on the hills and higher ground. This mode of battle was continued until dark, when we were obliged to stop and go into camp with a strong guard all around. In the morning not an Indian was in sight. It was learned afterward that there were some eight thousand warriors engaged and that they lost three hundred and eleven killed and six hundred or seven hundred wounded. Our losses were nine killed and about one hundred wounded. The battle was named "Waho-chon-chaka" and was the last fighting we had with the Indians for that summer.

Mrs. Arabella Merrit—1859.

My father's family were among the early pioneers in Martin county, Minnesota. I well remember an emergency that tried our wits and I suppose was equal to golf for developing arm muscle in a young girl—it certainly developed patience.

243

OLD RAIL FENCE CORNERS

Much snow had fallen during the winter of 1858-9 and the sloughs of which there were legions in that country, had frozen up in the fall, full of water. Toward the last of February, the snow began to melt. A heavy rain setting in on February 28th caused it to melt very rapidly until at last the whole prairie was flooded, making it impossible for us to leave our homes for any great distance. It was during this time that the flour and meal gave out. What could we do? Bread we must have! At last I thought of the coffee mill (one of the old fashioned kind, fastened to the wall.) I filled it with wheat and went to work. Never shall I forget those long hours of grinding to furnish bread for five in the family. Never bread tasted sweeter. Some of the time I would grind corn for a change and make meal, not, to be sure, the fine meal of today, but we pronounced it good then. Our coffee was parched rye. While I was grinding the wheat we had bread only twice a day. At noon, for three weeks, there was nothing on the table except baked potatoes and salt. Finally the salt gave out and for four meals we had only potatoes. At last the flood abated and my father started for Mankato, forty miles distant, to procure some provisions. The roads were something awful, but after three days he returned with flour, meal and other needed supplies. What a rejoicing to see him safely back! I was glad to be released from my job as miller.

On Aug. 21, '62 a messenger came through our little settlement situated on East Chain Lakes in Martin County, telling us there seemed to be trouble at the Indian Agency. It was feared it might prove serious. Our settlement consisted of six families. As there was scarcely any ammunition in the neighborhood one of the men started to Mankato, forty miles distant, to procure some. When he reached Gordon City, half way, he was told that it would not be safe to proceed. Even if he did he could get no ammunition, as Gordon City could not secure any and Minnesota was short. The massacre had begun on outlying

country round New Ulm. Our little settlement awaited anxiously his return. He had left Saturday morning, Aug. 22nd. Late in the afternoon of that day my
father and mother were away some little distance
from the house. I was alone. Chancing to look out I
saw twenty mounted men coming across the prairie.
My heart stood still. Where could I hide? At last I
decided to run to our nearest neighbor's about a quarter of a mile away, warn her and we could die together.
She and her three little children were alone, as it was
her husband who had gone for ammunition. I ran,
glancing back once, I could see the horsemen were in-
creasing their speed. I reached her house and rushing in said, "Mrs. Fowler, the Indians are coming!"
Calmly, she stood up and with a white face said, "Well
we can die here as well as anywhere." Just then her
little girl of eight years with a child's curiosity ran out
and peeped around the corner of the house. She came
running back saying, "Why, they are white men."
The reaction nearly took all our strength. I stepped
out. Just then two of our friends from Winnebago
City, twenty miles east of us, rode up. They had seen
me running and hurried after me guessing my fear
that they were Indians.

I went back home where there were twenty mounted men from Winnebago City, their objective point being Jackson, fourteen miles west of us where there was
a small Norwegian settlement. My mother and I got
supper for them and they went on their way. During
the night a messenger came from Winnebago asking
how long since they had left. He said there were orders for them to go to Madelia. He found them before morning and turned their course for Madelia. Had
they gone to Jackson they would have been in time to
prevent the massacre of fourteen persons which took
place where they were holding church services. A
few escaped and told that it was a band of five Indians
that did that awful work of killing and mutilating.
We were not aware of that cruel work so near us on
that bright Sabbath day.

OLD RAIL FENCE CORNERS

Early in the spring, a son of Dr. Mills of Red Wing came, bringing with him his pretty wife and two children, two and three years old. They had taken land six miles north of us and with the exception of an old trapper, who resided alone near them, our settlement was their nearest neighbors. On that morning my mother said to father, "I think it would be best to go up and bring Mrs. Mills and children down here for a few days." When father reached the Mills' home he found that Mr. Mills had gone out on the prairie that morning to look for his yoke of oxen that had strayed away during the night. Mrs. Mills left a note for him telling where she and the children had gone and gladly came to our home. About four o'clock our neighbor returned saying there was no ammunition to be had and that we must all leave our homes at once. It was not safe to stay. In those days every settler had hoops and canvas for his wagon, as those were what he had come into that part of the country with. So with all haste the "prairie schooners" were prepared. With true eastern forethought for her family my mother put in food enough for several days, a bed and trunk of clothes. One wagon, we found, would not hold all our goods and us too. Meantime no word came from Mr. Mills. We left our home just at dusk, a sad band of six families. We took Mrs. Mills and family with us, she not knowing what might have been the fate of her husband, but bravely and quietly going with us. Every farmer drove his herd of cattle and horses. It was all they could move.

One of our neighbors, Mrs. George Fowler, sister of the late Mrs. J. J. Hillmer, was confined to her bed with a babe two weeks old. She had to be carried on a bed in their wagon. Mr. Fowler's father, mother and sister from New Haven, Conn., were spending the summer in the west with their son. We started for Winnebago City, our nearest town east. We traveled all night to make that twenty miles, making slow progress with our heavy wagons, poor roads and herds. That country was full of sloughs at that time. Often during the night, the wagon would become stuck, and the men would unhitch the horses, we would walk out on the tongue of the wagon to more solid ground, then they would hitch chains to the end of the tongue and pull it out. We reached Winnebago in the morning and found the people had fled in fright like ourselves. There were only a few men left to guard the post office and store. We could not find safety there. We felt more fright. Thinking we were left behind to danger, we continued our course east all that day. From all cross roads wherever the eye turned we could see wagon loads of people and herds of stock coming. Ask anyone where they were going, the answer would be, "Don't know. Going where the crowd goes." On our second day out Mr. Mills found us and his wife and children. I often wonder how he did in that crowd.

At night the women and children slept in the wagons while the men lay under the wagons and kept guard. Every settlement we came to was deserted, every farm house empty, desolation everywhere. We traveled on until the afternoon of Aug. 25th when we reached the town of Albert Lea. Much to our joy we found this not deserted. There were five hundred of that frightened crowd camped near Albert Lea that night. We camped near a farm house on the outskirts of the town. We found there some fine people who kindly took Mrs. Mills and children into the house. Five days after our arrival at this farm house, Mrs. Mills gave birth to a fine boy. We stayed here several days when the news came that it was thought the trouble was over and it would be safe to return. Only three families returned to our settlement, the others going to relatives farther east.

On the second night after reaching home we were awakened toward morning by our neighbor saying, "There are buildings burning on the farms west of us." We arose and dressed, lighting our lamps. My father and the neighbor, Mr. Holmes Fowler, said they would creep up carefully and see what it meant. Mother and I were left alone. Father returned shortly saying, "The vacant houses are all burned. I shall send you and mother, Mrs. Fowler and her three children to Winnebago to get men to come to our rescue. We will stay here and guard our stock." **Four miles** east and near our road leading to Winnebago lived two young men. Said father, "You stop there and send one of the neighbors for help." We started just at break of day. When two miles from home a sight met our gaze that surely froze the blood in our veins. There, a short distance from the road, quietly grazing in the tall slough grass, were three Indian ponies. Every moment we expected to see their riders rise from the grass and make a dash for us. Quietly we drove on feeling more dead than alive, expecting every moment to hear that awful Indian yell. But nothing happened.

During the winter, six months before, a band of one hundred Sioux braves, their squaws and papooses camped six miles west of our home. Often several of them at a time came down to the settlement. We always gave them food and never thought of being afraid of them. When they broke camp they camped one night near our house. How well I remember taking out a milk pan of doughnuts and passing them around. I wonder if those doughnuts left an impression! Two miles from Winnebago we had to ford the Blue Earth River. The banks were quite steep. One of our horses was a high spirited full blood Morgan mare. She always made it a point to kick when going down those banks, often coming down astride of the tongue of the wagon. My brave mother was the driver that day. We reached the bank. Carefully, with steady, dainty steps, head proudly raised, she slowly took us down that steep bank and across the river bringing us safely upon the other side. I say she, for so much depended upon her, for her good mate was always gentle. Fully she seemed to realize the situation and fully demonstrated her love, and realized the responsibility placed upon her one mate. Just before entering Winnebago we met a company of ten mounted men going to the help of the three men we had left. They returned that day accompanied by father and his two neighbors bringing their herds of stock. After being in Winnebago a few days we received word that a company of fifty mounted men from Winona were coming. They had enlisted for thirty days. They were called the Winona Rangers. After a few days they came and we were escorted home by them. They built a barracks in our settlement and guarded a portion of that section of country for their enlisted term.

The Government sent the Twenty-fifth Wisconsin regiment to Winnebago where barracks were built. Portions of companies were distributed throughout the adjoining counties, a company of them taking the place of the Winona Rangers when their time was up.

Owing to my mother's ill health we removed to Homer, where her brother lived. Two hundred and fifty miles we went in our covered wagon, through the cold and snow of November. My father had made the trip weeks before and driven our stock down. In our wagon was stored what little we could bring of our household goods, the rest was left. On Thanksgiving day of 1862 we reached my uncle's house in the neighborhood where we now live.

OLD RAIL FENCE CORNERS

MISS MARION MOIR

Mrs. Gideon Pond—1843.

On the tweny-third day of August, 1842, I was married to Robert Hopkins. He was preparing to come to the Northwest as an assistant missionary in the Dakota mission, and in March 1843, we started on our long journey from Ohio to Fort Snelling, sent out by the American Board. We came down the Ohio and up the Mississippi in a steamboat, stopping off for Sabbath and had to wait a long time for a boat at Galena after spending Sunday there. We reached Fort Snelling in May after a tedious journey. From Fort Snelling we started up the Minnesota River in an open boat propelled by oars. At night we camped on the banks and cooked our supper. In the party were Mr. and Mrs. Steven Riggs and their two children and his wife's brother. Dr. Riggs was just returning from the east where he had had some books printed in the Dakota tongue.

We also had three men to row the boat. We suffered much from the myriads of mosquitoes. We baked our bread each day. It was simply flour and salt and water baked in a frying pan before a smoking camp fire. It was very distasteful to me and I determined to have a loaf of light bread. I had some home made yeast cakes in my luggage as bought yeast cakes were then unknown. I soaked one of them in a pail of river water, stirred in some flour and soon had some nice light yeast. I mixed a loaf of bread and set it where the hot sun would keep it warm. At night it was ready to be baked and I used a little Dutch oven which was on the boat to bake it in. The oven was like a black iron kettle flat on the bottom and standing on three little legs about three inches long. We placed coals under the oven and a thick iron cover heavier than any you ever saw, we heated in the fire and placed over the oven to bake the bread on the top, while to bake it on the sides we turned the oven around. I attending the baking of my bread with great solicitude and care.

While it was baking an Indian man came into the camp and sat down by the fire. I paid no attention to him but attended to my loaf, just as I would have done if he had not been there. Mrs. Riggs said, "You should not have let that man see your bread." I said, "Why not," and she answered, "He may come in the night and steal it," which I thought was preposterous. In the morning I fried some bacon, made coffee, spread the breakfast on the ground and went to get my bread and it was gone. So the breakfast had to wait until I could mix some of the bread I disliked so much and bake it. I remember well I thought "So this is the kind of people I have come to live among."

At the point called Traverse de Sioux we left the river and made the remainder of our journey nearly one hundred miles in wagons which had been sent from the mission at Lac qui Parle to meet us. A new station was to be started at Traverse and Mr. Riggs and two of the men remained there to build houses for us.

We were four or five days going from Traverse to Lac qui Parle and had many thrilling adventures. Dr. Riggs had been east a year and had taken with him three young Indian men that they might see and learn something of civilized life. They were returning with us on their way to their homes. The last morning of our journey two of them proposed to go ahead on foot and reach their friends, as they could go faster so, than in wagons. The other, being sick, remained with us. We had an extra horse and later he was told that he might ride on to meet his friends. After some time he came tearing back. He excitedly told us that his only brother had come to meet him and had been murdered by ambushed Ojibway Indians.

We soon came to where the scalped and bleeding body lay, right across the road. The men of our party carried the body gently to one side and covered it with a canvas. In a short time we met large numbers of Indian men armed and very much excited, in pursuit of those who had murdered their neighbor and friend. I could not understand a word they said, but their gestures and words were so fierce that I expected to be killed. They fired at our team and one of the horses was so seriously injured that we had to stop. Mrs. Riggs and I walked the rest of the journey, five miles, she carrying her fifteen months old baby. This was July 4, 1843. My first baby was born on the 10th of the following September.

On this last five miles of our journey, Indian women came out to meet us. Some of them had umbrellas and held them over us. They seemed to know that this was a terrible adventure for us. One of them put her arms around me and tried to help me on and was as kind as any white woman. They offered to carry Mrs. Riggs' baby, but the little thing was afraid of them and cried so that they could not. Mrs. Riggs kept saying over and over again, "Fear not, little flock, for it is your Father's good pleasure to give you the kingdom."

The Indians seemed to me very poor, indeed. They had for many years depended upon the buffalo but now these were growing very scarce and no longer furnished a living for them. The Indian women each year planted small patches of corn with only their hoes for plows. They raised only small amounts and they had no store houses. Sometimes they buried their supply of food for the coming spring in holes in the ground, but dared not mark the place for fear of having their supplies stolen, so they were not always able to find it when it was wanted. In the fall they gathered wild rice which they threshed by flailing it in buffalo skins. In the spring they made a little maple sugar. They were often very short of food and suffered from hunger.

OLD RAIL FENCE CORNERS

One day I cooked a squash, putting the parings in a swill pail. An old Indian woman came in and made loud cries of dismay when she saw my wastefulness, saying, "Why did you throw this away?" She then gathered them carefully out of the pail and carried them home in her blanket to cook. Pies that were set out on the window sill to cool disappeared also.

This first winter was spent at Lac qui Parle, or Medeiadam, (med-day-e-a-da) "The lake that speaks," in both tongues. I was told that it was so named from a remarkable echo about the lake. I kept house in a little room on the second floor of a log house. Dr. Williamson and his family lived on the lower floor.

One day as I was alone sitting at my table writing, the door of my room opened and a hideously painted Indian came in. His face, as nearly as I can remember, was painted half red and half black with white streaks across. A band around his head contained a number of large feathers, indicating the number of enemies he had killed. He evidently hoped to frighten me terribly. I determined I would try not to let him know how frightened I was. I sat still at my table and kept on with my writing and in a short time he went down stairs again. This Indian was the famous Little Crow, the leader of the outbreak of 1862. Afterwards my second husband, Mr. Pond, tried to teach Little Crow to read music and he told me that he had double teeth all around. Little Crow learned to sing and had a fine voice. He was a fine looking fellow without his paint; tall, slender and strong looking.

In the spring of 1844, April 4, we started on our journey back to Traverse de Sioux. We had a snow storm on the way but reached our new home in peace and safety. This was a one room log cabin with a little attic above. The Indians here were not quite as friendly as those at Lac qui Parle and seemed to wish we had never come among them.

OLD RAIL FENCE CORNERS

I had a class of all the little Indian girls that I could persuade to come to school. Their parents seemed very much opposed to having their children learn to read, sew, cook or anything else. I think they had an idea that in some way we would be paid for our trouble in teaching them and that it would be to their disadvantage when they sold their land. At any rate only a few girls came to school. In order to make my task of teaching them less unpleasant I provided basins, towels, soap and combs and requested them to use them each day as they came in. Contrary to my expectations they seemed to delight in these morning ablutions, especially if I brought a mirror so they might see themselves.

One of these girls was an especial favorite of mine. She came quite regularly and seemed interested in trying to learn all she could. She was about fifteen years old. The girls had to walk about a mile through the deep snow to reach the school. One day this favorite girl was absent. I asked why she was not there, but the other girls did not know. The next day again she was absent and the other girls told me the reason was because she did not wish to marry a man who had bought her and had three wives already. That day her parents went for food from a store of provisions which they had, leaving her at home to care for the younger children. While they were gone she committed suicide by hanging herself.

The Indian tents were heated by making a fire on the ground in the center, the smoke partially escaping through a hole in the top. On each side of this fire they drove a forked stick into the ground and laying a pole across these sticks hung on it their utensils for cooking. To this pole this poor Indian girl had tied a rope attached to a strap about her neck and, the pole being low, had lifted her feet from the ground and hanged herself rather than marry a man she did not love.

One day when I was alone in my house at Oiuwega or Traverse de Sioux an Indian man came softly in and sat down by the stove. I soon saw that he was drunk, which frightened me a little. I said nothing to him except to answer his questions because I did not wish to rouse his anger. Presently he reached to the stove and lifted a griddle and I thought he was going to strike me. The griddles on the cook stoves then, each had its handle attached instead of having a separate handle. I slipped out of the door and soon he went away. Later he came back and said, "They tell me I was going to strike you the other day. I was drunk and that is my reason. I would not have done it if I had been sober." I accepted his apology, thinking it a good one for an unlearned Indian.

The treaty between the U. S. government and the Dakota Indians was made in July of 1851. The commissioners of the government three in number, came in June. Their chief was Luke Lee. There were no houses where the white people could be entertained, so they camped in tents on the bluffs of the Minnesota river near an old trading house, occupied at that time by Mr. Le Blanc. The bluff was not an abrupt one, but formed a series of terraces from the river to the summit. The camp was on one of these terraces. There was a scarce fringe of trees along the river but from there to the top and as far back as the eye could see, perhaps for two miles back on the bluff, there was not a bush or tree.

A great many white men assembled, Gov. Ramsey, Gen. Sibley, Hon. H. M. Rice, editors also from some of our newspapers, among them Mr. Goodhue of the Pioneer Press, were there. Traders, too, came to collect debts from the Indians when they should receive the pay for their land. Mr. and Mrs. Richard Chute of St. Anthony came. Accidentally their tent had been left behind and they found a boarding place with me. The Indians were there in great numbers. Many of them were from the far west and these were much more uncouth and savage looking than any who lived around us. Some of their women wore no garment but the skin of animals which formed a skirt reaching from a few inches above the waist to the knee and hung from the shoulders by straps. The Indians pitched their tents on different terraces of the bluff some little distance away from the white people's camp.

Daily the Indians had their feasts, dances and games of different sorts. They seemed a little afraid to treat, were afraid of being wronged and were very cautious. The commissioners were very kind to them and treated them with great respect. They prepared for a great celebration of the Fourth of July. The mission families, Hopkins and Huggins, were invited to be present. Mr. Hopkins was asked to make an address and lead in the opening prayer. He rose early that fair beautiful morning and went, as was his custom, for a bath in the river. I made haste to prepare breakfast for my family of seven. My youngest child was seven weeks old that day. But the father never came back and the body was found three days later.

There were four white women at the place at that time, Mrs. Huggins, the wife of the other missionary, Miss Amanda Wilson, a mission school teacher, Mrs. Chute, a fair, beautiful young woman visitor and myself. We were just a short distance from the old crossing called by the Dakotas, Oiyuwega, (O-e-you-way-ga) and by the French Traverse de Sioux.

In September I went back to my mother in Ohio with my three little children. Mr. and Mrs. Riggs were going east, too, for a visit, and again I journeyed with them. As there was a large party of us and the American board which paid our expenses was not wealthy, Mr. Riggs thought we ought not to travel first class, so we went in the second class coaches. The seats were hard, like benches. My daughter, Sadie, then two and a half years old, was taken sick and cried and begged for water but there was none. I was in the deepest distress at not being able to give the poor sick little thing a drink. In the night the train stopped somewhere for water and a young man whom I could not remember ever having seen before got off and bought a cup of water for twenty-five cents and gave it to the poor, sick baby. If I have thought of that young man once I have thought hundreds, perhaps thousands of times of him and wished that I could thank him again and tell him what a beautiful thing he did.

I remained with my mother till I was married to Mr. Pond in April 1854. Again this northwest became my home. The Indians had sold their land to the government and been sent farther west. The country was filling up with white settlers. Bloomington has been my home ever since.

When I came to Bloomington as a .bride there were seven motherless children of the first Mrs. Pond, the eldest being about fifteen years old. I brought with me my three fatherless children, so our family numbered twelve. Our home was a log house of six rooms. There were no schools anywhere within our reach. Every morning our children and some of our neighbor's gathered about our long kitchen table which was our dining table as well, for their lessons taught by the mother or one of the older children. There were no sewing machines to make the numerous garments necessary for our family, no lamps, no kerosene. We made our own candles as well as our own bread and butter and cheese and soap. Our lives were as busy as lives could be.

In the summer of 1856 we made bricks on our own place with which we built the house where I have lived ever since. Mr. McLeod was our nearest neighbor. North of us I cannot remember that we had any nearer than Minneapolis. Down toward Fort Snelling lived Mr. Quinn in a little bit of a house.

One night Mr. Pond was at the Old Sibley House at Mendota when a number of traders were there. During the evening as they told stories and made merry, many of the traders told of the joys of sleeping out of doors with nothing between them and the starry sky; how they never minded how hard the bed was if they could only see the green trees around them and the stars above. Mr. Pond, who also had had experience in outdoor sleeping, said that he liked nature too, but he preferred to sleep, when he could, with a roof over him and a good bed beneath him. After some laughter and joking on the subject, the traders, one by one, stole out and gathering up all the feather beds the house afforded, heaped them upon the bed in the attic which Mr. Pond was to occupy, thinking that he would at once see the joke and return their beds to them. Instead, he climbed upon the mountain of feathers, laughing at the joke on his would-be-tormentors and slept comfortably all night while they had to spend the night on hard boards. He loved to tell this story of how the laugh was on them.

Mrs. E. R. Pond—1843.

After the Indian outbreak the different tribes were broken up and outside Indians called to the leadership. A little, wavy-haired Indian named Flute was one of these. He had never learned to wear the white man's foot gear. With a number of others he was taken to Washington. He went as a chief and soon after his return came one day to my door. He was a keen observer and, I knew, would have something interesting to tell of his journey, so I was glad to ask him about it. He began by saying that when he had seen the young Indians all dressed up in suits of store clothes, especially in long boots, he thought, they must be very comfortable. He was very glad when he reached Yankton, to put on a suit of white man's clothes. He said all those who were going on the trip were put into a car where there was not room to lie or sit down and were in it for two nights. When he got off at Chicago he found his feet and legs were very sore from his new boots. When he saw all the people in Chicago he thought, "It seems very strange that Little Crow should be such a fool as to think he could conquer the white man. Little Crow had been to Washington and knew how many men 'Grandfather' (president) had." He knew he had a great many soldiers but he also knew he was having a big war.

"There were so many people in Chicago that I thought he must have summoned the young men from all over the country that we might be impressed by their number. And they were all in such a hurry. No one had time to stop anywhere. We finally reached New York and were taken up, up, in a building and allowed to stay there and rest several days. We wondered a good deal what they would do in case of fire, but supposed they never had any. We asked the interpreter about it. One evening there was an unusual noise. It was always noisy, but this was everything noise. Then the interpreter came and said, 'Come quick now and see how grandfather fights fire.' We went downstairs quick and every man was calling as loud as he could. All of a sudden we heard a great bell ringing and there were a number of those little men with horses hitched to something that looked like buffalo's paunch with entrails rolled around it. They had a great many ladders and how they did it I don't know, but they went to work like squirrels and climbed, one ladder above another, until they reached the top. White men are wonderful. They ran up just like squirrels and took the buffalo entrails with them. Threw water, zip! Pretty soon, all dark! Fire gone!"

"We stayed in grandfather's country three or four weeks. Tobacco was plenty, very strong, no good! We walked about in Washington a good deal. One day we saw some red willow on little island. Little bridge led to island. We thought we could cross over and get some red willow to go with strong tobacco. Two or three went over to get it. After they began to cut it one looked up and said, 'Why grandfather didn't want us to come here,' and there were men with little sticks and they just made a few motions and broke the bridge. Then we saw a boat coming. As soon as it got through and the bridge was mended we thought we had better start back, so we started over and pretty soon a train of cars was coming. We couldn't go back, were afraid to stay on bridge, so dropped down and held on to beam while train went by. Bridge shook dreadfully. We hurried back and thought we would use white man's tobacco as it was."

All the while Flute was telling this story he was gesticulating with motions appropriate to the story and often reiterating "Little Crow is a fool," and crying, "Hey!"

Mrs. John Brown—1852.

The Sioux Indians did not often give a child to be brought up by white people, but Jane Williamson— "Aunt Jane" took little Susan and David, two very young Dakota children, to see what environment would do for the Indian. Later they were placed in other families.

Little Susan, though a Sioux Indian, was dreadfully afraid of Indians having always lived with the white people. One day in 1852 when all the men about the two places were busy plowing the field back of our house, Mrs. Whalen, with whom little Susan lived, felt nervous as a number of Indians had been seen about, so she took little Susan and come to spend the day with me, her nearest neighbor. The house was just a small temporary board one. Little Susan asked for a piece of bread and butter and went out and sat on the Indian mound by the house to eat it. Here the Indians must have seen her, for soon after she went back into the house, twenty Indians came into the yard and up to the open doorway—the door not yet being hung. Twelve Indians filed in and filled the room. My baby was in the cradle by the door. Little Susan, Mrs. Whalen and I were also in the room. The braves began to ask questions about little Susan, "Is she good squaw? We are Sioux and love little Sioux girl. We want to shake hands with her." They passed her along, one handing her hand to another, till the one nearest the door pushed her out. The Indians out doors shot her through the arm and breast and she fell forward. I seized my baby from the cradle and looking out the door, saw that five or six of the Indians had their feet on little Susan's breast, scalping her. I screamed for the men who were hidden from view by the trees between the house and clearing. When they reached the house the Indians—Chippewas, were gone. For months afterwards arrow heads and other things which they had dropped in their flight were found about the place. One large bundle was found in the yard. There is a stone in memory of little Susan in the Bloomington cemetery.

Often as I came up the hill from the spring with water, an Indian would softly cross the path in his moccasined feet and give me such a start that I nearly dropped my pail of water. This spring is the one from which the Minneapolis Automobile club, situated on the Minnesota river draws its supply. Just a little west of the club house is the place where little Susan was killed, also an Indian mound and the marks of an old trail.

One day an Indian walked into my house and asked me for a whetstone. I gave it, not daring to refuse him. He sat down and sharpened his knife, feeling its edge and pointing often and looking significantly at me.

A Shakopee Indian once said to Mr. James Brown, keeper of the ferry, "Our Pond's a good deal better man than your Pond. Your Pond preaches for nothing, but our Pond preaches for nothing and gives a good deal to the church."

Mr. Pond once met a Shakopee Indian on the trail and neither would turn out for the other. They ran into each other "bump." Indian said "Ho." Mr. Pond said, "Ho." Each continued on his way.

OLD RAIL FENCE CORNERS

ROCHESTER CHAPTER

BELLE BOYNTON WELCH
(Mrs. E. A. Welch)

MISS IDA WING

Marion L. Dibble—1855.

After a tedious journey alternating between steam boats and railroad cars, we arrived at Red Wing. Here father left us and went on foot to his new home. Procuring a yoke of oxen from a kind neighbor, he returned to Red Wing and brought us there. Our first work was to cover our bark roof with sods taken from our future garden, and to build a stone fireplace to warm our house and cook our food.

The country was wild prairie with some strips of timber along the branches of Zumbro River, which ran about a mile east of our house, along the banks of which river could be seen the remains of Indian tepees and their paths crossed the country in all directions.

Game and fish were very plentiful. During our first winter, we had a deer hung on every rafter on the north side of the house. Our supply of meat for the first year or two depended upon our success as hunters and fishermen.

Mr. M. G. Cobb—1857.

In July 1857, I walked from High Forest to Austin to record a deed. The distance was thirty-five miles, and as there were no roads, I was guided by my compass. I passed only three houses on the way. I found no one at home, and was unsuccessful in my endeavor to get a drink of water. I made the journey on Sunday, and a hot July day. There was no means of getting water from the wells, as there were no pumps. Water was drawn from the wells by a rope and bucket. I looked into the window of one house and could see the bucket and rope in the kitchen, but the houses were locked. So I traveled wearily on until I reached Austin, when my tongue fairly hung out of my mouth, and was so swollen that I could not speak aloud for two hours. I made this trip in one day. I could have mailed the deed, as there as a stage coach carrying the mail once a week, but I was a young man and thought I could easily walk that distance, and then be sure that my business was attended to properly.

Two rival stage coach lines went from Chatfield to Winona. It took a whole day to make the trip, a stop being made for dinner at a village called Enterprise. The regular fare for the trip was $2.50. The stagecoaches started from Madarra Hotel, Chatfield. This hotel is still there, and is called by the same name.

Walker & Co. ran one of the lines. It was Mr. Walker who first accosted me and said, "If you will go with me, I will take you for 50c." I answered that I had a lady friend who was going on the same trip, and Mr. Walker at once agreed to take her also at the same price—50 cents.

A little later I was accosted by Mr. Burbank, who had established stage lines on the most important routes in Minnesota and he was endeavoring to run out his rival, Mr. Walker. He asked me to go with him. I told him that Walker had agreed to take me for 50 cents, wherewith Mr. J. C. Burbank declared, "Well, I will take you for nothing and pay for your dinner besides."

Judge Lorin Cray—1859.

In the early spring of '59 my father and brother-in-law started with teams of oxen and covered wagons from our home near Oshkosh, Wisconsin, to seek a location in the West, where homes could be had "Without money and without price," in the great new state of Minnesota.

In October of '59 all of the earthly belongings of my father, being my mother, seven children and a handful of household goods, were loaded into a wagon drawn by a pair of unbroken steers, and we started for our new home with great anticipations. Our two cows were driven behind the wagon. My elder brother drove the steers attached to the wagon, and we, the younger children drove the cows, and in the short period of precisely thirty days we reached our new home in the western part of Shelby county. Now we make the trip in twelve hours. But our loads were heavy for the teams we had, and through Wisconsin sand and good Minnesota mud, we made scarcely more than ten miles a day, camping at night in and under our wagons.

The year had been a peculiar one in Wisconsin. There had been severe frost at some time in every month during the entire summer and corn and other produce was badly frost bitten. By October first all vegetation was brown and dead. But there had been much rain in Minnesota, evidently preventing frosts, and when we crossed the great Father of Waters at La Crosse, much swollen and turbid, we were greeted by green foliage and the freshness of spring. Vegetation was rank, grass tender, crops good, foliage magnificent, and boy-like, I at once fell in love with Minnesota.

We entered Blue Earth county near the southeast corner, and went as nearly directly west as possible, passing Minnesota lake near the north shore, camping for the last time very close to the north shore of Lura lake, where we spent the night.

My recollection of the southern part of this county, is that it was mostly low and level, with a wonderful growth of wild grasses. The lands were nearly all taken and there were seen here and there settlers' shanties, and in some places quite comfortable homes, until we crossed the Blue Earth river west of Shelbyville, when, after leaving the settlers' cabins in or near the river timber, the picture was wild and dreary to the very limit. Save a few cabins and claim shanties in the vicinity of the Mounds, one could look from the river west, southwest and northwest, and not a sign of human life or habitation could be seen.

We were four miles from Shelbyville, and to get our mail we must go this distance, and cross the Blue Earth river, either in a canoe or by fording. I remember one occasion in the very early spring, when the river was scarcely free from ice, and was badly swollen, filling its banks, five or six of us, neighbors, started for Shelbyville on foot to get our mail, and to hear the postmaster read the news from the weekly St. Paul paper which came to him, there being at that time, I think, no newspaper taken west of the river. We reached the river. The ice had gone out, and the boat was on the other side. We agreed to draw cuts and decide who should swim the river and get the boat. The lot fell upon Jonah, and I have had chills ever since. I am not quite certain that the cuts were fairly held.

Father's claim was not a very desirable one. Soon after he had taken it a man named Sam Tait came into the country and "jumped" a claim which adjoined ours upon the east, and was the making of a much more desirable farm than ours. He succeeded in holding the claim. A few days after our arrival a prairie fire came from the west and with a brisk wind swept the whole country with a very besom of destruction. We came near losing everything we had. Sam was a loser, quite a quantity of his hay was destroyed. Very shortly after the fire he made us an informal call and in language not the most polite but very emphatic, declared his intention to leave the country at once and offered to sell us his claim. We bought it, one hundred and sixty acres of land, three acres broken, a small stock of hay not burned, his sod stable and board shanty. For the purchase price we gave him a shot gun and hauled two loads of his goods to Mankato.

This was my first visit to Mankato. We removed our shanty to our new purchase at once. Two years ago my brother and I sold the farm for $9600, and it was well worth it.

OLD RAIL FENCE CORNERS

It seemed at first in those early days impossible to have social relations with anyone. Neighbors as we had known them, we had none. The nearest settlers were a mile distant from us, and there were but four or five families nearer than two or three miles distant. But we soon learned that we had neighbors even though the distance was considerable. First one neighbor and then another would extend to every family in the vicinity an invitation to spend an afternoon or an evening. Someone would hitch his oxen to his wagon or sled, and going from house to house, gather up a full load well rounded up and then at the usual gait for such conveyances, we rode and visited and sang until we reached the appointed place, where perhaps, eight, ten or a dozen persons spent the afternoon or evening, in the one little room, where the meal was being prepared and the table spread. There were no sets or clans, no grades of society, all belonged to the select four hundred, and all were treated and fared alike. Friendships were formed which were never broken, and when recalled always revive tender memories.

August 18th, 1862, the Sioux Indian troubles began. There were no railroads, no telegraph or telephone lines, but one stage line, and I could never understand how the reports of these troubles traveled as rapidly as they did. On August 19th this whole country had reasonably reliable information of the uprising. A neighbor came to our house in the night, neighbor went to neighbor and so the news traveled. The men were in a fury of excitement and anxiety, the women and children were quaking with fear. Wagons were hastily loaded with women and children, and a little food, animals were turned loose to provide for themselves; houses were left unlocked, oxen were hitched to the wagons, and a general stampede was started toward the east, with all eyes turned toward the west. No one knew whither they were going, they only knew that they dare not stay.

OLD RAIL FENCE CORNERS

A halt was made at Shelbyville, the strongest buildings were selected for occupancy, the women and children were placed inside, and the men acted as pickets. In our whole country there were scarcely a dozen guns. The reports came worse and worse, and another pellmell stampede began for the east, some stopping at Wilton, Owatonna and Rochester. After waiting two or three weeks, and hearing encouraging reports, some of the more venturesome returned to their homes with their families, only to remain a few days, and to be again driven away by the near proximity of the Indians, and the sickening reports of their savage murders.

This condition continued until late in the fall, when, under the general belief that the Indians would not move on the warpath in the winter, the greater number of settlers returned to their homes to save what they could of their nearly destroyed and wasted crops. Some never returned. With feelings of partial security, and encouraged by their escape from slaughter thus far, the settlers remained at their homes, under an intense strain of anxiety, but nearly undisturbed until 1864, when the rumblings and rumors of Indian troubles were again heard; but the settlers were not so easily terrified as before, and held their ground.

On the 11th day of August, 1864, after quite a long period of comparative repose and freedom from Indian disturbances, a party of six or eight Indians suddenly appeared in the edge of the timber on the east side of the Blue Earth, near the town line of Shelby and Vernon, and taking wholly by surprise Mr. Noble G. Root and his two sons, who were stacking grain, shot and killed Mr. Root and seriously wounded one, and I think, both of his sons. These Indians then crossed the river in a westerly direction, reaching the open country where the Willow Creek cemetery now is. On that day Mr. Charles Mack of Willow Creek, with his team and mower had gone to the farm of Mr. Hindman, a short distance southwest of Willow Creek to mow hay for Mr. Hindman, and in exchange Mr. Hindman had gone to the farm of Mr. Mack to assist Mr. Jesse Mack in stacking grain.

Mr. Mack and Mr. Hindman were loading grain directly across the road from the cemetery, when, on looking toward the road, but a few rods away, they saw some Indians coming directly toward them. They both hastily got upon the load and Mr. Mack whipped his horses into a run, when in crossing a dead furrow Mr. Hindman was thrown from the load, pitchfork in hand, striking upon his face in the stubble and dirt. Rubbing the dirt from his eyes as best he could so that he could see, he started to run and when he was able to open his eyes he discovered that he was running directly toward the Indians. He reversed the engines somewhat suddenly, put on a little more steam, and made splendid time in the other direction toward the creek bed, less than a quarter of a mile away. Once in the creek, the water of which was very shallow at that time, he followed the bed of the creek for nearly a quarter of a mile, and then stopped to rest and to wash the blood and dirt from his face. Soon he left the stream and started up the bluff on the opposite side, which was quite steep and covered thickly with timber and brush. When nearly at the top of the bluff he came to a little opening in the brush, and looking ahead about one hundred feet he saw those Indians deliberately watching his approach. Utterly exhausted and unnerved, he dare not run; he paused, and in a moment a burly Indian drew a large knife and started directly toward him. Concluding that his day of reckoning had come Mr. Hindman took the position of a soldier, with his pitchfork at "charge bayonets" and awaited the approach of the Indian. The Indian came to within a very few feet of Mr. Hindman and stopped. Each stood, looked, and waited for the other to open the meeting; finally the Indian turned as if to retreat, and Mr. Hindman turned again toward the creek.

He then followed the creek bed down to the house of Mr. Charles Mack, where he found a pony belonging to himself, which he had ridden there that morning, and started with all speed for his own home, where he arrived just before dark. His children were gone, his house ransacked, nearly everything broken or destroyed, and in the meadow a short distance from the house was the dead body of Mr. Charles Mack. By this time darkness had set in. His wife had gone that day about two miles to the house of Mr. Jesse Thomas to attend a neighborhood quilting. He again mounted his pony and started across the prairie for that place. When about one-half the distance had been made, his pony looked sharply through the semi-darkness in the direction indicated and there about three hundred feet away were the Indians; four of them were mounted, the remainder on foot. Mr. Hindman put whip and spur to his pony and ran him for about a mile, then he stopped in a valley to listen for the Indians, but he did not hear or see them.

On arriving at the house of Jesse Thomas he found it deserted, ransacked and nearly everything destroyed.

It proved that his children saw the Indians attack Mr. Mack, and ran from the house and secreted themselves in the very tall grass of the slough in which Mr. Mack was mowing, and escaped with their lives. The ladies at the quilting had a visit from the Indians; they saw them approaching from a belt of timber but a few rods away, and escaping by way of a back door to a cornfield which came quite up to the house, all of their lives were saved. The Indians secured the horses of Mr. Root, and also those of Mr. Charles Mack, and those of Mr. Stevens whose horses were at the place of the quilting.

No more honest men, kindhearted and generous neighbors, or hardy pioneers, ever gave their lives in the defense of their property and their families, than were Charles Mack and Noble G. Root.

A man was asked, why did you return to the west, after having gone back to New York and having spent two years there? His answer was. "Neighbors. Would you want to spend your life where the people twenty feet away do not know your name or care whether you live or die? We used to have neighbors in the west, but when our baby died in New York, not a person came near us, and we went alone to the cemetery. We thought we would come back home." How very many have had nearly the same experience. In the congested districts it seems to be everyone for himself. On the frontier a settler becomes ill, and his grain is sown, planted and harvested. Who by? Neighbors. A widow buries her husband and again the neighbors come. It is no light thing for one to leave his own harvest and go miles to save the crop of another, but it is and has been done times without number by those who are tried and true neighbors and the sentiment which prompts such kindly acts counts for something some time, and it means something in making up the sum total of happiness in this short life of ours.

What did we have to eat that first year? Potatoes and corn. No flour, no meat, some milk. I doubt whether there was a barrel of flour within three miles of our home. No wheat had been raised, no hogs had been fattened; corn and potatoes were the only food.

Mr. M. R. Van Schaick—1860.

I cast my vote for Abraham Lincoln in 1860 in New York and immediately after, with my family, started for Minnesota, arriving in Rochester late in the season. Our household goods were lost for some time, but were recovered at La Crosse and hauled by oxen to Rochester.

One night a man rode into Rochester bearing the news that a thousand Indians were on their way to massacre all the people west of the Mississippi river. Great excitement prevailed and most of the farmers and their families rushed into town. I sent my family into town, but my brother and I decided to stay in our homes.

After barricading the doors and windows and loading our muskets, we went to bed. About midnight, we heard a stealthy step outside and a moment later someone entered the loft overhead. We sat the rest of the night watching the stairs, but the Indian did not appear. Just at daylight, I saw him drop silently down by the side of the house and glide away in the shrubbery. The reason of his visit was never known.

Another time, my near neighbor, Mr. Jaffeney, who was living alone in a log house was visited by twelve Indians on a cold stormy night. At first he saw a dusky face appear at his window, then the form of an Indian who silently raised the sash and crept in. He was wet to the skin and his clothes were frozen to his body. He made no sound but sat down on the floor near the fire; soon eleven more followed his example. The man was much frightened, but felt more reassured when the Chief lighted a pipe passing it to each of the twelve, and then to the Pale Face.

At the first peep of day, they silently passed through the window and were lost in the shadows. In the early spring when they were breaking up their camp, they left a large deer on his door step to pay for their lodging.

Wolves and bears were plenty at this time, as well as Indians. Cattle ran at large, and once when I was yarding my cattle, I was followed for over a mile by wolves.

Mrs. Conrad Magnus.

Several homes near New Ulm had been burned by the Indians. The women and children left without homes were all sheltered in a warehouse in town. At night the men were on guard. They lacked ammunition, so I sat up all one night melting lead in a teaspoon to make balls.

During the night an infant cried incessantly until finally we were afraid it would cry itself to death. There was no milk to give it. At three o'clock in the morning I said I would go out and milk the cow if the men would guard me. Several men, with loaded guns, stood around the cow while I got a cupful of milk for the baby.

OLD RAIL FENCE CORNERS

Mrs. Orin Pike—1864.

We left Buffalo late in September, 1864 for Rochester. As we went on, soldiers came on board the train returning to the country's service, as they said, after a brief furlough at home; votes were then taken from time to time to ascertain the most popular candidate for the presidency resulting, as I recall it now, each time in a large majority for Lincoln. This seemed to greatly disturb an elderly man and when apparently he could stand it no longer, he denounced the government as despotic, the draft unconstitutional, the Emancipation Proclamation as an effort on Lincoln's part to flood the whole North with "niggers," characterizing Lincoln as a tyrant, who ought to be shot.

Then there stepped out into the aisle a fine looking young man, who wore shoulder straps and in distinct tones said, "There are three things in this world that I hate—a thousand legged worm, a rattlesnake and a copperhead. A copperhead is the meanest of all." Then turning to the old man he went on, "Your gray hairs have been your protection while you abused the government. This is a land of free speech, but if you traduce Abraham Lincoln farther, I will not be answerable for the consequences." Votes were afterward taken but the old man was silent contenting himself with looking mad.

Our train was gone when we reached Chicago. We stayed all night, going on early in the morning, reaching La Crosse at dusk and leaving the cars to take the boat for Winona. The Mississippi was very low and the night was spent ere we reached Winona.

Monday morning we again took the cars for St. Charles. The railroad then called Winona and St. Peter, was not completed beyond that point. Looking from the car windows, we saw sleds and low looking wagons with one and sometimes two large barrels in them which those who knew, said were for hauling water. The stage took us safely to the "American House" at Rochester.

OLD RAIL FENCE CORNERS

MONUMENT CHAPTER
Minneapolis
MARY FRANCES PARTRIDGE
(Mrs. M. E. Partridge)

ANNA MACFARLANE TORRANCE
(Mrs. Ell Torrance)

Mrs. Mary E. Partridge—1854.

The pioneers were brave souls, able to cope with emergencies of many kinds. In them, the adage was verified, "As thy days so shall thy strength be." In 1854 I left Wisconsin, a bride, with my husband, to begin life on a government claim in Minnesota. As we passed through what is now the beautiful city of Faribault, there was only one frame house, which belonged to a half breed from whom the town was named. We settled eight miles beyond in the township of Medford in a small log cabin with bark floors, as there were at that time no saw mills in that locality. Soon our simple house was crowded to the utmost with relatives and friends looking for claims in this rare section of the state. There was a scarcity of neighbors, no schools nor places for church or holiday meetings. It was years before I heard a sermon preached.

It was plain living in those years of self-denial. Only necessities could be gotten, but soon all this changed. Neighbors began to settle near. All were willing to share, ever solicitous for the other, all were on a level, simplicity and cordiality prevailed. There were hardships, hard labor and trials of many kinds, but these developed strength of character. All were in the prime of life, of strong manhood and joyous womanhood. "How beautiful is youth, how fair it gleams, with its illusions, aspirations, dreams." There were no complaints or murmurs. Children were wel-

273

comed gladly. To my home came three before the oldest was four years old.

In 1857 came the hard times. Indian corn was the staple food. Few things the farmer raised would bring money. We went without many comforts heretofore deemed indispensable.

A little later this first home was sold and another in a southern county better adapted to cattle raising was bought and thither we moved. With a good beginning in horses and cattle and an experience in farming, better than all else, the future held high hopes and bright promises, but, alas for human expectations, the Civil War come. Already one call had thinned the county of the younger and unmarried men. The second call sounded. The call was urgent,
"Cease to consult, the time of action calls.

War, horrid war, approaches to your walls."
All able-bodied patriots enlisted, my husband among the number, with a promise from the stay-at-homes to take care of the crops and look out for the interests of the family.

Then came harships and troubles to which pioneer life could not be compared. I was obliged to see crops lost for lack of help to harvest them; cattle and horses well nigh worthless as there was no sale for them, neither was there male help sufficient to cultivate the farm, which went back to former wildness. The government was months behind in paying the soldiers, who at best received only a beggarly pittance. One night, alone with my children, I was awakened by a knock on the window and a call, "Hurry! Leave at once. The Indians are upon us, scalping as they come." With the little ones I fled across the fields to the nearest house, a half mile away, later, to find this a false alarm. Another time the alarm was given and again it proved false, but was no easier borne for it was believed the truth. All night long we were kept to the highest pitch of terror expecting every minute to hear the awful war-whoop. The night dragged on without this culmination.

OLD RAIL FENCE CORNERS

My husband died just before the war closed. His nurse at the hospital wrote me of his serious condition and I started at once for the hospital in Louisville. There were no railroads in the country at that time, stages and boats were the only means of reaching that point. To show the contrast between traveling then and now, it took me over two weeks to reach Louisville and when I arrived at the hospital found that my husband had been buried a week before my arrival. The nurses and officials at the hospital, while exceedingly busy, were most kind and sympathetic in relating to me pleasant recollections of my husband's last days.

I recall only two pleasant instances in the otherwise unhappy experience of our separation occasioned by the war. These were the furloughs which brought him home, one while he was stationed at Fort Snelling lasting for a few days, and later when he was sent home for two or three months as a recruiting officer for his regiment.

Does the luxurious life men and women of today enjoy, develop character, consideration for others, generosity and sympathy towards the less fortunate neighbor as did the trying pioneer days? If not, where lies the blame? What is the cure?

Judge Loren W. Collins—1852.

In 1853 my father visited Eden Prairie. On arriving they found a lynch court in session. A man named Gorman who had squatted upon a very desirable piece of land had gotten into an altercation with a squatter by the name of Samuel Mitchell. These men were Irishmen, Gorman a Catholic and Mitchell a Protestant. Gorman had filled Mitchell's left arm full of shot, and the court gave its judgment that Gorman must get out of the country with his family, within twenty-four hours. He had staked out the claim, had built a log house and had ready for crop about two acres of land. My father had $100.00 in gold with him, probably more money than any other man in the community possessed at that time. Gorman sold out to him for the $100.00 and father took possession.

There were then a dozen or fifteen settlers in that vicinity, among them the Goulds, the Mitchells, Mr. Abbott and Mr. Gates. There came about that time, Mr. Staring, who lived immediately east of us.

During that summer some fifteen acres were broken up and the two acres which had been previously made ready for seed by Mr. Gorman, were planted to corn and potatoes. Father hired a yoke of oxen to use during the summer and kept one cow.

Father returned to Massachusetts and in the winter we came to Buffalo by rail. In early May we embarked on the steamer "Nominee," which was then the fastest boat on the river. At the head of the flagstaff was a new broom which indicated that the boat had beaten every other vessel then running on the river north of Galena. The Captain was Russell Blakeley who for many years commanded the best boats belonging to the Packet Company.

We reached St. Paul about ten o'clock on May seventh and I remember very well that the thing which attracted my attention more than any other was the newly trimmed cupola of the Territorial Capitol building. There were at least fifteen steamboats at the lower levee when we arrived there, all busy in unloading. They were packed with passengers and freight coming up the river, but going down they carried very little, for there was nothing to ship. The first shipments of any consequence were potatoes in the spring of 1855. For two or three years after that nearly all the flour and grain used in the territory was brought from Galena.

Father took a pair of oxen and his wagon from the boat and we made our way up a very steep hill from Jackson Street to Third. From there we went up Third to the corner of Wabasha, where father bought some flour and feed and we drove back to the boat. About five o'clock in the afternoon the Nominee steamed up the river as far as Fort Snelling, taking at least one-fifth of its passengers and freight. We tied up at the ferry boat landing, at the foot of the hill under the old fort, and began to take off our cattle and freight. The hill was very steep leading up to the fort and father, aided by the boys, began to take our goods in small wagon loads to the top of the hill, so that we could properly load them. Uncle William, my mother, Aunt Isabel and the small children had been transferred at St. Paul to a small steamboat called the "Iola," which was to take them up the Minnesota river to Hennepin Landing, a mile or two from our claim at Eden Prairie.

One of the wagons was left at the top of the hill while father went back for more of the goods. I was told to take care of the cattle. Among the cattle was a white heifer, a very wild animal. Father put a rope around her horns and gave me the rope to hold, while he went down the hill. I put the rope around one hind wheel of the wagon thinking I could hold the animal that way. While I was standing there in the twilight, six or seven soldiers came out of the fort for guard duty and when they passed me the heifer became frightened, gave a jerk upon the rope and necessarily upon the wheel. The wagon had not been properly coupled, and when the animal at one end of the rope and myself at the other brought pressure upon the wheel, the hind wheels separated from the front, and the wheels, the heifer and the boy, went very hastily to the foot of the hill. Part of the time the wheels were off the ground, some of the time it was the heifer, but it seemed to me it was the **boy** who filled air space the greater portion of the period consumed in the descent. This mishap created great consternation not only among the representatives of Uncle Sam, but among the people who had just left the boat. It was my first encounter with the United States Army and I was badly scared.

About ten o'clock after we landed, we started three wagons with a pair of oxen for each and about **ten** head of cows and young stock. It was a beautiful

277

night, with full moon and after traveling a mile to what was known as Bloomington Creek, we stopped to graze the cattle and to rest. We all got more or less sleep and it was eight in the morning before we were able to start the cavalcade. We arrived in sight of our future home, under most auspicious circumstances. The weather was mild and the sun shining brightly when we came to a place from where father pointed out the log house in the edge of the woods, with a stove-pipe through the roof and the smoke coming out. My uncle Sherbuel had remained an occupant of this house all winter, that he might hold this claim of my father's and the one next to it, which had been seelcted for my Uncle William. Uncle Sherbuel was something of a hunter and trapper, and had made good use of his time during the winter and had a good assortment of furs, otter, wolf, mink, fox and those of smaller animals. He had killed several deer and was tanning the hides at the time we arrived. He had also caught and salted several hundred pounds of bass, pike and pickerel.

Father had little money left and we were without seed, except potatoes, for about three acres of our land. Potatoes were of very little value and it was doubtful if it would pay to plant them, but as we had nothing else to put into the ground father concluded that he would seed the three acres with potatoes, of which he had plenty of the kind known as Irish Reds, a round potato of exceedingly fine variety. He sowed a few acres of wheat, two or three acres of oats and planted two or three acres of corn and of course, we had a garden. We had to build a yard for the cattle at night, some sort of shelter for them, and we also had to build pig-pens. Lumber was almost unobtainable so these structures were largely of logs. They had to be very well built, strong as well as high, in order to keep cattle and hogs out of the fields. I remember that we had one hog that would climb anything in sight and what she could not climb she would dig under. Many a time in the summer of '54 and '55 did I chase that animal and her offspring back into the pig-pen.

I had a most tremendous appetite. Our food consisted mostly of potatoes, bread, wheat or corn, beans and plenty of game. Ducks, chickens or fish could be had by going a few hundred feet in almost any direction. We had no well and all the water we used was hauled from the lake, nearly a half mile distant. Father rigged up a crotch of a tree upon which was placed a water barrel and this was dragged back and forth by a yoke of cattle. Starting from the lake with a full barrel we had good luck if we reached the house with half of it.

In the summer when the corn began to get into the milk stage, we had a great fight with the blackbirds. They would swarm down upon the fields and picking open the heads of the ears, would practically spoil every ear they touched. Scare-crows were of no service in keeping the birds off, and finally the boys were put into the fields, upon little elevations made of fence rails, with guns loaded with powder and shot. We killed hundreds of birds in order to save the corn and had good crops of wheat and oats and we also had a most remarkable yield of potatoes; so large in fact, that we had to build a root-cellar in the hillside out of logs. We dug potatoes and picked them up that fall until I was nearly worn out, but in the spring the demand for potatoes was so great that father sold bushels at $1.05 a bushel. This gave him a large amount of ready money and he bought a pair of horses.

There were plenty of Sioux Indians living in the vicinity of Shakopee. A reddish colored stone, about two feet high stood a half mile west of our place on the Indian trail leading from Minnetonka to Shakopee. Around this stone the Indians used to gather, engaged apparently in some religious exercise and in smoking kinni kinic.

My cousin William and I raised that summer a quantity of nice watermelons, the seeds having been brought from Springfield. In the fall we loaded up two wagons with them and with oxen as the motive power started one afternoon for St. Anthony. We had to make our way down towards Fort Snelling until we came within two miles of the fort. Then we turned towards our destination. It was a long and tedious trip. We camped out over night and did not reach the west bank of the Mississippi River opposite St. Anthony until three o'clock the next afternoon. We fed our cattle in a grove not far from where the Nicollet House now stands, then started for the ferry, which swung across the Mississippi River about where the stone arch bridge now is. The island was heavily timbered and the road ran across at an angle, coming out at a bridge on First Street South. We got up onto the street just about the time the men were coming out of the mills, sold our watermelons and went home with $10.00 each, the proceeds of our first farming. It was a three days trip and a very tiresome one for the boys as well as for the cattle.

A friend by the name of Shatto and I took up a claim but were hailed out. When the storm ceased, I crawled out and looked around. My stove was broken, everything was water soaked, except some provisions which I had in a bucket which had a cover and my cattle had disappeared. I considered matters for a few minutes and concluded that the only thing I could do was to start for the hotel at Kenyon, some three miles away. I was drenched. My boots, all wore boots in those days, were soaked with water and very soon hurt my feet so I had to take them off. I made my way into Kenyon and there saw the great destruction which had been done by the hail. There was not a whole pane of glass in the little village and the inhabitants were engaged in patching up their windows with boards and blankets, as best they could. The crops were entirely destroyed. Many people had suffered by being struck by hailstones, some of which were as large as hens eggs.

EARLY SOLDIERS AT FORT SNELLING.
(See pages 19 and 158.)
Presented by Mrs. P. V. Collins.

OLD RAIL FENCE CORNERS

I had in my pocket $1.50, and I told the landlord, Mr. Bullis, my condition and that I wanted to stay all night.

When supper was ready I went to the table and much to my surprise met a Hastings lawyer with whom I had some acquaintance, our Seagrave Smith. Smith urged me to give up the idea of becoming a farmer and take up the study of law. So it was this hail storm that made me a lawyer.

In the fall of 1858 I secured a school and was initiated as a country school-master. The school house was a log building, about two and a half miles up the river from Cannon Falls. The neighborhood was largely Methodist and the pupils were all boys, about twenty-five in number. There was not at that time in the district a single girl over six years of age and under sixteen. Mr. Hurlbut had one boy Charles about fourteen years of age. Very soon after my school commenced for a four months term the Methodists concluded they would have a revival. They used the school house every evening for that purpose and on Sunday it was occupied all day. Nearly all of the pupils attended these meetings, began to profess conversion and in three or four weeks had become probationists.

I had adopted the New England custom of having each pupil read a verse from the New Testament at the opening of school in the morning, and in a short time Deacon Morrill and Elder Curray came to me with the suggestion that I open the school with prayer. I replied that it would not be just the thing for me to be very active in this for I was not a professor of religion but that I had considered the matter and if the boys were willing I should be very glad to call upon them in alphabetical order for a prayer each morning. I submitted this question to the pupils and found that, without exception, they were anxious to adopt the plan. I then said that if it was adopted it would have to be followed to the end of school, no matter what their wishes might be.

OLD RAIL FENCE CORNERS

I made out a roll, putting the names down in order and called upon one boy each morning for prayer. This worked well for a few weeks, but one evening Mr. Hurlbut said to me that Charlie had told him, while they were feeding the cattle, that night, that he would refuse to pray next time I called upon him. I had found it unnecessary to inflict corporal punishment upon a single pupil up to that time, but had in my desk a good stout switch. A few mornings afterwards when it was Charlie's turn to open the school with prayer, I called upon him and met a point blank refusal. I directed his attention to what had been said at the outset about continuing this as a school exercise when once adopted, and he still refused. It became necessary for me to stop the insurrection without delay. I took the switch, seized Charlie by the coat collar, as he was attempting to get out of his seat, switched him around the legs pretty smartly and the rebellion was at an end. Charlie prayed briefly, but fervently. After that there was no more trouble but many of the boys had somewhat fallen from grace before school ended. Yet they kept up their devotional exercises without any urging on my part. Mr. Hurlbut was something of a scoffer at religion and my prompt action with his boy made me extremely popular in the district.

I boarded around as was the custom in those days and built my own fires in the schoolhouse. Some of the pupils are still residents of that neighborhood and I rarely meet one who does not remind me of my whipping Charlie Hurlbut until, as they say, he dropped on his knees in prayer.

For my four months teaching I received a school district order for $60.00 and in the fall of '59 with this as my sole asset, I commenced the study of law in Hastings, with the firm of Smith and Crosby. It is hardly necessary for me to say that we were all poor in those days. There was no money and no work except farming, but in this way we could earn enough to live upon in a very humble manner.

OLD RAIL FENCE CORNERS

I first saw the late Judge Flandrau at Lewiston, he was then Indian agent and was making his way on horseback from Faribault to Hastings. He had a party of twelve or fifteen men with him, all full blood or mixed blood Indians, and they stopped for dinner. Judge Flandrau was very tanned and clad in the garb of the Indian as were his associates, it was with difficulty that I determined which one of the party was the white man Flandrau.

OLD RAIL FENCE CORNERS

MISS STELLA COLE

Mr. Elijah G. Nutting—1852.

My father's hotel, the Hotel de Bush, as we derisively called it, was the first hotel in Faribault. It may perhaps be called a frame house by courtesy, rather than technically, as it was made by placing boards vertically side by side, battened together by a third board. On the first floor were the family apartments, separated from the dining room and the "office" by partitions of cotton cloth hung on wires. The office, ten feet by twelve, boasted an improvised desk, a stool and a candle. The second floor was called the "school section," a large apartment filled with bedsteads rudely made of boards and supporting straw, hay or coarse grass ticks. Here the fortunate early bird took his rest, fully clothed, even to his boots, protected from the snow, which blustered in at the unglazed windows by his horse blankets. Later comers took possession of the straw ticks on the floor and made no complaint next morning when, after a breakfast of salt pork, black tea with brown sugar and butter so strong it could seldom be eaten, they were presented with a bill of $2.00. In one corner of this "school section" was a tiny enclosure, screened with a cotton cloth partition, containing a bed and two soap boxes, one for a dressing table and the other for a chair. This was called the "bridal chamber" and was to be had at a suitable price, by those seeking greater privacy. We had bread and pork for breakfast, pork and bread for dinner, and some of both for supper.

A large sheet iron stove down stairs was kept red hot in the winter and a man was employed to prevent people, coming in from the icy out-of-doors, from rushing too near its heat and thus suddenly thawing out their frozen ears, cheeks or noses.

When in 1858 or '59 my father sold the hotel, its purchaser mortgaged it, paying an interest rate of twenty-four per cent a year.

On July Fourth, 1856 the Barron House was formally opened on such a scale of splendor that the days of the Faribault House were numbered.

The Scott brothers built the first saw mill in Faribault. It was located on the spot where the new addition to the shoe factory now is. The machinery was brought in from St. Louis and came up by boat to Hastings at an enormous cost and it took twelve yoke of oxen to haul the boiler from that point. They were a long time getting it from Cannon City, as they had to cut a road through the dense woods. A party whom they met after dusk, when he saw the huge cylinder, exclaimed, "Well that is the largest saw log I ever saw."

Mr. J. Warren Richardson—1854.

I came with my father and mother from St. Anthony where we had lived for a short time, to Faribault and settled in Walcott where we secured a log house and a claim for $75.00. This was on Mud Creek. While at St. Anthony my father had made us such furniture as we needed. From the saw mill he got plank fourteen feet in length, which he cut into strips. He then bored holes in the corners and inserted pieces of pine, taken out of the river, for legs, and thus we were provided with stools. For tables we used our trunks. We slept on ticks full of prairie hay on the floor. These were piled in the corner daytimes and taken out at night.

Our house on the farm contained one room twenty feet square and as my father used to say "A log and a half story high." We were ourselves a family of five besides three boarders and a stray family of three appearing among us with no home, my mother invited them also to share our scanty shelter. At night she

divided the house into apartments by hanging up
sheets and the two families prepared their meals on
the same cookstove. We made our coffee of potatoes
by baking them till there was nothing left in them but
a hole, and then crushing them. It was excellent. In
winter my father cut timber for his fences. He loaded
it onto the bobs which I, a ten year old boy, would
then drive back, stringing the logs along the way
where they would lie till spring when father split them
into rails and built the fence. I have often chased the
timber wolves with my whip as I drove along. They
would follow the team and then when I turned around
to chase them they would turn and run in front of the
team.

Finding that the snow blew in through our covered shake roof, we cut sod and covered the roof with
it. The following summer, my father being away, I
planted some popcorn, which we had brought from
the east, in this sod roof. It grew about fourteen inches high and my father, upon his return, was greatly
puzzled by the strange crop which he found growing
on his roof.

When kindling was needed, my father would
raise the puncheons which made our floor and hew
some from these.

Our clothing consisted of Kentucky jeans and
white shirts for best, with overalls added for warmth
in winter. We also wore as many coats as we had left
from our eastern outfit. These had to be patched
many, many times. The saying always was "Patch
beside patch is neighborly; patch upon patch is beggarly." I never had underwear or an overcoat until
I enlisted.

One day I was plowing with a double yoke of ox-
en. I was driving while Mr. Whitney was guiding the
plow. Mr. Whitney's brother was across the river
hunting for a lost horse. For a long time we heard
him shouting, but paid no attention until at last we
saw him retreating slowly down the opposite bank
before a big bear. He called for help. We got over

there in short order. Mr. Whitney said that the bear had three small cubs up a tree, but when we reached there she had disappeared with one cub. He climbed the tree while his brother and I kept guard below. He caught the two cubs by their thick fur and brought them down and kept them.

In 1856, we came into town and I often played with the Indian boys, shooting with bows and arrows in "Frogtown," which was lined with Indian tepees. They always played fair.

Our log schoolhouse had rude desks facing the sidewall.

Mrs. Henry C. Prescott—1855.

My father, Dr. Nathan Bemis, came to Faribault where his father and brother had already settled when I was eight years old. We went first to the Nutting House, but as there was only the "bridal chamber" with its one bed for the use of women, Mr. John Whipple, although his wife was ill, invited my mother, with my baby sister, to stay at his house, which was across the street. My sister, and a young lady who had come with us, slept in the bed in the "bridal chamber." My father and brother laid their straw ticks on the floor outside and I occupied a trundle bed in Mrs. Nutting's room.

We soon moved out to the Smallidge House, east of town, where our family consisted of our original seven and four men who boarded with us. There was but one room, and only a small part of the floor was boarded over and on this, at night, we spread our cotton ticks, filled with "prairie feathers" or dried prairie grass, and the men went out of doors while the women went to bed. In the morning the men rose first and withdrew. The ticks were then piled in a corner and the furniture was lifted onto the floor and the house was ready for day-time use. Gradually by standing in line at the sawmill, each getting a board a day, if the supply held out, our men got enough boards to cover the entire floor.

The next winter General Shields offered us his office for our home, if we could stand the cold. He, himself, preferred to winter in the Nutting Hotel. This winter was a horror to us all. We all froze our feet and the bedclothes never thawed out all winter, freezing lower each night from our breath. Before going to bed my brother used to take a run in the snow in his bare feet and then jump into bed that the reaction might warm them for a little while. All thermometers froze and burst at the beginning of the winter so we never knew how cold it was. Someone had always to hold my baby sister to keep her off the floor so that she might not freeze. At night my mother hung a carpet across the room to divide the bedroom from the living room. Dish towels hung to dry on the oven door would freeze.

That winter my father's nephew shot himself by accident and it was necessary to amputate his leg. My father had no instruments and there were no anesthetics nearer than St. Paul, so my cousin was lashed to a table while my father and Dr. Jewett took off the leg with a fine carpenter's saw and a razor. He was obliged to stay in bed all winter for fear the stump would freeze.

Later we lived, for a time, in a log house. The rain penetrated the chinks, and I remember once when my sister was ill the men had to keep moving the table around, as the wind shifted, to screen her from the rain.

There was no butter, eggs, milk or chickens to be had; no canned things or fresh vegetables. My mother once bought a half bushel of potatoes of a man who came with a load from Iowa, paying $3.00 a bushel. When she came to bake them, they turned perfectly black and had to be thrown away. The man was gone. Again my father bought half a hog from a man who brought in a load of pork, but my mother had learned her lesson and cooked a piece before the man left town and, as it proved to be bad, my father hunted him up and made him take back his hog and refund the money.

OLD RAIL FENCE CORNERS

The first Thanksgiving my mother said she was going to invite some young lawyers to dinner who boarded with "Old Uncle Rundle". What she had I can not remember, except "fried cakes" and rice pudding made without milk or eggs, but the guests said they never had eaten anything so delicious.

Judge Thomas S. Buckham—1856.

In 1856 three or four hundred Indians on their way to the annual payment, camped in the woods between town and Cannon City. One evening we went, in a body, to visit them and were entertained by dancing. However, too much "fire water" caused some fear among the guests.

We had several courses of lectures during those early years. One year we had as lecturers, Wendell Phillips, Douglas, Beecher, Tilton and Emerson; following them came the Peake family, bell ringers and last of all, a sleight of hand performer from Mankato, Mr. Wheeler, who astonished his audience by swallowing a blunt sword twenty-two inches long.

At another time we had a home-made "lecture course" in which Mr. Cole, Mr. Batchelder, Judge Lowell, myself and others took part.

One of our first celebrations of the Fourth of July ended rather disastrously. We had planned a burlesque procession in which everybody was to take part. It started out fairly well. Dr. Jewett delivered an oration and Frank Nutting sang a song called "The Unfortunate Man," but the enthusiasm was shortly quenched by torrents of rain which in the end literally drove most of the participants to drink.

After the panic of 1857-8, I was sitting idly one day in front of my office on Main Street, as there was absolutely no law business. No other man was in sight, and there hadn't been a dollar seen in the town in months, except the "shin-plaster" issued by banks, which must be cashed on the instant lest the bank in question should fail over night. Suddenly I saw a stranger walking down the street, and as very few strangers had come to town of late, I watched him idly. As he came up he asked, "Young man, do you know of a good piece of land which can be bought?" I spoke of a farm south of town of which I had charge, which was for sale for $2100.00 or $12.50 an acre. He said, "I'll go and see it." Two or three hours later as I still sat dreaming, as there was no other business of any kind for any one to do, the man returned and after asking about the title of the land which its owner had preempted, said that he would think about it and went into the bank. Having made some inquiries as to my responsibility, he shortly reappeared with a bundle of greenbacks of small denominations and counted out the $2100.00. They were the first government bank notes I had ever seen and such a sum of money as had not been seen in Faribault in many months. My client then said, "Now young man, you'll see that land worth $25.00 an acre some day." Today it is part of the Weston farm and is valued at $150.00 an acre and is the nicest farm in the county.

The first political machine in the State was organized in Faribault the year Minnesota became a State. Five or six of us young men decided to put a little new life into politics and we prepared a slate. It was five or six against a hundred unorganized voters and we carried the caucus and were all sent as delegates to the Convention. Here also our modern method produced a revolution, but such a fight resulted that the Convention split and some of them went over to vote the Democratic ticket. However, we elected a fair proportion of our candidates and defeated those who had been holding the offices by force of habit.

Mrs. Rodney A. Mott—1857.
We came to Faribault, I think, the nicest and easiest way. We drove from Illinois in a covered immigrant wagon. At first we tried to find lodgings at night, but the poor accommodations and the unwillingness to take us in, led us at last to sleep in the wagon, and we came to prefer that way. After we got

away from the really settled country, everyone welcomed us with open arms and gladly shared with us everything they had.

We came up through Medford. I begged to stay there, but Mr. Mott insisted on going to Faribault as they had planned. Our first house was a little cabin on the site of the present cathedral and later we lived in a house where the hay market now stands, but this was lost on a mortgage during the hard times in 1857.

Mrs. Kate Davis Batchelder—1858.

As Kate Davis, a girl of ten, I came with my brother, a lad of eighteen and a sister fourteen, from New York to Wisconsin. Our father was in Fond du Lac, Wisconsin, where his business as a millwright had called him, and it was thought best to have us go out to be with him. We came in a wagon drawn by a team of spirited horses. We came over the thousand miles between New York and Wisconsin, fording unfamiliar rivers, stopping in strange cities, through prairie and forest, with only rough wild roads at best, never doubting our ability to find our father at our journey's end and perhaps because of that unquestioning faith, we did find him. What a journey to remember. We camped in Chicago when it was no larger than Faribault is now, on the spot near the Lake front where the Congress Hotel now houses the most exclusive of Chicago's mob of humanity. Milwaukee as we passed through it was a tiny hamlet.

When I went to visit my brother who had taken the farm on the east shore of Cannon Lake, I made the trip to Hastings in a boat, and from there in a wagon. As we were driving along, I saw coming towards us, three figures which instinct told me were Indians. On coming nearer, I saw each of them had scalps dripping with blood, hanging to his belt. They reassured me by telling me they were only Indian scalps.

Mr. Berry, afterward a Judge on the Supreme Bench, started out on foot from Janesville, Wisconsin with Mr. Batchelder and after prospecting around and visiting St. Paul, Shakopee, Mankato, Cannon Falls and Zumbrota, they finally walked in here. Fifty years afterwards Mr. Batchelder went out to Cannon Lake and walked into town over the same road that he had come over as a young man, and he said that while, of course, the buildings had changed things somewhat, on the whole it looked suprisingly as it had the first time he passed over it. Mr. Berry and Mr. Batchelder opened a law office in a little one story frame building in the back of which they slept. While coming into town, they had met O. F. Perkins, who had opened a law office, and business not being very brisk, he had turned a rather unskillful hand to raising potatoes. At $2.50 a bushel he managed to do well enough and eked out his scanty income from the law. It was while he was carrying the potatoes to plant that he met Mr. Berry and Mr. Batchelder and having become friends, they all, together with Mr. Randall and Mr. Perkins' brother, started bachelor's hall back of Mr. Perkins' office, where they took turns cooking and washing dishes. I have heard Mr. Batchelder say that "hasty pudding" or what we call corn meal mush, was his specialty and I believe, partly in recollection of those old days when lack of materials as well as unskillful cooks compelled the frequent appearance of this questionable dainty, partly perhaps, because he had learned to like it, "hasty pudding" was served Monday on his table for all the later years of his life.

During one winter I attended several dances in a rude hall whose walls were lined with benches of rough boards with the result that my black satin dress was so full of slivers that it took all my time to pick the slivers out.

We always wore hoops and mine were of black whalebone, covered with white cloth. One day, when at my brother's house, my hoop skirt had been washed and was hanging to dry behind the stove and I was in the little bedroom in the loft. My sister called to me that some young men were coming to call and I was forced to come down the ladder from the loft, to my great mortification without my hoops. There they hung in plain sight all during that call.

At Cannon Lake, near my brother's cabin was a place where the Indians had their war dances. One night after we had gone to bed in the little loft over the one down stairs room, I was awakened by my brother's voice in altercation with some Indians. It seemed the latch-string, the primitive lock of the log cabin had been left out and these Indians came in. They wanted my brother to hide them as they had quarreled with the other Indians. This he refused to do and drove them out. The next morning the tribe came by dragging the bodies of those two Indians. They had been caught just after leaving the house. The bodies were tied over poles with the heads, arms and legs trailing in the dust.

Mrs. John C. Turner—

The Nutting Hotel was the scene of many a dance when settlers came from miles around to take part in quadrilles and reels to the music of violin. We used to bring an extra gown so that after midnight we might change to a fresh one, for these dances lasted till daylight.

When sliding down the hill where St. James School now stands, it was rather exciting to be upset by barricades erected near the foot by mischievous Indian boys, who greeted the accident with hoots of joy.

OLD RAIL FENCE CORNERS

JOSIAH EDSON CHAPTER
Northfield

EMILY SARGENT BIERMAN
(Mrs. C. A. Bierman)

Mr. C. H. Watson—1855.

One hundred and fifty soldiers were sent out from Fort Ridgely in 1862 to bury those in the country around who had been massacred by the Indians. I was acting as picket out of Fort Ridgely and was first to hear the firing sixteen miles distant at Birch Coolie. It was the Indians attacking the burial party. I notified those at the fort and a party was sent out for relief. As they neared Birch Coolie they found they were outnumbered by the savages and Lieut. Sheehan returned to Fort Ridgely for the rest of the regiment. Then I accompanied them. They finally came to the small band of soldiers, who had been attacked by the Indians, to find twenty-three dead, and forty-five wounded out of the one hundred and fifty-three men. The soldiers horses had been tied close together to a rope to feed. There many of them had been shot, and being so close together many were still standing, or had fallen down on their knees—dead, but they served as a breast-work for the men. The twenty-three soldiers were buried on the spot and the wounded taken to Fort Ridgely.

I was also at Camp Release, under command of Gen. Sibley, where a great many Indians were taken prisoners. These Indians had killed many whites, and had some sixty women and children, prisoners. The soldiers managed to secure the Indians' guns and then released the women and children, finally taking the Indians prisoners, placing them in a log house, where they were carefully guarded. These, together with others secured at Yellow Medicine were chained together and taken to Mankato, where, in December, thirty-eight were hanged.

The Old Trail afterward Stage Coach road, known as the Hastings-Faribault Trail, passed through North-field along what is now Division Street. Going north it followed the Stanton road. At the entrance of Mr. Olin's farm it passed along in front of the house—and along through his pasture—east of the pond—on down onto Mr. Alexander's land—following between two rows of trees, still standing, and crossed the Cannon river just above where the Waterford dam now stands. Thence along what is still known as the Hastings road. Through Mr. Olin's pasture there is still about fifteen or twenty rods of the Old Trail and road left.

Mrs. Augusta Prehn Bierman—

In the spring of '55 several of us German families, consisting of the Prehn's, Bierman's, Drentlaws and Sumner's, came to Minnesota from a settlement fifteen miles west of Chicago. We settled on claims near the present city of Northfield. We were on the way eleven and one-half weeks. We came by way of Joliet, ford-ed the river at La Crosse and came up here by way of Rochester and Kenyon. We carried enough provi-sions with us to last most of the trip. We had some sixteen yoke of oxen, many cows, calves, and six colts. We slept in the wagons and we baked bread in iron kettles by burying them in hot ashes.

Our first home and the Prehn's was built in this way: We dug down in the earth four feet, very much as we would today for a cellar, but into a side hill. Above these four feet, logs were built up, plastered together with mud. For a roof, logs and branches of trees were placed across the side walls and then plas-tered together with mud.

Coming up through Kenyon we saw many In-dians camping along the road. The colts and oxen were deathly afraid of them and would turn way out of the road when passing, keeping just as far away as possible.

OLD RAIL FENCE CORNERS

Among the earliest marriages recorded in Rice county is that of William Bierman and Augusta Prehn 1857.

Mrs. Ann Alexander.

My husband with his father and a brother, Jonas, came in '54 and took up claims adjoining the present site of Northfield. They drove two ox teams and brought cattle, a couple of sheep and some pigs.

My husband's parents kept boarders and had some sixteen or eighteen all of the time and each day brought many extra from the stage coaches plying between here and Hastings and here and St. Paul.

Every mouthful of food consumed that first year was brought from Hastings, twenty-eight miles away, and it kept one man and an ox team on the road all the time.

Pork was purchased by the barrel and it would seldom last a week.

By the following spring, '55, when I was married and came to Minnesota some of the land had been broken, so small gardens were planted and potatoes and other vegetables raised. I believe it was about the time of the civil war that butter sold as low as 5c a pound and eggs 3c a dozen.

In these early days the Indians received annuities at Red Wing and on their yearly pilgrimages they would often camp in this vicinity as long as five or six weeks. The chiefs spent their time in hunting and fishing. The west side of the river was then not settled at all and there they had their camps. The squaws would come to the settler's homes, set their papooses up against the side of the house and walk into the house to beg. I have seen the large living room of mother's boarding house lined with Indians, smoking one pipe—each man taking a few puffs and then passing the pipe along. In those days the mosquitoes were very thick and if anyone was out doors they would literally be eaten alive. Mother's boarding house would be filled and people would be begging to be allowed to come and sleep under the tables—anything to get in away from the pests.

Mr. J. W. Huckins.

I enlisted from Minneapolis in Captain Strout's company which was sent to guard the frontier at the time of the Indian outbreak. We went up the Mississippi, then west to Litchfield, then to Glencoe and Hutchinson and were finally at Acton, where the first blow fell. The place was thirty-five miles northwest of the Lower Sioux agency, in Meeker county.

We soldiers found that our cartridges were not the right calibre. Some of the men had personal rifles, and one was found who had a pair of bullet molds of the right size. We took the bullets from the cartridges and busied ourselves, making them over the right size, using the powder and balls separately. During the engagement near Acton, the Indians managed to completely surround the soldiers. The captain ordered his men to dash through the Indian lines. The men ran for their lives, and those on horseback were ordered, at point of guns, to wait for men on foot. This sudden action took the Indians unawares and they were so surprised they forgot to keep up the fire. Most of us effected an escape. Out of sixty men but three were killed, though some twenty were wounded. We fell back to Hutchinson where there was a stockade. The Indians were getting quite fearless and would come in closer and closer to the stockade. One man had a very rare, long range gun and killed an Indian at the distance of a mile, after which the Indians kept a better distance.

Mrs. C. W. Gress—1855.

We landed in St. Paul in April '55, making the trip in about three weeks. We started on the boat, Minnesota Belle, but because of low water our household effects had to be transferred at Davenport, Iowa, to a small boat. There was a siege of cholera on the first boat, and two bodies were taken ashore and buried in the sand.

OLD RAIL FENCE CORNERS

During the time of transferring the baggage, I had to carry the money for safe keeping. I made a wide belt with pockets of different lengths suspended from it. Here, and in the pockets of my skirt was gold of all denominations and some silver, of such weight that for three days I was ill from carrying it. After spending a few days in St. Paul we moved to Minnetonka Mills where we bought a relinquishment for $600 and paid $200 to prove up—making $800 for one hundred and sixty acres or $5 an acre; that land fifty years later was well worth $100 an acre. For three years we were eaten out by grasshoppers.

While here at Minnetonka Mills I often had Indians come to my house. On one occasion I stood churning when an Indian stepped in and took the dasher from me indicating that he wanted some of it. I was not afraid of him and took the dasher from him and pushed him aside with my elbow. I had just finished baking and so gave him a large slice of bread, spreading it generously with butter. He dug the center out of the piece crowding it into his mouth, throwing the crust on the hearth. This angered me as my crust was soft and tender and I picked up a broom and started toward him yelling "puck-a-chee" (get out) and he rushed for the door and disappeared.

We then concluded, after such bad luck with our crops, we would move back to St. Paul, where Mr. Gress could work at his trade, that of a shoe-maker.

Mr. Gress would bring home work at night when I would assist him. We made a very high, cloth, buttoned shoe, called a snow shoe. I would close the seams, front and back, all by hand, as we had no machine; open seams and back, stitch down flat, and would bind the tops and laps and make fifteen or twenty buttonholes, for 50c a pair. The soles would then be put on in the shop. For slippers I received 15c for closing and binding the same way. During the war I made shirts and haver-sacks for the soldiers. The shirts were dark blue wool and were well made and finished. I broke the record one day when I made six of these garments and took care of four small children.

Mr. Alvin M. Olin—1855.

We came to Minnesota in 1855. We brought with us four yoke of oxen, thirty-five head of cattle and three hogs. We, with a family of three sons and a daughter, were four weeks on the way. We crossed the river on a ferry at Prairie du Chien and came up through Rochester and Cannon Falls and camped at Stanton while I went to a claim near Kenyon, that I had taken up the fall before, to find it had been jumped so I came on to Northfield and took up a claim on the Cannon River. We had with us two covered wagons —known as prairie schooners. In these we had our provisions, composed of flour, smoked meats and a barrel of crackers. We also had our furniture, chairs and chests and two rocking chairs for the mother and daughter. Here all of their leisure time, while on the move, was spent industriously applying their knitting needles, meanwhile singing to themselves to the accompaniment of the thud, thud of the oxen.

Each day was opened with the family prayer, after which we had the morning meal and then the boys took turns starting on ahead with the pigs, this extra time being needed because of the pigs' obstinacy. One morning the boys found they had started back in the same direction from which they had come and had traveled six miles before they found it out. We purchased a barrel of crackers in Milwaukee and our noon-day meal consisted of crackers and milk, and as milk soured, we fed it to the hogs. Butter was made on the way, and bread and biscuits were baked in a kettle.

When we staked out our claim, we laid a floor and placed a tent over it where we lived till logs could be procured. These we got on the west side of the river, then government land. For shingles we drove to Trim Mill ten or twelve miles the other side of Prescott, Wis. At one time that summer two hundred Indians were camped near our farm for two days on their way to St. Paul.

OLD RAIL FENCE CORNERS

Mrs. Pauline Hagen:—

I was four years old when my parents settled in Hastings. Mother was obliged to return to Wisconsin to see about our goods which were delayed in coming, and father wintered here and took care of us three small children. Our house had no floor and very little furniture, and this hand-made, save for a small sheet iron stove through the cracks of which the fire could be plainly seen.

At bed time father placed us in sacks, firmly tied around our little bodies, and put us on straw beds on the ground and then covered us with straw for warmth. We had no other covering. Our food that first winter consisted mostly of corn meal, made up in a variety of ways. But mother on her arrival in the spring with our lost household goods, found her family fat and rugged and none the worse for the severe winter of '55-'56.

Mrs. Catherine Meade:—

We were at Fort Ridgely at the time of the outbreak. At the fort were gathered all the women and children of the settlers for protection We could hear the Indian war whoops in the distance. The confusion was terrible and twelve of the women were prematurely confined during the first twenty-four hours. I helped Dr. Miller, post surgeon, and for forty-eight hours I had no sleep and hardly time to eat. Finally, completely exhausted I fell asleep on the floor, with my little daughter by my side. When aroused by my husband, saying "The Indians are near at hand," I declared I might as well die one place as another. I could not go on and remained where I was. The alarm was a false one and we were all saved.

One woman by the name of Jones told me she took part of her children into the stockade and returned for the rest. She found herself confronted by two stalwart Indians. She rushed into a small closet, and bracing herself between the wall and the door kept it closed in this way until help came. She was nearly exhausted and gave birth to a child before morning.

OLD RAIL FENCE CORNERS

Another woman told me that instead of going into the stockade she fled with her two children into a corn field, pursued by an Indian. He lost track of her and as one child started to scream she almost smothered it in her effort to conceal their hiding place. The Indian after half an hour gave up the search.

The stockade at Fort Ridgely had four entrances —one at each corner, at which a cannon was placed. There was but one man who could load the cannon, Sargeant Frantzkey, and as he had only unskilled help he was kept very busy running back and forth between the four guns. Ammunition was scarce and we had to use everything; nails, screws, sharp pieces of iron and steel were saved and the cannons loaded with this mixture called Sharp Nails. This was considered much more deadly than cannon balls, for when fired, it would scatter and fly in all directions.

The block house—where the ammunition was stored—was located outside the garrison and stockade, as a protection from fire. The only way to replenish the supply was to make a trip to the block house. So a guard was stationed at each end, and one man ran as fast as he could, secured a supply and ran back, of course at the risk of his life. The women also helped secure this ammunition, filling their aprons, while men filled gunny sacks.

After the first fight, when the excitement had calmed down, the women busied themselves making bullets and were obliged to remain until help came from St. Paul—nearly two weeks.

OLD RAIL FENCE CORNERS

GREYSOLON DU LHUT CHAPTER
Duluth

MARIE ROBERTSON KEITH
(Mrs. Chas. Keith)

Mr. Glass—1848.

I came to Minnesota in 1848 and was later pur-
veyor to the Indians. An Indian trail extended from
Fond du Lac to St. Paul. It ran from Fond du Lac by
trail to Knife Falls, Knife Falls by canoe on St. Louis
river to Cloquet, from there to Hoodwood, from there
to Sandy Lake, portage from there to Grand Rapids,
from Grand Rapids by way of the Mississippi river to
St. Paul.

Mr. John W. Goulding of Princeton.

My first knowledge of Indians was when I was
about ten years of age. We lived on Rum river about
three miles above St. Francis, where a canoe load of
Indians landed and camped near us. Mo-zo-man-e
who was then a chief, was said to be sick and his
squaw came to our house asking by signs for pills, of
which my sister gave her a box. She was afterward
afraid that the Indian would take the entire box at one
dose and we would be killed in consequence. The
taking of the whole box at one dose was probably the
fact, as the empty box was at once returned and the
patient reported to be cured, but no evil results came
to us.

In 1856 my father, who had been engaged with
McAboy in the construction of the Territorial road
through Princeton to Mille Lacs Lake, thought it best
that the family remove to Princeton and we came with
a six ox team. Princeton at that time with the outlying settlements of Estes Brook, Germany and Battle
Brook, had perhaps one hundred and fifty people. In-

dians in blankets and paint were a daily, almost hourly sight.

They outnumbered us many times, but gave us no trouble. In the summer of '57 two Sioux warriors came in by the way of Little Falls to the falls in Rum river just above the mouth of Bradbury brook, where they shot and scalped "Same Day" brother of Kay-gway-do-say and returned home to the Sioux country south of the Mississippi. Soon after this occurrence one hundred and twenty-five Chippewas came down Rum river on foot armed and painted for war. They stayed with us in Princeton over night and had a war dance where Jay Herdliska's house now stands, which was witnessed by the entire population then here.

Among the Indians were Mo-zo-man-e, Noon-Day, Kay-gway-do-say, Benjamin, Keg-wit-a-see and others. The next morning they killed Dexter Paynes' cow for beef and took their departure down the east side of the river. In about twenty days they came back in a hurry somewhat scattered and badly licked. They had found the Sioux at Shakopee and had been defeated, it was said with the aid of the whites living near there, which was probably so, as we should have aided the Chippewas under similar circumstances.

I remember nothing more worth repeating until 1862, the year of the Sioux massacre. We, at Princeton, had heard of that outbreak, that the Chippewas had been urged to join, that "Hole-in-the-day" had been sending runners to Mille Lacs asking that band to join with him in extermination of the whites, and we were all getting nervous. Finally all the people in the outlying settlements came into Princeton and camped in and about the old log hotel near the big elm (which still stands, the largest and most beautiful tree in the city.) Captain Benedict Hippler, an old soldier who had seen service in Germany, took command, and men and boys armed with all sorts of guns were drilled continually by the Captain, who was a martinet and at one time threatened to shoot me and a companion for sleeping on our post. It was found that Stevens the Indian trader at Mille Lacs had a large stock of powder, and H. A. Pemberton was sent to haul it away, which he did with Stevens mules, bringing it to Princeton where it was stored in my brother's cellar. About this time it was determined to build a stockade fort. I hauled the poplar logs from which it was built with my father's oxen from just across the East Branch, and I made many loads in a day. We moved a small house within the enclosure for the women and children and had the fort, such as it was, about completed when one day as Captain Hippler was putting us through one of his drills an Indian face appeared at a port hole and Kay-gway-do-say said, "What you do here, this no good, pooh!" He then told us that Hole-in-the-day had sent his runners to Mille Lacs urging war and that the Mille Lacs band had held a council and that "some young men" had urged war but the older heads led by Mun-o-min-e-kay-shein (Ricemaker) and others had counseled against it and that there would be no trouble.

This eased our minds somewhat and the settlers gradually returned to their homes. Soon we were reinforced by Co. F. of the Eighth Minn., who stayed with us two winters in "The old quarters" across the river, but, save their effect in overawing the Indians, their mission was peaceful. That same fall, '62, the Government concluded to make a display of force at a delayed payment to be made to the Chippewas at Mille Lacs and an Iowa regiment was sent with several cannon to accompany the paymaster to Mille Lacs.

Stevens, the trader at Mille Lacs had a large stock of Indian goods at Princeton and just before the payment my father sent me, then sixteen years of age, with four oxen and a wagon to haul these goods to Mille Lacs some fifty miles over what was then and for twenty years afterwards, was one of the worst roads in the state. After several days on the road I was reaching the trading post at night and as I neared there, was puzzled by the great number of lights to be seen. Finally as I approached the post I passed through a line of torches on each side, held by Indians who had heard that oxen were coming for beef and were ready to make beef of my team, had not the trader Stevens explained to them that their share would come later.

The next morning I set out on my return. Night found me at the upper crossing of Rum river where I drew my wagon a few rods out of the road, tied my oxen and tried to sleep, but was disturbed all night by drunken Indians "going to payment." The next day I met the paymaster and an escort, who, after inquiring if I were not afraid passed along up river. That evening I met the troops at the lower crossing of Rum river encamped on the east bank.

The quartermaster at once told me that in the morning I must turn about and help draw his supplies to Mille Lacs and upon my refusal I was placed in a tent under guard. The next morning after we had again discussed the matter, I partially assented and gained permission to drive my oxen unyoked to the river for water, which, as soon as they had drank, they waded and struck out for Princeton and no one could head them. The quartermaster then used my yokes and wagon for four of his beef oxen and went his way allowing me to come home. After some days, with much labor the troops reached Mille Lacs, where, it was said, the discharge of the cannon into the lake made a great scattering among the Indians, it being the first cannon they had ever seen. Upon the return of the troops to Princeton the quartermaster returned my yokes and wagon and paid for the use of them.

I have spoken several times in this story of Kaygway-do-say, who was always a great friend of mine and of the whites in general. During the Sioux war he served with others, as a scout, was always a great friend of Captain Jonathan Chase, whom he always spoke of as "Me and Jock." He visited in my father's family many times and one of my sisters tried to teach him to read. It was not a success but he was much amused at his own mistakes. A few years before he died he visited me, inquired for my sisters, hunted them out and visited them, and on his return said to me "Be-she-ke-o-ge-ma," my Indian name, "you and your sisters seem just like my own folks." Poor old "Kaig," like about all his associates has gone to the "Happy Hunting Ground." Peace to his ashes.

Mrs. Colbrath.

My father, Roswell P. Russell came to the region of Mendota as a boy and was employed by Gen. Sibley. At one time, Mrs. Sibley sent him on on an errand to St. Paul and he ventured to make the trip on the ice, with a horse and cutter. Coming suddenly upon a crack in the ice, he lashed the horse, thinking he might spring over it, but the poor animal was caught and swept under the ice, while he and the cutter remained on the ice and were saved. This narrow escape made a great impression, naturally and the story was handed down to his children.

My father married a Miss Patch of an old family of pioneers and they were the first couple married at the Falls of St. Anthony.

OLD RAIL FENCE CORNERS

MISS EMILY BROWN

Mrs. Mary B. Aiton—

When the treaty was made at Mendota in 1851, the Indians who ceded the land gave up their settlement at Kaposia, (South St. Paul), leaving behind them their dead, buried on the hill, and the land endeared to them by association. With them, when they moved westward to Yellow Medicine, went their faithful missionary and teacher, Doctor Thomas Williamson. That same year his sister, familiarly know as "Aunt Jane," made a visit to her old home town in Ohio, where I lived, and her interesting accounts of her experiences so filled me with missionary zeal that I went west, with her, as a teacher to the Indians.

With "Aunt Jane," I landed at Kaposia, and after a short rest, we began the overland journey to Yellow Medicine. The last night of our journey, two of our horses strayed away, and in the morning the ox-teams with the freight, and us women went on, leaving Dr. Williamson to search for the runaways. When we rode down into the valley, we saw ahead of us, the missing horses. We two women volunteered to go back to tell Dr. Williamson, and the rest of the party went on. We found the doctor, and to save us fatigue, he suggested that we take a short-cut across country to the agency, while he followed the road to rejoin the travelers.

Somehow we failed to follow directions and traveled all the rest of the day, coming at night to a river. Here on the bank we decided to rest. In the distance we could see a prairie fire, gradually eating its way towards the river; but we felt safe near the water and lay down to sleep. Just after we fell asleep, I was awakened by a loud call, and I realized the joy of knowing that we were found. The men who had been sent in search of us were calling, in hopes that we would answer and we continued our journey without further incident.

One morning in the spring of 1851, our little mission house at Kaposia was full of bustle and confusion, for we were busy preparing for an Indian wedding. The prospective bride was a pretty Sioux maiden, and her fiance was a white trader. Everything was in readiness for the ceremony, but no groom appeared. The hours wore on; the bride wept; but no news of the groom came until late in the afternoon a rumor reached us that he was celebrating the occasion by a drunken revel, and was not in condition to take his part in the ceremony. A white mother would have wept over daughter's grief, but not this Indian mother. When told that the ceremony must be postponed, she replied with stoical Indian patience: "It is well; I like his white skin; but I hate his drunken ways.

Dr. A. C. Daniels—

When I was agency physician at Lac qui Parle, I often saw the humorous side of Indian life. One day when the Indians had received their government allowance, a party of them too freely indulged their appetites for liquor; and one, a big brave, who had adopted the patriotic name of George Washington, led a band of Indians to the home of the Catholic sisters, and demanded food. The sisters saw the Indians' condition, barred the door, and told the braves to go away. George, however, was insistent in his demands, and finally put his giant strength against the door, and splintered the upper part. He had put his head into the opening, and was about to crawl through it, when one of the sisters seized a rolling pin, and rained sturdy blows upon his head and shoulders. He raised a yell that brought me to the spot just in time to see a funny sight. Just as George was about to beat a retreat, his squaw came running up and began to belabor him from the rear, while the nun continued the assault.

OLD RAIL FENCE CORNERS

There he was with part of his body in the house and part of it out, crying out in a manner most unseemly for an Indian brave. When the women desisted, he was both sober and repentant.

In early days, the Indian agent at Lac qui Parle hoisted the American flag each morning over the agency. During a serious drought, the Indians conceived the idea that the Great Spirit was displeased at the sight of the flag, and begged the agent to take it down. The patriotic agent tried to reason with them but to no avail, so one afternoon he took the flag down for a time. In a little while, a black cloud appeared and then a heavy downpour of rain followed. The Indians, as you know were very superstitious, and they were firmly convinced that the flag was a true barometer, so the agent had to be cautious in his display of the flag.

Mr. Z. S. Gault—

One morning as I rode a horse down to the Minnesota River to water it, I noticed a stolid looking Indian, with a gun by his side, sitting on a boulder by the river bank. Just as my horse began to drink, the Indian raised his gun and fired; the horse kicked up his heels, and I promptly became a Baptist by immersion. I can still show you the boulder, but you will have to imagine the Indian.

When I was a small boy, a party of Sioux Indians returned to Traverse from an attack upon the Chippewas at Shakopee, and proceeded to celebrate the event with a scalp dance. This dance and the whoops of the Indians attracted spectators from Traverse and St. Peter; and with boyish curiosity, I was as near as possible to the dancers. Suddenly I spied one brave, dancing about, with a skunk skin tied to his heel and trailing on the ground behind him. Obeying a mischievous impulse, I jumped upon the trailing skin, and stopped the wild dancer. The savage wheeled, quickly raised his tomahawk, and was ready to strike; but when he saw a white boy, he merely kicked me out of the ring, and kept on with the dance.

OLD RAIL FENCE CORNERS

Mr. J. C. Bryant—

When Governor McGill, came to St. Peter as a young man, he was obliged to practice strict economy to make both ends meet. The revenue he derived from teaching was so very meager, that he had to do without some of what we regard as actual necessities. Late in the fall he was passing Jack Lamberton's store, when the warm-hearted proprietor noticed that the school-master wore no overcoat. He guessed the reason; but he asked Mr. McGill why he wore no overcoat. "Well, I haven't one, and I am not able to buy one yet," he replied with sturdy honesty. "Just come right in, and help yourself to one, and pay for it when you can," said Mr. Lamberton with characteristic generosity. This kindness was a bond that made the two men friends for life, although later they were often arrayed against each other politically.

When certain men in the state were trying to steal the Capital from St. Peter for St. Paul, Captain Dodd is said to have traveled on foot from St. Peter to St. Paul between sunrise and sunset in the interests of St. Peter. This feat would seem to me a physical impossibility, but it was a story current when I was a boy in St. Peter. It is a matter of history, too, that all the attempts to save the Capital were futile, and the indomitable Captain Dodd had his long walk in vain.

Captain Dodd was considerable of a mimic and an actor. During a political campaign, he took the platform against a certain Tom Corwin of Ohio, who was considered a great political orator. On one occasion Corwin was the first speaker, and to emphasize his speech, he danced about on the stage, gesticulated freely, and made a great impression. When Mr. Dodd's turn to speak, came, he arose, and without a word, gravely gave a pantomimic reproduction of the orator's acts and gestures. Then he sat down amid roars of laughter, that completely spoiled the effect of his opponent's speech.

310

OLD RAIL FENCE CORNERS

Mrs. Nancy Kiethley Bean—

When Edward Eggleston, the author of the "Hoosier Schoolmaster," was obliged to come west for his health, he was, for a number of years, a resident of Traverse, and St. Peter. Here on week days he engaged in the humble occupation of soap-making, and on Sundays he went out to the country communities to preach the gospel. His church was often the one room of some farmer's log cabin, and he missed the pulpit upon which to pound, to emphasize the points in his sermon in the good orthodox style of the exhorter. One Sunday early in his ministry, he came to our home near Cleveland, to preach, and that day he strongly felt the need of a pulpit. "Why can't you make me a pulpit?" he asked my father after the service. "I can and I will before you come again," father replied. Father went to work, and from the trunk of a tree, he hewed out a rough pulpit! The young preacher exhorted with such fervor from his new pulpit that I was the first convert of the man who afterwards became famous.

In the fall of that same year, the annual Methodist conference was held at Winona, and Mr. Eggleston prepared to go. Before he went my father met him, and asked him whether he was going to the conference. "Yes," was the reply, "I am going." Now father knew that money was scarce and that Mr. Eggleston's preaching and soap-making yielded him little revenue, so he went to one of the brethren, a certain Mr. Arter, who had recently come from the east, bringing with him gold coin, and told of Mr. Eggleston's desire to go to Winona. Mr. Arter was interested and offered Mr. Eggleston five dollars to help defray the expense of his trip, but was met with a polite but none the less firm refusal.

"I shall not need money," said Mr. Eggleston. "I can walk part of the way, some one will give me a lift now and then and the brethren will give me food and lodging when I require it."

However, Mr. Arter insisted that he should take the gold, and he finally prevailed, but Mr. Eggleston started on foot for the conference. Upon his return, he gave the gold to its original owner, for with sturdy pioneer independence, he had traveled the distance to Winona on foot, except for an occasional lift from some traveler, driving a slow ox team.

Mrs. Mary Davis Fenton—

One summer morning in 1852, a man on horseback rode rapidly up to the door of our farm house, shouted the news of the uprising of the Indians, and then rode on to warn others of the danger. We hastily gathered together a few necessary articles, and fled to St. Peter. When we returned home after the danger was over, we found that our house had been looted, and father discovered that his pet razor had disappeared.

"I will never shave again," he declared, "until the man who stole my razor, brings it back."

Naturally the thief failed to return, and to the day of his death in 1911, father wore his patriarchial beard, and kept his vow never to shave again.

OLD RAIL FENCE CORNERS

NATHAN HALE CHAPTER

St. Paul

GRACE RANDALL LYMAN
(Mrs. G. C. Lyman)

GERTRUDE KAERCHER
(Mrs. A. B. Kaercher)

Mrs. Frederick Penny.

We lived about four miles from Shakopee, at what was called Eden Prairie. My father was William O. Collins. The Sioux Indians' old camping ground and home was on the river bottoms at Shakopee. Three miles below our place was Hennepin Landing where the boats landed coming from St. Paul. The trail of the Sioux led directly past our house, so we saw a great deal of the Indians.

At one corner of my father's land was a big boulder called Red Rock, held sacred by the Indians. Whenever the Sioux were going into battle against the Chippewas, they came to this rock and if they were successful, they brought their trophies of war and placed them on the rock. There was room for one Indian to lie down close to the rock. The others would dance around or sit in council. As soon as they had gone, the white settlers would take everything of value.

One thing we were taught was never to show fear of Indians. They knew very quickly and loved to scare anyone who showed they were afraid. Chaska and five of his men had been out duck hunting and stopped at our house for supper the night before the outbreak in 1862. The Indians were always friendly with all members of my father's family, and never asked for a meal unless they were willing to pay with ducks or in some way. Next morning after Chaska had supper with us, a man came riding from St. Peter

313

telling everyone to flee. Twenty families (ours among the others) remained.

My oldest brother had enlisted and the very day after Chaska was at our house, he was ordered back from Fort Snelling to go to Fort Ridgely.

The most disgraceful thing to an Indian is to be struck with a whip or a stick. One day I was holding the baby in my arms when an Indian put his head in through the window close to my face before I knew anyone was near. I was so frightened I ran to my mother. The Indians thought we were afraid so started for the garden to destroy the melons, squash and pumpkins growing there. My mother put on father's coat, took a big cane and went after them saying, "Get out, these are to feed papoose" over and over. There were forty in the party but they went without further trouble.

One day on my way to school, I heard the children calling to me to run, but the grass was so high I could see no one and did not know an Indian was near. When I saw him, I was not afraid. I went on to the school house door, but the teacher was so frightened she had locked the door and I could not get in. I stood waiting, and the Indian patted me on the head and said, "Heap brave papoose" and went on down the trail.

One family by the name of Dorr and another by the name of Horner were both very well to do. When a man rode to their places at the time of the outbreak telling them the Indians were coming, they took what they could in wagons and started for Eden Prairie where the Dorr family stayed with the Neals. Mrs. Dorr was a Neal girl. The Horners stayed with us until the trouble was over. The Dorr house and barns were burned to the ground, but the soldiers stopped the Indians before they reached the Horner place. Both families went back and rebuilt what had been destroyed, living there for many years.

OLD RAIL FENCE CORNERS

Mr. James Clark of St. Peter.

I came to St. Peter in March 1856. I was in the livery business, so was among the Indians more or less until the outbreak in 1862. I made the first trip from the Agency to Faribault with Bishop Whipple. Also the last when we took a number of Indian girls from Faribault to the Sioux Agency in August 1862.

I had enlisted and was with my company in line at Fort Snelling, being sworn in when a man came riding in to tell us the Indians were on the war path. We were ordered to St. Peter at once and found the families all sheltered in stone houses and the men barricading the town with cord wood and digging rifle pits in the bluffs. But none of the families was molested within a radius of about seven miles. Everyone who was left in town had to help. All the lead pipes were taken out of the wells and slugs were cut from pieces of iron.

Jim Powell, a young man left in charge of the cattle at the Agency, waiting for the Indians to receive their pay, said to me when I came up on my last trip, "Jim, I am afraid there will be trouble. The Indians are getting ugly. They shot an ox and skinned it and we can't say a word." When the outbreak came Jim Powell was sitting on a mule at the Agency. Five Indians shot at him. He tried to make his mule go down to the ferry. He would not go, so Jim slipped off and ran for the ferry. The boat had started across to Fort Ridgely, but he swam out and climbed on. He went across, then the twelve miles to the fort and enlisted. Before this the Indians were driven to beg for food, their rations had been so slow in coming from the government.

I often think there is many a man that should have a monument to commemorate his brave deeds. There was Duncan Kennedy of St. Peter, one of the bravest men I ever knew. During the outbreak he carried messages back and forth from St. Peter to Fort Ridgely, alone. When asked why he did not take someone with him, he said it was safer alone for if he saw an Indian he would know what to do; he would lie down and be quiet. If some one was with him, he would have to tell them to be quiet.

*Mrs. John Crippen was an early settler in the country, coming here by way of the Morris trail. There were two trails, one by way of Hutchinson, and the other following along the Minnesota River, the latter being the trail used during the Sibley Expedition.

Mr. and Mrs. Crippen, with a baby about a year old, came to their homestead not far from Big Stone lake where they endured many privations the first few years. The first year the grasshoppers took all the garden and grain. After the first year new settlers began to come in and Mr. Crippen assisted them in locating claims, and in that way managed to live until another crop was raised. In relating some of the experiences Mrs. Crippen states that they had a house 10x12 and the first shingled roof in this country at that time. At one time, two gentlemen from Minneapolis, Messrs. Hyde and Curtiss, had occasion to stay over night with them so they gave these parties their only bed, making one on the floor for themselves, hanging a curtain between. While preparing breakfast she heard one of the gentlemen say—"Hello, little fellow, what are you doing with my toe?" Her baby had awakened and gone over to their bed. It was over a year before they had any chickens or cow; she used to hunt plover's eggs and several times was without flour, having to grind wheat and corn in a coffee mill. The nearest railroad town was Morris forty miles northeast.

The first 4th of July celebration was held near the lake at a place now called "Point Comfort." The flag staff is still where they placed it. A Mrs. Tyler roasted a small pig, which they used as a center piece at the picnic dinner, minus the apple in its mouth.

One of the young gentlemen, whose father was a

---

* Mrs. Kaeroher's work begins with Mrs. Crippen.

minister in Minneapolis, had him send him sermons which he read on the Sabbath in the school-house.

C. K. Orton, the founder of Ortonville took a homestead adjoining Big Stone Lake. In the spring he returned for his family consisting then of his wife and child, Clara, together with several neighbors. They started in the month of July, following the old trail via New Ulm, thence to Montevideo. When they reached Montevideo they discovered the bridges had washed away, so they were obliged to ford the Chippewa river which was very deep and rapid. Mr. and Mrs. Orton rode side by side, he carrying a sack of flour which he lost while endeavoring to hold her, but which he afterward recovered. It took the party several days to get their belongings, which consisted of cattle, horses, oxen, etc., on the west side of the river.

They were badly frightened a few months later, which was after they had settled in their new home, by a Mr. Movius, of Big Stone City, who came to them with a report that the Indians, five hundred in number, from the Sisseton reservation were on the war path and were headed their way. Mrs. Orton and another woman, being alone with the children, say that they had a flat bottomed boat which they had planned to get in and get out into the middle of the lake and that if overtaken by the Indians, rather than be tortured as they had seen other people near New Ulm and other towns, would drown themselves and children, but luckily it was a false report.

Mr. Orton was the first postmaster of this place, the mail being brought once a week from Appleton, twenty-five miles east, by Mr. Lathrop, who had a wagon train hauled by oxen by which he carried flour and provisions to the settlers along the lake shore.

There is a log cabin still standing in Big Stone City, which was built in the year 1857.

A. B. Kaercher has in his possession the Government Patent given in 1855 and signed by Franklin Pierce to his father, John Kaercher, for 160 acres of land in Fillmore County, Minnesota, where John Kaercher founded the Village of Preston, and erected the second flouring mill in the Territory of Minnesota.

Lyman R. Jones of Ortonville has a stove door taken from the ruins of the Presbyterian mission, built in 1838 and which was destroyed by fire March 3, 1854.

Mr. Roberts, an old timer here, has the powder horn which Little Crow carried through the Sioux massacre.

OLD RAIL FENCE CORNERS

DAUGHTERS OF LIBERTY CHAPTER
Duluth

FRANCES ANGELINE POOLE WOODBRIDGE
(Mrs. W. S. Woodbridge)

Mrs. Nettleton.

My husband and I came to this region in 1854. At first we lived in Superior, Wis., but in September of that year we went down to Madeline Island to the Indian payment when the government bought the Duluth property from the Indians. My husband got title to the best of Minnesota Point. This was the same payment where they gave Chief Buffalo his four square miles of land in Duluth.

Minnesota Point is a narrow neck of land seven miles long and about a quarter of a mile wide projecting from the mainland in Duluth and separating Lake Superior from St. Louis Bay. One day we had a picnic party of Superior people over on Minnesota Point. Among them were Mrs. Post, Orator Hall and his wife, my husband and the Rev. Mr. Wilson from somewhere near Boston and a number of others. During the picnic various names for the new town started on Minnesota Point were proposed and Mr. Wilson at last proposed "Duluth." He named the city in honor of the first navigator and explorer who ever came up here. When the other proprietors came here and made preemptions and had obtained land they wanted to call it "Portland." My husband said "No that his property was in Duluth and it should stay in Duluth." I had never been in Duluth at that time unless it was for a picnic on Minnesota Point.

We moved across the bay to Duluth in 1858. My husband and his brother William had a contract for carrying the mail from Superior to St. Paul. Sometimes the mail was carried by team and sometimes the men packed it on their backs. In the spring and fall the roads were so bad that the use of the team was impossible. Letters were delivered once a week and papers once a month, perhaps. The military road had been commenced but not finished.

Mrs. W. S. Woodbridge.

While the experiences of the early days could be considered a hardship for the men it was ten times more annoying to women. The hardships of housekeeping, for instance and home making, keeping the home tidy and comfortable, not to say attractive, were much greater than any hardships the men were called upon to endure. The first year or two, there was no mirror at the head of the lakes. Those who were fortunate enough to have a new tin boiler, or new tin dishes could get along very well. One of the early settlers has told me that he had frequently seen the women combing and arranging their hair by their reflection in the wash boiler or dish pan. Ribbons, perfumes and fancy articles were wholly unknown. An old settler who came with his family told me "Our whole outfit comprised a feather bed and a lunch basket in which were a knife, fork and two small china dishes. I also bought a single mattress and a pair of blankets in Cleveland on my way to Duluth. We built our bedsteads out of green tamarack poles peeled, using the bark for ropes to hold it together and made a table of two boards which were found floating in the Bay. Bed clothing consisted of Indian blankets and moccasins answered for shoes, while curtains, carpets and upholstered furniture were unknown."

The postoffice was in a small building on First Street and First Avenue East. The postmaster, Mr. Richard Marvin was a member of the Fire Brigade. His friend, Mr. Melvin Forbes, who had just started in the paper and stationery business opposite, spent the night with him. The milkman was in the habit of bringing milk to the door in the morning. A lady who had come up by boat and was leaving by train in the early morning for St. Paul knocked on the door of the postoffice to inquire if any mail had been forwarded to her there. Mr. Forbes, supposing the milkman was at the door, leaped out of bed, caught Mr. Marvin's fireman's helmet and put it on his head, opened the door wide with a flourish and making a profound bow in his short white night shirt said, "Good morning." Not until he raised his head did he see the lady. I have often wondered what opinion she formed of Duluth in her short stay here.

I used to watch the Indians who were a common sight in those early days in Duluth, especially in the winter, when they would come into town with their dog teams, the sledges laden down with skins which they exchanged for provisions. The dog teams were very interesting with their intelligent well trained Indian dogs. There were usually three or four dogs driven tandem with a simple harness consisting of a collar and a strap around the body of each. The driver always ran or walked by the side of the sledge never sitting on it. We see pictures of dog teams in Alaska, for instance, with a dozen or more dogs, but that would have been impossible in a heavily wooded country as this was in those days.

The Indians did not know the use of a door bell, neither did they stand on ceremony, but if they found the door of a house unlocked they walked in without knocking. I remember that one New Year's Day we found on going into the sitting room after dinner, that six Indians had quietly taken possession, two men and four squaws. They advanced, offering to shake hands and saying, "'Appy New Year, ten cents." "'Appy New Year, ten cents." It was all the English they could speak but they knew well what it meant and did not leave until each one had received a gift. We were glad enough to see them go and to open the windows.

I well remember a funeral which occurred in the early days. The coffin was placed in a wagon which was drawn by one horse and the mourners followed on foot. I also remember how very muddy the roads were, consisting of sticky, tenacious red clay which clung to our rubbers and sucked them off our feet as we walked.

We bought water by the pailful which was carted up from the Lake and placed in a barrel in the kitchen and often on a cold winter morning, we were obliged to chop it out and melt it in the tea kettle. The windows in our house were always covered with half an inch of frost. I remember on one very cold night I was awakened by a fire bell. The windows were red with light from some burning dwelling near and I rushed from window to window trying in vain to see out and locate the fire.

OLD RAIL FENCE CORNERS

Mrs. Martin Jay Clum.

I accompanied my husband, Martin Jay Clum, a member of Company "D," Second Minnesota Volunteers to Fort Ridgely in 1862. There were left at the fort but few men to guard it, as the greater number of them had been ordered to the frontier to quell the Indian outbreaks.

My daughter, Victoria Maria, nine months old, was ill, getting her teeth and although the night was hot and sultry the windows of our quarters had to be kept closed on account of the mosquitoes. It was impossible to obtain any mosquito bar so I walked the floor nearly all night with her on my arm fanning her constantly as the heat was almost unbearable.

Toward morning, I paused for a few seconds to look out of the window and as I did so, fancied I saw tiny dark objects moving around a huge straw stack some distance away. You can scarcely imagine my horror as the dawn disclosed the truth of my fears.

I put down my dear baby—rushed outside— called to a herder to go at once and find out what those objects were, moving about the stack. Hastily mounting a mule he made a detour of the straw stack and reported. "If there's one Indian there, there's fifty with their ponies buried in and around the stack." He at once gave the alarm but before the guard reached the stack there was not an Indian to be seen. Interpreter Quinn soon sent his son, Tom, to warn me not to leave the garrison as I had been in the habit of taking walks with my baby in her carriage.

Later in the day, the pickets and scouts came in and reported a large camp of over four hundred Indians on the opposite bank of the river, waiting, no doubt, as Interpreter Quinn said, a chance to make a raid, capture and maybe massacre everyone of us. He also told me that while the Indians might not perhaps harm me they would be likely to take my baby and it would be as bad to be frightened to death as to be scalped.

Mr. August Larpenteur—1843, Ninety-three years old.

The first day I came, in 1843, I had dinner with Mrs. Jackson. It was a fine one—ducks, venison, and vegetables raised by the Selkirk refugees. Here I first tasted pemmican. It was most excellent. The bread was baked in a Dutch oven.

New Year's Day, Mr. Jackson, Luther Furnell and I took a yoke of oxen to make some New Years calls. We first went to Mr. Gervais' where we talked, took a drink, kissed the girls and then to Vital Guerin's. Next we went up to Mrs. Mortimer's where we made a sedate call. She lived where the police station now stands. Last, near present Seven Corners, we called on the Irvine's. By this time the OXEN were tired. We began to feel drowsy, so we returned and took a rest.

The Indians always called on us on Christmas, went through much handshaking and expected a present.

INDEX

The names of persons and places known to be misspelled in the text are corrected in this index. If there is wide variance, the misspelled word appears in parenthesis in the index entry. In many cases first names have been added to surnames. All place names not located by state are in Minnesota.

Brownton, 84
Bryant, J. C., 310
Buck, Cornelius F., 237
Buck, H. L., 237–239
Buckham, Thomas S., 289
Buckwheat, 62, 195
Buell, Salmon A., 122–126
Buffalo, 71, 157, 166; as food, 12, 157, 252; cataloo, 18; and Red River carts, 34; used for coats, 36, 129, 194; and Indians, 252
Buffalo, Indian chief, 319
Buffalo (N.Y.), 157, 217, 272, 276
Buffalo gnat, 69
Buffalo Grove, Fillmore County, 71, 72
Bullis, ———, Kenyon, 281
Burbank, James C., 263; stagecoach line, 139
Burchineau, ———, Minneapolis, 28
Burdick, C. A., 104
Burdon, ———, Lake Minnetonka, 202
Bush, Mrs. ———, Lafayette, 140
Butter, 33, 77, 188, 257; and bread, 20, 260, 298; decorated, 57; made while traveling, 116, 299; price of, 126, 154, 296; and Indians, 159, 298

CAKE, 81, 130, 131, 132, 226
Caledonia, 153
Calico, 90, 129, 137, 199
Camden Place, Minneapolis, 67, 75
Camp, Mr. and Mrs. George A., 226
Camp Pope, 221
Camp Release, 220, 294
Canada, 119. See also Winnipeg
Candles, 40, 99, 141, 215, 257
Candy, 198
Cannon City, 73, 114, 285, 289
Cannon Falls, 114, 281, 291, 299
Cannon Lake, 291, 292, 293
Cannon River, 295, 299
Canoes, 12, 43, 99, 137, 186
Carimona, 71
Carli, Dr. Christopher, 30

Carpenters, 32, 97, 103, 178, 194, 212, 223
Carpets, 130, 157, 166, 195, 225, 288, 320
Carver, 103, 130, 234
Cass Lake, 137
Catholics, 164, 275, 308
Cattle, 140, 188, 276, 277, 279; in Red River Valley, 15; at Lac qui Parle, 15, 22; and Indians, 16, 140; drovers, 16, 21, 24, 242; milking, 21, 83, 116, 166, 271; and turnips, 76; value of, 94, 274; running loose, 103, 106, 133, 271; brought by settlers, 22, 116, 134, 165, 173, 264, 295, 296. See also Oxen
Central Avenue, Minneapolis, 184
Central Hotel, St. Paul, 40
Central Market, Minneapolis, 67
Chaffee, Rev. James F., 216
Chairs, 99, 225, 299; homemade, 19, 70, 86, 190, 285; purchased, 106, 115
Champlin, 186, 187, 220
Charles, Miss———, schoolteacher, 234
Chase, Jonathan, 305
Chaska, Dakota Indian, 313
Chaska, 140
Chatfield, Carrie Secombe, 182
Chatfield, 263
Cheese, 152, 257
Cheever Tower, Minneapolis, 183
Cherries, 131
Chicago, 31, 47, 75, 217, 272, 291, 295; Indians' view of, 35, 258
Chickens, 118, 140, 194, 288, 316; brought by settlers, 116, 188; price of, 126, 154
Children. See Games, Indians, Schools
Chilton, ———, Wayzata, 97
Chippewa Falls (Wis.), 24
Chippewa Indians, 29, 82, 84, 136–138, 261, 304, 305; warfare with Dakota, 10, 20, 30, 44, 49, 54, 65, 82, 102, 107, 116, 163–165, 168, 186, 198, 233, 251, 291, 303, 309, 313; in Sioux War of 1862, 303. See also Indians, specific names
Chippewa River, 317

Cholera, 41, 223, 297
Christian Science Monitor, x
Christmas, 27, 141, 158, 195, 198, 226, 324
Church, Mrs. Calvin, 222
Churches, in St. Paul, 22, 158; in Minneapolis, 58, 103, 115, 216; in Bloomington, 92; in Richfield, 185; in Brooklyn, 188; in St. Peter, 311, 317. *See also* Indians and Christianity, Missions and missionaries, specific denominations
Chute, Mrs. Richard, 65–67, 135
Chute, Richard, 66, 67, 255
Cincinnati (O.), 165
Civil War, 82, 83, 131; boats, 33; effect on women, 117, 133, 143, 274; economic effects, 155, 173; and Sioux War of *1862*, 162, 175, 219, 230, 240, 314, 315
"Clarion," steamboat, 160
Clark, James, 315–318
Clarke, Edwin, 136
Clay, ———, Wayzata, 204
Cleveland (Minn.), 311
Cleveland (O.), 320
Clifford, Elizabeth, 64, photo opp. 144
Clifford, Louise, xii
Clock, 166
Cloquet, 302
Cloth, 71, 97, 141, 187, 188. *See also* specific fabrics
Clothing, 48, 95, 117, 187, 257. *See also* Indians, Red River carts, drivers of, and specific clothing items
Clouse's Creek, 49
Clum, K. Maude, 323
Clum, Mr. and Mrs. Martin Jay, 323
Clum, Victoria Maria, 323
Coats, 36, 105, 140, 286, 310; of buffalo fur, 36, 129, 194; lack of, 71, 95; price of, 129
Cobb, M. G., 262
Coffee, 131, 226, 251; substitutes for, 71, 115, 117, 131, 199, 244, 286; and Indians, 80; mills, 142, 195, 244, 316

Coffins, 103
Colbrath, Mrs. ———, Duluth, 306
Cole, Gordon E., 289
Cole, Stella, 284
Collins, Loren W., judge, 275–283
Collins, William O., 313
Congregationalists, 39 (Methodist), 123, 184
Connolly, Alonzo P., 212–216
Consumption, 20, 48, 58, 120
Cook, ———, Glencoe, 130
Cooper, Peter, 105
Cormack, ———, Minneapolis, 30
Corn, 23, 75, 104, 127, 128, 131, 172, 181, 184, 270, 276, 278; and Indians, 40, 137, 252; price of, 69; meal, 70, 95, 117, 118, 131, 142, 195, 244, 292, 300, 316; sweet, 154; and blackbirds, 171, 279; Indian, 274
Corwin, Tom, 310
Cowan, Mr. and Mrs. William, 120, 122, 126
Cows. *See* Cattle
Crabapples, 71, 154, 196
Crackers, 12, 165, 299
Cradles, 99, 225, 261
Cranberries, 20, 91, 131, 137, 141, 154, 187
Cray, Lorin, judge, 176–178, 263–270
Crazy Jane, Winnebago Indian, 179
Cressey, Rev. Timothy R., 22
Crippen, Mr. and Mrs. John, 316
Crocheting, 106
Crooks, William, 214, 221
Cross Lake, 25
Crow River, 144
Crow Wing Valley, 2
Crowe, Isaac, 191
Crystal Bay, 202
Cunningham, John, 72
Curray, ———, Cannon Falls, 281
Curtains, 320
Curtis, Orin, 215
Curtis, Theodore, 110
Curtiss, Charles C., 316
Cut Nose, Dak'ota Indian, 95

334

335

Martin County, 243
Marvin, Richard, 320
Maryland, 126, 139
Masonic order, 226
Massachusetts, 217, 222, 276, 279, 319
Massolt, Mary, 134
Matches, 215
Maxfield, George, 160, 165
Maxfield, Mrs. ——, Dodge County, 110
Maxwell, Delilah, 202–206, 211
Maxwell, Jeanette Thompson, 237
Maxwell's Bay, 202
Meade, Catherine, 300
Medford township (Steele County), 273, 291
Meeker County, 297
Melons, 314
Mendota, 9, 12, 42, 257, 306, 307
Merchants' Hotel, St. Paul, 164
Merrill, Elijah W., 184
Merrill, Mrs. E. A., 77
Merrit, Arabella, 243–249
Methodists, 123, 216, 281, 311
Mice, 189
Mickel, Mrs. ——, Fort Ridgely, 144
Middle Lake, 127, 128
Miles, ——, Champlin, 186
Milk, 14, 21, 77, 112, 124, 130; and Indians, 92, 148; lack of, 148, 288, 289; delivered, 320
Mille Lacs Lake, 136, 138, 302, 303, 304, 305
Miller, Gov. Stephen, 177
Miller, Mary, 206
Mills, Dr. ——, Red Wing, 246
Mills, Minard, 160, 166
Milwaukee (Wis.), 55, 291, 299
Milwaukee Railroad, 106
Minneapolis, ix, xvii, 11, 27–29, 33, 36–40, 43, 47, 56–58, 74, 75, 77, 88, 102, 135, 142, 182–184, 190–192, 212–216, 280. *See also* Churches, Falls of St. Anthony, Ferries, Hotels and halfway houses, Roads and trails, Sawmills, Schools

Minneapolis Automobile Club, 261
Minneapolis Journal, quoted, xix
Minneapolis Sunday Tribune, quoted, x
Minnehaha Creek, 184, 227
Minnehaha Falls, 11, 48, 52, 159, 214
Minneiska, 139
Minneopa Falls, 169
Minnesota, population, vii; historic sites marked, xvii, xviiin
"Minnesota Belle," steamboat, 297
Minnesota Outfitting Co., St. Paul, 182
Minnesota Pioneer, St. Paul newspaper, 40, 255
Minnesota Point, Duluth, 319
Minnesota River, and land trails, 5, 59, 78, 316; boats on, 42, 116, 140, 166, 172, 235, 250; during Sioux War of *1862*, 139, 230, 234, 235
Minnesota Territory, population, vii; capital of, 25, 229, 276; penitentiary, 25; legislature, 41
Minnetonka Mills, 54, 207, 208, 298
Minnewashta Lake, 97
Mirrors, 320
Missions and missionaries, 12, 42, 47, 250, 256, 307, 318. *See also* specific names
Mississippi River, xvii; water levels, 264, 272. *See also* Ferries, Steamboats
Missouri River, 221
Mitchell, Gen. Henry Z., 138
Mitchell, Samuel, 275
Mittens, 77, 105, 106, 210
Moccasins, 61, 320; worn by Indians, 9, 82, 137; used by whites, 80, 96, 131, 185
Moir, Marion, 250
Molasses, 64, 130, 196
Moline (Ill.), 221
Money, 84, 215, 290; shinplasters, 33, 40, 289; interest rates, 170, 285; of Indians, 235. *See also* Gold, Panic of *1857*
Montana, 243
Montevideo, 220, 317
Moore, Alexander, 69
Moores, John, 60

Moose, 137
Morehart, Lillian Butler (Mrs. William J.), 160
Morgan, George N., 111; foundry, 88
Morgan, Jack, 30, 64
Morgan, Lucy, 113
Mormons, 16
Morrill, ———, Cannon Falls, 281
Morris, Jonathan, 94
Morris, James T., xiv, xviii
Morris, Lucy L. Wilder (Mrs. James T.), editor and compiler, ix, 6, 9; biographical sketch, xiii-xix; as author, xiv; in D.A.R., xv-xvii, xix; park named for, xviii
Morristown, 93
Mortimer, Mrs. Richard W., 324
Mosquitoes, 69, 97, 98, 130, 156, 202, 213, 296; on boats, 13, 43
Mott, Mrs. Rodney A., 290
Moulton, Isaac, 138, 143
Mound, 199, 264
Mousseau (Merceau), Charles, 223; family, 56
Movius, ———, Big Stone City, 317
Mo-zo-man-e, Chippewa chief, 302, 303
Mud Creek, 285
Mules, 202, 304, 323
Müller (Mueller, Miller), Dr. and Mrs. Alfred, 144, 150, 300
Mun-o-min-e-kay-shein, Chippewa Indian, 304
Murphy, ———, Shakopee, 233
Murphy, Dr. John H., 34, 57
Muscatine (Ia.), 201
Music, 126, 130, 224, 253
Muslin, 50
Musser, ———, Muscatine, Ia., 201
Mutton, 154
Myrick, Andrew J., 145

NAILS, 26, 103
Nash, Z. E. B., 216
National Citizens Bank, Mankato, 176

Nauvoo (Ill.), 16
Neal, ———, Eden Prairie, 314
Neill, Edward D., 42
Neill, J. D., 157–159
Neill, Minnesota, 157–159
"Nelson," steamboat, 26
Nettleton, Mrs. ———, Duluth, 319
Nettleton, William, 319
New Auburn, 87
New Hampshire, 182
New Haven (Conn.), 246
New Ulm, in Sioux War of 1862, 80, 124–126, 167, 176, 179, 181, 245, 271; trail to, 317
New Year's Day, 192, 226, 321, 324
New York, 157, 217, 276; settlers from, 48, 170, 188, 197, 270, 272, 291
New York City, Indian view of, 259
Newton, Rep. Walter H., xvi
Nichols, William, 83
Nicollet, Joseph N., 42
Nicollet, 119, 121
Nicollet Avenue, Minneapolis, 133, 155
Nicollet Hotel, Minneapolis, 112, 153, 280
Nicollet Island, 29, 39, 228
Niemann, Mrs. W. L., 196–199
Ninth Minnesota Regiment, 178
Noble, Mrs. ———, Brownton, 88
Noble, Rev. Frederick A., 138
"Nominee," steamboat, 56, 163, 165, 276
Noon-Day, Chippewa Indian, 303
North, Mr. and Mrs. John W., 224
North, T. E. B., 226
North Dakota, 240, 243
North Mankato, 171
"Northern Belle," steamboat, 85
Northfield, ix, 114, 295, 296, 299
Northrup, Mrs. ———, 57
Northup, Anson, 104
North West Co., 61
Norwegians, 106, 245
Nutting, Elijah G., 72, 284
Nutting, Frank, 289
Nutting House, Faribault, 80, 284, 287, 288, 293

337

Sault Ste. Marie (Mich.), 196
Sawmills, 24, 25, 33, 35, 64, 82, 169, 188, 285, 287, 299; built by government, 10, 11, 22, 43, 64, 110, 112; at Marine, 29, 182, 197; at Minneapolis, 33, 34, 38, 47, 52, 74, 143, 225, 226
Schaick, R., 270
Schmidt, Mrs. Mary, photo opp. 144
Schools, xiii, 49, 72, 90, 160, 167, 186, 188, 257, 281, 287, 310, 314; in Minneapolis, 37, 38, 39, 55, 57, 112, 113, 183, 186, 190, 214; for Indians, 254
Scots, 11
Scott, ———, Faribault, 285
Scott, ———, St. Paul, 158
Scott, Harvey, 285
Scrimgeour, ———, Minneapolis, 111
Seamstresses, 89, 95
Seccombe (Secomb), Rev. Charles, 39
Second Minnesota Volunteers, 323
Seeger, ———, St. Peter, 123
Selkirk Colony, 11; settlers from, 324
Seven Corners, Minneapolis, 324
Seventh Street, St. Paul, 106
Seward's Mill, Mankato, 175
Shakopee, Dakota chief, village of, 9, 63, 232
Shakopee, and Indians, 9, 18, 63; boat stop, 13, 42; trails to, 58, 60, 63, 119; and Sioux War of 1862, 61, 234; trading post, 232; sacred stone at, 232, 279, 313
Shatto, ———, 280
Shaver, B. F., 206–212
Shaw, J. B., 226
Shawboshkung, Chippewa chief, 138
Shawls, 40, 90, 137, 143
Sheehan, Lt. Timothy J., 231, 294
Sheep, 36, 72, 141, 296
Shelbyville, 264, 265, 267
Shepley, Caroline Rogers, 222
Sherrard, Mrs. ———, Shakopee, 236
Sherwood, Lucy Leavenworth, 5
Sheyenne (Chien) River (N. Dak.), 213
Shields, Gen. James, 288
Shingle Creek, 57, 58

Shirts, 71, 77, 95, 213, 286, 298
Shoes and boots, 19, 20, 50, 61, 69, 213; shoemaking, 19, 32, 71, 95, 298; price of, 128, 298; and Indians, 258
Shortening, 51, 130
Sibley, Henry H., 10, 12, 37, 66, 120, 306; house, 9, 257; and Little Crow, 43, 45; in Sioux War of 1862, 139, 152, 221, 234, 294; and 1851 treaty, 255; leads 1863 expedition, 316
Sibley Park, Mankato, 176
Sidewalks, 34, 36, 55, 113, 162
Sidle, Jacob K., 215
Silk, 50, 51, 90, 132
Silver Lake, 77
Sinclair, Daniel, 138
Sioux City (Ia.), 161
Sioux Indians. See Dakota Indians
Sioux War of 1862, 120, 124–126, 139, 144–152, 175, 179–181, 219–221, 230, 233–235, 240–243, 244–249, 266–269, 294, 297, 300, 315, 318, 323; and Little Crow, 45, 46, 149; and friendly Indians, 61, 62, 82, 94, 120, 140, 145, 161, 233; refugees of, 61, 83, 124–126, 127, 134, 139, 175, 180, 233, 240, 246, 266, 271, 274, 314; and Chippewa, 83; causes of, 109, 145, 210, 230, 233, 315; ammunition shortage in, 150, 151, 244, 246, 271, 297, 301; and Winnebago, 163; aftermath of, 221, 242, 243, 267–269. See also Fort Ridgely
Sisters of Charity, 164
Sisseton Indians, 317
Sisseton (S. Dak.), reservation, 317
Sixth (Fifth) Minnesota Regiment, 214, 220
Slaymaker, ———, Minneapolis, 224
Sleds and sleighs, 75, 238, 306
Sleepy Eyes, Dakota chief, 180
Slocum, Frank, 114
Smallidge House, Faribault, 287
Smith, Harris, 230
Smith, Hiram, 186
Smith, Joseph, Mormon leader, 16
Smith, Mary Staring, 133

Thompson, Susie, 49
Thorne, Martha, 78–80
Tibbetts, Mrs. ———, Minneapolis, 153
Tobacco, 118, 137, 258
Todd, Anna, 135, photo opp. 144
Tomatoes, 128
Torrance, Anne MacFarlane, 273
Tourtelotte Hospital, Mankato, 160
Towels, 141
Trails. See Roads and trails
Traverse, Mrs. ———, Little Canada, 20
Traverse des Sioux, 120, 122, 123, 126, 254, 311; boats to, 12, 14, 42, 60, 65, 251; on way to Lac qui Parle, 12, 14, 58, 251, 253; mission, 15, 251, 253; trail to from St. Paul, 58, 60; Indian dance at, 116, 309. See also Treaties
Treaties, at Traverse des Sioux, *1851*, 65, 109, 255, photo opp. 64; at Mendota, *1851*, 307
Troutmere (Wis.), 49
Troy (N.Y.), 48
Trunks, 78, 139, 217, 246
Turner, Mrs. John C., 293
Turnips, 107, 119, 130, 141
Turtle Mountain (N. Dak.), 137
Turtles, 108
Tuttle, Calvin A., 52, 55, 183; sawmill, 33, 52
Tuttle, Clara, 55
Tuttle, Luella, 55
Twenty-fifth Wisconsin Regiment, 249
Tyler, Emma J., 224
Tyler, Mrs. ———, Big Stone Lake, 316
Tyler, Samuel, 229
Typhoid fever, 224

UNION SCHOOL, Mankato, 160
Union Station, Minneapolis, 11, 64, 77, 207
University Avenue, Minneapolis, 135, 183
University Hill, St. Paul, 56, 183
University of Minnesota, xvii, xviii, 103, 108, 183, 190, 192

Upper Sioux Agency, 120, 233, 234, 294
Utensils, 14, 109, 141, 159

VAN BRUNT, GEORGE M., family, 160
Vander Horck, John, 51, 240
Van Sant, Ruth Hall, 182
Van Sant, Gov. Samuel R., 199–201
Veal, 200
Vegetables, 66, 95, 128, 141, 184, 213, 324. See also specific types
Velvet, 132
Venison, 36, 95, 154, 195, 324
Vermont, 70
Vernon Center, 105
Vinegar, 95, 100, 130
Violins, 29, 119, 155

WABASHA STREET, St. Paul, 276
Wagons, 56, 60, 139. See also Oxen, Prairie schooners, Red River carts, Stagecoaches
Wakefield, Dr. and Mrs. J. L., 234
Wakefield, Warren, 94–97
Wales bookstore, Minneapolis, 74
Walker, M. O., stagecoach company, 263
Walker, Mrs. T. B., 115
Walker & Co., stagecoach line, 263
Wallpaper, 49, 86, 120
"War Eagle," steamboat, 26, 182
Warren, ———, Mankato, 160
Washburn, W. D., 154
Washburn Park, Minneapolis, 184, 185
Washington, George, Dakota Indian, 308
Washington Avenue, Minneapolis, 133, 153, 155
Washington Avenue Bridge, Minneapolis, 110
Washington, D.C., Dakota Indians at, 258, 259
Wass, Mrs. ———, Minneapolis, 53
Water and wells, 111, 135, 149, 231, 262, 279, 322
Waterford Dam, Northfield, 295
Watermelons, 279

343

Watertown, 142
Watson, C. H., 294
Waukopee, 70
Wauqaucauthah, Dakota Indian, 160
Way, Georgiana M., 116–118
Wayzata, 94, 202, 204, 207
Webb, Luther, 50
Weddings, 19, 46, 50, 306; newlyweds, 27, 51, 59, 69; Indian, 254, 308
Weeks, Mary, 76, photo opp. 144
Weiser, Dr. ———, Shakopee, 235
Welch, Belle Boynton, 262
Wells, George, 144
Wells, Kate, 164
Wells, Henry T., 34, 133
West Mankato, 177
Weston, ———, Faribault, 290
Whalen, Mrs. ———, Bloomington, 260
Wheat, 21, 79, 117, 172, 173, 278, 279; in Red River Valley, 15; cracked, 70; and grasshoppers, 128; price of, 129, 171, 199; lack of, 270. See also Flour
Whipple, Bishop Henry B., 94, 138, 315
Whipple, John, 287
White, Mrs. William J., 84–88
White Lodge, Dakota Indian, 180
Whitney, ———, Faribault, 286
Whitney, Oat, 229
Whittle, ———, Minneapolis, 34
Wilder, Mrs. ———, Morristown, 93
"William Crooks," locomotive, 214
Williamson, Dr. Thomas S., missionary, 9, 14, 58, 59, 61, 253, 307
Williamson, Jane (Mrs. Thomas), 60, 260, 307
Willoughby Co., stagecoach line, 182
Willow Creek, 267
Wilson, Amanda, 256
Wilton, 267
Windows, 18, 135, 207, 223, 284, 322
Windom, 173
Wine, 123, 152
Wing, Ida, 262
Winnebago City, 169, 245, 246, 248

Winnebago Indians, 35, 104, 167, 168, 178, 235, 236; and Dakota, 163, 167, 170, 175. See also specific names
Winnebagoshish Lake, 137
Winnipeg (Man.), 1, 28, 51, 52, 105
Winona, ix, 123, 138, 230, 237, 263, 272, 311. See also Winona Rangers
Winona & St. Peter Railroad, 272
Winona Rangers, 239, 249
Winslow Hotel, Minneapolis, 37, 212, 224
Winter, Mrs. James A., 107
Wisconsin, settlers from, 169, 263, 291, 299, 300, 319
Wolves, 20, 52, 60, 71, 80, 86, 87, 117, 203, 208, 213, 271, 286
Women, xx, 51, 53, 77, 320; birth of children, 53, 78, 118, 191, 223, 247, 300; during Sioux War of 1862, 83, 126, 127, 144–152, 175, 180, 220, 234, 245–248, 271, 274, 300, 323; care of infants, 88, 207; during Civil War, 117, 133, 143, 274. See also Dakota Indians
Wood, Maj. Samuel, 230
Wood Lake, 1862 battle at, 220
Woodbridge, Frances Angeline Poole, 319
Woodbridge, Mrs. W. S., 320–322
Woodcock, 52
Woodmans' Hall, Minneapolis, 155
Woods, Mrs. Newman, 99–101
Wool, 71, 95
Worms, 100
Wright, ———, near Alexandria, 105

"YANKEE," steamboat, 31, 42
Yeast, 250
Yellow Medicine, 307. See also Upper Sioux Agency
Yorktown (Va.), national military park, xvi

ZUMBRO RIVER, 139, 262
Zumbrota, 292